D0025084

Old Age in a
Bureaucratic
Society

WITHDRAWN

Old Age in a Bureaucratic Society

THE ELDERLY, THE EXPERTS, AND THE STATE IN AMERICAN HISTORY

EDITED BY
David Van Tassel and
Peter N. Stearns

CONTRIBUTIONS TO THE STUDY OF AGING, NUMBER 4

GREENWOOD PRESS
New York • Westport, Connecticut • London

HQ
1064
.U5
O38
1986

Library of Congress Cataloging in Publication Data
Main entry under title:

Old age in a bureaucratic society.

(Contributions to the study of aging, ISSN 0732-085X ;
no. 4)
  Bibliography: p.
  Includes index.
  1. Aged—United States—Social conditions. 2. Old
age pensions—United States—History. 3. Aged—United
States—Family relationships—History. 4. Gerontology—
United States—History. I. Van Tassel, David D.
(David Dirck), 1928– . II. Stearns, Peter N.
III. Series.
HQ1064.U5O38   1986   305.2′6′0973   85-14662
ISBN 0-313-25000-6 (lib. bdg. : alk. paper)

Copyright © 1986 by David Van Tassel and Peter N. Stearns

All rights reserved. No portion of this book may be
reproduced, by any process or technique, without the
express written consent of the publisher.

Library of Congress Catalog Card Number: 85-14662
ISBN: 0-313-25000-6
ISSN: 0732-085X

First published in 1986

Greenwood Press, Inc.
88 Post Road West, Westport, Connecticut 06881

Printed in the United States of America

The paper used in this book complies with the
Permanent Paper Standard issued by the National
Information Standards Organization (Z39.48-1984).

10 9 8 7 6 5 4 3 2 1

FEB 1 2 1987

Contents

List of Tables and Figures

PETER N. STEARNS
DAVID VAN TASSEL

Introduction

Themes and Prospects in Old Age History

Since the mid-1970s, the history of old age has risen from virtual non-existence to its current status as a promising and provocative subfield of social history. Old age now commands a complex literature in terms of new factual knowledge and new analytical frameworks. This growth has been doubly fueled, by the general interest of social historians in probing new facets of ordinary life and new groupings among ordinary people, and by the rising visibility of the elderly and the magnitude of their economic and medical problems in, and for, American society—recent developments that beg for historical context.

Historians of old age have advanced knowledge of the elderly on several fronts. To begin with, we now know that the simplest kind of historical framework—positing a sharp dichotomy between traditional societies, which are benign to the elderly, and modern societies, which turn vicious—is inaccurate. Understanding that there never really was, at least in Western society, a "golden" age of old age is not only a gain for accuracy; it also suggests the difficulty of dealing with certain contemporary old age problems that are not merely modern artifacts and which cannot be resolved by returning to an imagined utopian past.

Historians have also pointed to key changes in the more purely modern experience of the elderly. Changes in family position, the advent of mass retirement, partial alterations in social policies, and, perhaps especially in the United States, a more disparaging cultural image of the elderly mark stages in the nineteenth- and twentieth-century experiences of older people. Despite gaps in historical findings and some vigorous ongoing debate, we now know that old age has a rich and varied past and that understanding the conditions of the elderly in times past sheds significant light on key periods in our social history.

Old age and the elderly, understood historically, affect our grasp of the evolution of modern society beyond their function as life stage and an "inarticulate" grouping to add to the arsenal of the social historian. The way a society treats its elderly offers a window on larger social values and institutions, telling us a good bit about how that society operates quite apart from the specific treatment offered older people. For example, the famous American penchant for youthfulness, an artifact of the nineteenth century, gains new meaning and offers new kinds of assessment when compared to the ways old age was viewed and elderly people viewed themselves during the same period. More specifically, the position of older relatives sheds new light on the structure and functions of families. Attention to the elderly, or lack thereof, adds a dimension to the history of the modern state. Age groupings, including older ages, must now be included with ethnic, gender, and class distinctions in the assessment of the modern work experience and, at least in our own century, the modern experience of leisure as well. In sum, old age history enriches the interests of social and political historians not just as an independent subfield with its own topical concerns and interpretive dynamics, but also as a revealing illustration of wider social processes. Understanding trends in the position of the elderly can illumine and give human context to broader developments, such as the rise of a capitalist economy and a bureaucratic state.

Finally, old age history becomes increasingly necessary as an ingredient of current policy inquiry. The unavoidable realization of the importance of old age issues in contemporary politics has opened up new channels for the investigation of past social policy, in which the elderly turn out to have figured prominently. Broader understanding of trends in the conditions and expectations of the elderly themselves and in the view of old age held by the non-old can only enhance our appreciation of current policy dilemmas, such as social security financing and medical policy, which bid fair to be as inescapable as they are politically intractable. We bring to such policy issues a fund of historically evolved ideas about what old age is and should be, and explicit consideration of the origins and past impact of these ideas must be part of the process of policy evaluation.

Fortunately, while a definitive history of American old age has yet to be written, a variety of historians have recently sketched some of the key contours of the past experience of the elderly and its relationship to present conditions. Since the field of inquiry is new and its findings only beginning to penetrate beyond specialist ranks, it is particularly important to make available the discoveries and concepts, as well as the limitations and future research agendas, of old age history. This includes works by a large number of the historians who have thus far contributed much to American old age research and summarizes the leading approaches to date while pointing to additional tasks before us. Both its summary and agenda-setting features will aid in the dissemination of the historical component of the evaluation of old age. They will also encourage and guide ongoing study in what remains one of the more exciting and open-ended branches of American social history.

This book grew out of papers that were first presented at a conference, "Old Age in a Bureaucratic Society," held at Case Western Reserve University in April 1983, funded by the Rockefeller Foundation, and sponsored jointly by the Department of History and the Center of Aging and Health of Case Western Reserve University. The third in a series that began in 1974, this conference had three major purposes: to encourage the continuing historical analysis of old age, to focus new research efforts on the problems of bureaucracy and social policy, and to bring the power of historical knowledge and analysis together in addressing the challenges posed today by the crisis of the welfare state. In bringing together scholars of different generations, disciplines, and ideological bents, the meeting underscored issues that have developed in the literature and that now divide policymakers on matters affecting the elderly. This volume presents findings in the historical development of several key interrelationships between the elderly and the modern world: in demography and family structure, in culture, and in policy. The chapters collectively offer some of the basic interpretive advances made by historians in recent years and, often explicitly, some of the current arguments as well.

The volume is divided into five parts. Part I offers a critique of the recent historiography, by Brian Gratton, and Gerald Grob's assessment of overall directions in interpretation. This is a starting point for further consideration, and a reminder also of important points of agreement as well as dispute among historians of old age. The complex relationship between modern and premodern old age, for example, is something that virtually all historical scholars now agree upon, even if they may quarrel about when the "modern" begins and exactly what it involves. This understanding has important implications as a context for gerontological research as well as broader social history and even bears on policy issues, opposing some simplifiers who evoke a utopian past for the elderly to which we should strive to return.

Part II focuses on attitudes toward the elderly. This topic has received particular attention from old age historians, many of whom see key changes in the cultural valuation of old age in nineteenth-century America. Here, interestingly, echoes of the more traditional distinction between premodern and modern society still resound, with the contention that in the American context (not, most historians would argue, in the European, where the traditional culture was less benign) the elderly moved from a position of considerable cultural veneration in the colonial period to increasing scorn at some point during the nineteenth century. Thomas Cole uses changes in religious outlook to suggest the most sweeping kind of alteration, in which old people became the model for degeneration and decay. Carole Haber deals with a more limited change, in medical outlook, but a crucial one because of the growing importance of physicians in dealing with the elderly population. Both Cole and Haber reflect a further assumption common to most cultural historians of American old age: that the new and nasty paradigms established in the nineteenth century continue without major disruption to the present day. They make a compelling case for regarding nineteenth-century developments as the crucible for some of the key problems of older people today.

Part III focuses on the social history of the elderly themselves, as their demographic and family position has altered. Here the emphasis is on twentieth-century change, and the evaluation of the quality of change is more open-ended than is the norm among the historians who have focused on nineteenth-century culture. In terms of family life, the elderly have gained as well as lost in modern times. Indeed, some structural changes may not be as significant as they seem statistically; Daniel Scott Smith notes that the changes have proceeded without an explicit sense of anguish, which suggests that they mesh with alterations in values of the major groups in question. In other respects, change can be cited without being easily evaluated in terms of quality. Thus Tamara Hareven notes that alterations in family experience have helped to highlight old age as a stage of life; whether to the benefit or detriment of those involved is not clear.

Smith and Hareven approach the social history of the elderly from rather different vantage points, to be sure. Smith relies on general statistical data, particularly changes in homeownership and household composition affecting the elderly. Hareven's approach stresses more qualitative evidence, changes in the life-course experience of the elderly and their subjective relationships with kin. It is important to note also that Smith and Hareven disagree on the household patterns of the elderly during the nineteenth century, with Hareven emphasizing much more nuclearity, much less coresidence (particularly dependent coresidence) with younger kin. Yet, in one key respect, Smith and Hareven reach complementary conclusions in emphasizing the importance of twentieth-century changes in the long-term experience of older Americans. Though they define change differently, both find significant alterations in the family situation of older people, especially the economic uses of the family, whether denoted by stated expectations concerning kin, as with Hareven, or measured by separate household formation, as with Smith. Smith's data may also parallel Hareven's findings that old age becomes an increasingly separate experience, in terms of the larger patterns of the family, as the old identify their status through the departure of younger kin and symbolize it by the maintenance of individual households. Both studies substantially modify the most common stereotypes of "modern" changes in old age, particularly in playing down the statistical or experiential significance of outright institutionalization. Questions remain unanswered, even as we learn more about the social experience of modern old people and the timing of historical changes; we have yet to learn enough about the affective links of older people to each other and to younger kin, despite or because of residential change. But both Smith and Hareven demonstrate that we already know a great deal about how the immediate environment of old age has shifted.

Part IV, which most directly involves the experience of older people in an increasingly bureaucratic society, takes up the theme of old age policy. Jill Quadagno traces the evolution of the treatment of elderly dependents by American society from colonial times through the establishment of Medicare. She shows some important continuities in both the problems the elderly have posed and the criteria policymakers have applied, but she also demonstrates the changing institutional context, from community to state to federal government. Andrew Achenbaum and John Myles treat the specific history of social security from different perspectives. Both see the Social Security Act as a major break in the history of old age policy, and both note a crisis in the social security approach since the 1970s. But the two scholars disagree substantially over the nature of the present crisis and the lessons offered by recent history as to its best resolution. William Graebner assesses the bases of disagreement and sketches his own sense of where the social security crisis fits in the evolution of contemporary American history. In his reply, Achenbaum evaluates the range of disagreement somewhat differently, while indicating the inevitability of ongoing debate as the bases of old age policy come under new scrutiny.

The final section of this volume is a comment on the empirical and conceptual bases for further research. In this chapter, Charles Rosenberg points to the extent to which old age history, already rich in data and generalization, remains open to additional insight, from the standpoint of history *per se* and also in terms of relating historical findings to other disciplines and policy analysis. It is a scholarly truism to claim that much remains to be done; but in the field of old age history, the recency of serious inquiry and the importance of the subject affirm it. As Rosenberg suggests, linkage between old age history and other topical inquiries, plus development of empirical case studies to supplement the rather sweeping efforts to date, offer promising approaches. Finally, a bibliography indicates major work in the field to date.

The topical organization of this book, combined with some frank disagreements among the authors, makes it obvious that old age history has not produced a single compelling synthesis. Yet while a universally accepted interpretive framework remains elusive—and several candidates are suggested in the following pages—there are in fact a number of important interrelationships among the approaches used here. One relationship is chronological: the focus of change in the conditions of the elderly seems to shift over time. Thus although changes in culture—the way the elderly were viewed—were probably more important than policy changes or alterations in family structure during the nineteenth century, the reverse is true in our own century. The chapters on demographic and policy change, indeed, establish the magnitude of relatively recent shifts in the experience and context of old age; the elderly have a lively mid-twentieth-century history, of interest in itself and of special importance to experts and policymakers in this field.

More direct connections link the topical emphases, in addititon to the chronological unfolding. Alterations in the demography of the elderly are closely tied to new policy dilemmas as the elderly have loomed larger in numbers and have gained a new sense of their distinctness, not only within families but also in the larger society. Changes in nineteenth-century culture, which almost all historians view as unfavorable to the prestige of old age, must be tested against twentieth-century developments. Do alterations of the position of the elderly in the twentieth-century family reflect adverse assumptions about the validity of old age, or do they reveal a more vital, optimistic, self-reliant subculture among the modern old? Certainly the nineteenth-century cultural deterioration affected twentieth-century policy decisions about the elderly, and may affect them still. The question is, how much? Have we escaped, indeed, can we escape, judgments about the elderly that reflect nineteenth-century assumptions? How many policy decisions, even benign in intention, have reflected the nineteenth century's tendency to view old age as peripheral, the elderly as useless? Even the advent of social security, for example, hailed as a major achievement, must be examined for its possible reflection of a tendency to relegate the elderly to the sidelines. And efforts to deal with the social security crisis may certainly reflect this tendency. Thus Myles argues for viewing the elderly as one dependent category among several, contending that the rise of old age dependency is being matched by the reduction in the percentage of dependent children—a twin development predicated on shifts in twentieth-century demographic structure. But we may not be capable of viewing elderly and young in the same light because of contrasting cultural assumptions about their value; and so the changes in balance among dependent groups may be more vexing than Myles admits.

We have not, to be sure, reached the point of easy unification of the various themes of old age history, and there can be no pretense that the chapters in this volume finally accomplish the task. But differences in thematic focus do not reflect complete anarchy, and historians of old age have been reasonably alert to relationships among the various facets of the old age experience in modern history.

Even when incompletely integrated, even when disagreeing in interpretation, historians of the elderly have moved the phenomenon of old age into the fabric of social change. Change is the historian's business—not the mere cataloging of the past for its own sake; and for the most part historians of old age have been quite conscious of this aspect of their task. Old age is not a timeless experience, though the biology of aging has certain enduring ingredients. Nor are the problems of old age brand new, without an ample baggage of cultural and policy precedents. The contributors to this volume share a concern for placing the old age experience in time, and for setting the present concerns of the elderly in this same temporal perspective.

Thus old age historians are clearly moving away from the simplest kind of historical context, which contrasts a relatively unchanging "then" with an equally static "now." In the first place, important continuities connect rather recent developments with patterns in the eighteenth century and earlier. Quadagno notes that half the major characteristics of the Elizabethan Poor Law of 1601 remain intact in approaches to old age welfare policies today—to wit, secular control, means-tested eligibility, and differential care for the "worthy" and "unworthy" poor; two other criteria, local tax responsibility and family responsibility, have been modified but persist and have been suggested recently by the Reagan administration as guidelines for services; and the sixth criterion, the residency requirement, was ruled unconstitutional only in the 1960s. In another area Haber, though stressing important changes in medical outlook during the nineteenth century, sees vital links to earlier medical views. Selective continuities, then, must inform any historical view of old age and must be recognized by anyone attempting even to assess the position of the elderly today.

A second complexity involves the nature of change—for historians do agree that changes have occurred. In important ways, the advent of modern social structures has complicated the lives of older people. Gratton reminds us of the shifts brought to the labor force participation rates of older people by the transition from agriculture to industry. Haber and Cole stress the decline in veneration that seems to be particularly noticeable in American culture. But other changes may have a happier ring. Changes in residence patterns may suggest some weakening of extended family ties, thus evoking a new or heightened loneliness for old age. But they also may suggest a fruitful conversion of older people to the possibility of greater individualism, greater independence of action—in short, productive adoption of values that have gained ground in modern American society. Official policies toward the elderly, especially as developed in this century, while not entirely free from older standards, certainly involve a more elaborate governmental commitment to old age and new political power for older people themselves. Change, then, has been multidirectional and has occurred at different times depending on the aspect of old age involved.

In stressing the significance of continuity and the complexity of change itself, historians are not simply scoring factual points. They are also working more seriously to integrate the elderly into our picture of social change, where complexities are regularly involved. And they are working, fairly consciously, to improve the sense of history on which present judgments can be made. This volume demonstrates a high concern—too high, perhaps, for some historical purists—for linking old age history to a humane approach to the problems of older people in the present. Old age history can thus be used as part of an evaluation of medical attitudes, of family outlook, and certainly of the policies of the state. Without question, historians have demonstrated that approaches to the elderly today cannot be formulated in the abstract. Trends from the past must be taken into account, to either build on or combat.

One final feature of old age history, as conveyed here, demands comment: the field of inquiry is in a decidedly intermediate stage. Basic misconceptions have been attacked. An important overview has been established. We know fundamental lines of development in terms of attitudes toward the elderly, relevant demographic changes, and state policies. We also have some notions, though they deserve more precise exploration, of relevant shifts in economic structure.

To push beyond this important intermediate stage, two elaborations are essential. First, we need further refinements on the points already established. Relatively little additional inquiry into general attitudes is required, though there are still some unresolved issues, particularly in terms of the comparative context for the American outlook. What we need in this area are more detailed examinations of key groups. Already, we know that the physician's outlook, though it may relate to some general cultural norms, has distinctive features. We need similar historical inquiry into the attitudes of others who deal with the elderly, including social workers, who have been rather left out of historians' research in this field to date. To push further on the impact of economic change, we need, as Gratton suggests, some local studies to establish certain specific cases in greater detail, providing grist for further and more precise generalization than is now possible.

The second desirable addition to the existing level of inquiry must involve a more direct examination of the elderly themselves. Here the field of old age history is rather like that of women's studies a decade ago. We know a great deal about attitudes and policies toward the elderly, but too little about the group itself. In the chapters that follow, the elderly are mainly acted upon—by the rise of factory industry, the attitudes of doctors and ministers, the policies of the state, which often derived from factors quite remote from the actual conditions of older people. And perhaps older people *are* more acted upon than some other groups. But we have learned through social history that most groups have their own field of action and their own outlook, and for the elderly this remains to be fully explored.

Changes in demography and family position provide an obvious entry to such inquiry, as we trace the ways in which older people viewed the alterations in family structure, and what they expected the family to provide. Smith and Hareven suggest important lines of study, though it would be good to have a clearer notion of whether the elderly have played a role in causing family changes, such as residential separation, or whether the initiative has come more from younger members. Policy history also, in evoking the impact of expectations by the elderly themselves as they acquire increasing political power, opens important questions about older people as active agents in history, or at least in recent history. Examination of geriatric medicine raises historical problems not only about what doctors did and didn't do, but about actual health conditions and medical expectations on the part of the elderly in major past historical periods. Changes in the emotional life of the elderly and their role in ties of affection also require exploration, one way of approaching historically the important topic of grandparenthood. In sum, the evolution of the elderly must be understood in terms of a double dynamic—the forces operating on the elderly, about which this volume has much to say; and the values and behavior patterns of older people themselves, which still constitute largely unknown territory.

This suggested advance into the real social history of old age must include careful linkage of old age with other periods of life. Mostly, historians in this field have treated their subject as a grouping more than as a stage of life. Hareven and others urge us to deal with the subject from the angle of life experience as well. Here, too, are some analogies from other topical fields in social history that have been developed earlier. Women's history, for example, has increasingly turned from an examination of women apart, to a larger framework of gender history in which interactions with men and with developments in the male outlook are crucial. Old age history has even more to gain from an overall framework of inquiry into stages of life. To date, historians have explored childhood, youth, and now old age as rather discrete entities—and no one has directly ventured a history of middle age at all. The opportunity now exists for a larger vision—which would seek to embrace the interactions among various age groups and the evolving definition and impact of stages of life—as a goal in itself and as a means of improving the grasp of the experience of particular segments like the elderly. The increasing tendency of modern society to categorize people by age—from age-graded nursery schools to retirement communities—has surely encouraged our impulse to take up age groups one by one, but even this process of age grading needs a wider framework for full understanding. And the phenomenon of increasing segregation of the elderly, discussed in this volume in terms of residential patterns and age-specific policies, ultimately requires a wider framework as well, to clarify its impact on all the age groups involved. How, for example, has the experience of old age been affected by the fact that most death is now concentrated among the elderly, whereas before 1900 children shared with the old the incidence of high death rates?

That important work still remains to be done can come as no great surprise. This volume establishes some definite conclusions that do not need additional study; sets some vital debates, such as the tension between cultural and economic factors in shaping the old age experience; and points directly to subjects for further research, as in the matter of filling in some of the blanks in the modern history of old people in families. It also works toward a vital need for dissemination in the field of old age history. The gains historians have made are not yet fully enough assimilated into other branches of gerontology; they have yet to penetrate the assumptions of many relevant policymakers and geriatric practitioners. Too many people, in short, remain unaware of the changing context for old age in modern society; the challenge not only of adding to the research storehouse but of disseminating its contents is a real one, and to that end the following chapters valuably contribute.

Amid all their disagreements and differences in emphasis, old age historians are united by a lively sympathy for the objects of their study. Various experts, and policymakers above all, particularly in a bureaucratized society like ours, have an obvious interest in routinizing their contacts with the elderly and applying increasingly simple formulas to them. Already gerontologists have told us that the elderly are in fact a

quite varied group, embracing—some contend—more diversity in behavior and personality than any other adult age category. In their own
way, historians contribute also to the essential battle against some of
the routinizing tendencies of a bureaucratic society, by showing the
strengths and sorrows of old age past and the complexities that have
accompanied moving the final stages of life from past to present.

PART I

THE STATE OF THE FIELD

The New History of the Aged: A Critique

Exploration of the history of the elderly has just passed that Colum-
bian stage when discovery by chance governs investigation. That phase
has made fundamental contributions to our understanding. Confidence
in the dominant paradigm, the "old world" of modernization theory,
has been shaken, and innovative hypotheses have been proposed to or-
ganize what has been discovered to guide future work. The new historians of aging have exposed the weaknesses of modernization theory, which once dominated what historical sense there was in this
subject; the great distinction in their work is their emphasis on attitudinal rather than structural change. Modernization explained the history of the aged in terms of the structural differences between traditional and modern societies. But the new history is informed by the
notion that ageism is an independent force; that "culture" powerfully
influences the status of the aged.

Modernization theory has long provided social gerontologists an explanation for the circumstances of the population they study. So it is
helpful to review the growing conflict over this interpretation, to assess the contributions of new works in the history of the American aged
from the seventeenth to the mid-twentieth centuries, and to suggest a
course for future research.

THE CRITIQUE OF MODERNIZATION THEORY

The application of modernization theory to the American elderly stemmed from early twentieth-century concern over old age poverty and dependency: it was presumed that the shift from an agricultural to an industrial nation was the source of the older American's plight. This interpretation of the decline of the aged was an intuitive construct: it appealed to common sense, nostalgia, and fear of industrialization and urbanization. The first advocates of old age pensions seized upon "modernization"—though they did not call it that—as a ready explanation for the pitiful state of the elderly in industrial America and as a justification for extraordinary remedial measures.[1]

In the 1950s, modernization flowered as a general scholarly theory when American intellectuals, faced with an emerging Third World, sought a Western model to explain the process of economic development.[2] This more refined concept dignified the intuition of the leaders of the social insurance movement, and reference to modernization theory among social gerontologists soon reached dogmatic proportions.[3]

Among numerous theses advanced in modernization theory's application to the aged, the following are the most consistent.[4] In stable agricultural societies, the aged enjoy relatively good economic circumstances and high status. This good fortune follows from five conditions. First, landed property is power in agricultural economies; the old tend to control such property, hence they maintain authority over a needy younger generation. Second, the family is the unit of economic organization, and the property rights of the older members result in a very direct and forceful influence over the lives of the younger members. Since the family is extended, patriarchal authority is quite broad and security in old age is guaranteed. Third, as farmers who control their own employment, old people continue to perform a work role that is useful and valued. Fourth, high fertility and high mortality result in a very small proportion of the aged in the population, a circumstance said to enhance their status. Finally, in such societies illiteracy is the norm, and the aged are repositories of wisdom born of long experience; it is they who pass on to the younger generation skills, knowledge, and traditions (including the veneration of age).

In modern societies, the economic circumstances and status of the aged are relatively low. Landed property is no longer the essential source of wealth and power in an industrial economy, and the family is no longer the unit of economic organization. Under these conditions, the aged lose control over younger family members because they have no compelling economic authority. The extended family disintegrates into nuclear units, which are more suitable for the geographic and economic mobility characteristic of industrial societies. As workers who sell their labor power, old people are not superior to other workers, and since they are often judged to be inferior, they suffer high unemployment (i.e., retirement). This low labor force participation implies both economic losses and status losses: the aged lose the work role necessary to normal status. The demographic transition characteristic of modern societies results in large proportions of the aged in the population, a condition that presumably lowers status. In a literate population, knowledge is greater among the young than the aged (who have received less and inferior schooling), and communication of information, skills, and tradition does not depend on the old-timers. Finally, as a result of these changes, large numbers of the elderly become impoverished and dependent, a "deviant" group.

Criticism of this theoretical view grew first out of a general distaste for its dichotomous shape.[5] No self-preserving historian appreciates uniformity among traditional societies, convergence of modern ones, and the inapplicability of findings in one upon the other. Social gerontologists objected to the convergence of contemporary societies and argued that cultural forces might overcome the impact of industrialization.[6]

But the most striking criticism sprang from the startling discovery that the nuclear household was the predominant form in preindustrial Western societies. This discovery led to the conclusion that the aged could not have exercised power through an extended family. Since social gerontologists had begun to find that the aged in modern societies maintain close contact with their kin, a sharp break between past and present seemed implausible. Other historical research tapped a vein of pronounced hostility toward the aged in traditional societies.[7] Some writers found changes in fertility before or well after industrial or urban development.[8] And American historians threw even more suspicion on structural interpretations by locating a shift from veneration toward vilification of the aged that was independent of industrialization, urbanization, and demographic transition.[9]

These criticisms exposed the weaknesses in the broad and vague generalizations characteristic of modernization theory. In the main, the criticisms attacked the structural dynamic of the theory: the new his-torians debunk the golden age, reject structural causation, and focus our attention on the force of ageism in the history of the elderly.

This attitudinal view is at best incomplete and at worst dead wrong. Nowhere in the literature of modernization theory can there be found a sustained analysis of the continued control of the means of production by the aged in agricultural economies, a structural condition quite independent of modernization's fuzzy generalities. Evidence of the impact of property possession can be traced in anthropological research and in historical studies of colonial America and peasant Europe. The anthropology of old age reveals cultural diversity within a cultural universe: where older people control resources necessary to satisfy the needs of younger people, the elders' status will generally be high.[10]

Such control is most likely in societies where property may be privately held. Family tensions and intergenerational conflicts—often cited as proof that the elderly were not well regarded in the past[11]—are actually symptoms of the power of older persons in the economic inheritance system. Historical study of peasant Europe and colonial America provides similar evidence of the authority available to elders in landowning economies.[12] Such status relied only indirectly on age, but its significance in age relations is obvious. In such societies, the natural lot of growing older was to come into possession of the means of production and, with that, to exercise some control over one's environment and over younger generations.

One would fully expect that an economic transition of the magnitude of industrialization, which undermined the previous economic system and its contingent age relations, would have a most direct effect on the place of the aged in society. But the most powerful new histories of aging in America explicitly reject this logic: they see the structural change from farm to factory as of little consequence. The decline in the elderly's status is connected to an independent force, ageism. Cultural attitude is found to have more importance than structure. It is on this presumption that the new history of the American aged has been written.

THE NEW HISTORY OF THE AMERICAN ELDERLY

David Hackett Fischer's Bland-Lee Lectures at Clark University led to the first new interpretation of the history of aging in America. Fischer

argued that American history demonstrated the failure of modernization theory because the decline in the status of the aged occurred *be-*
fore "industrialization, urbanization, and the growth of mass education . . . [before] 'modernization' in the ordinary meaning of the term."
Fischer proposed that a period of exaltation of the aged (1607–1820)
was shattered by a "new set of ideas" that resulted in a "revolution
in age relations" (1770–1820). American society was from this point
set on a "straight and stable" course toward the triumph of geronto-
phobia (1770–1970).[13] After initial enthusiasm, most scholars have come
to doubt Fischer's periodization if not his ideological determinism.[14]
The urban and cosmopolitan sources that figure so prominently in
Fischer's work are not strong proof for a transformation in the lives of
the mass of men and women in America, who as farmers were part of
a local, familial, and traditional network. A fine sense of this distinction is given in a remark made by the Reverend William Bentley of
Salem, Massachusetts, when visiting rural Andover in 1793. Bentley
noted that the country people gathered to dance "in classes due to their
ages, not with regard to their condition as in the Seaport Towns."[15]

In fact, Fischer's book provides an unintentional confirmation of one
part of the theory he attacks. In a fine account of seventeenth- and
eighteenth-century New England, he finds that this society's prescriptive literature cautioned the young to venerate their elders as wise and
as specially marked by God.[16] The aged often served in high office; as
owners of property, they exercised great authority over their sons and
daughters, such that "land was an instrument of generational politics"
and "youth was the hostage of age."[17] The preeminence of age created a disposition on the part of great numbers of people to report
themselves older than they were: in two large censuses taken in 1776
and 1787 (Maryland and Connecticut), the age bias revealed in the distribution of reported ages runs in the opposite direction of all known
modern censuses, showing a clear preference for greater age.[18] This is
a most exciting finding! The bias toward youth is so pronounced in our
time that we must conclude that the view Americans took toward age
was utterly different in the late eighteenth century. No more telling
piece of evidence exists in the social history of the aged.

When we combine Fischer's evidence with the numerous studies extant of the power and security attending the property-owning elderly in
America's agricultural, family based economy,[19] the picture of a "traditional" world is remarkably like that which modernization theorists

tried to paint; thus a father in colonial Virginia directs in his will: "Sons Michael, Rupert, and Matthew are to obey their mother and follow her orders or they are not to get their land."[20] It is a telling irony that a book so hostile to modernization theory will be remembered mainly for confirming that theory's argument about preindustrial society. This reading of early America is reinforced by other studies of old age, which find that respect for the aged in early New England reveals a "gerontocratic society founded . . . 'by patriarchs, which gave office to its elders, not its youth, and believed in hierarchy.' "[21]

Fischer's very convincing case for the exaltation of the aged in early America is not succeeded by a persuasive one for a sudden social revolution in age relations in the period 1770–1820. Deterioration of status did occur on the heavily populated Eastern seaboard during the eighteenth century, because farm holdings were too small for distribution among children. As Daniel Scott Smith has observed, "During most of the eighteenth century scarcity increased and the older matrix of values sustaining respect for the aged withered."[22] However, as James Henretta has argued, this was a long process, which began anew in each area of frontier settlement.[23] Most of the evidence that Fischer produced for sudden change has been effectively criticized.[24] Census data, which were powerful as a proof of the veneration of the aged in the eighteenth century, offer little evidence of a "deep change" in the period 1770–1820. Fischer presents only two reliable censuses, from 1776 and 1787. These show a pronounced preference for age. No census data whatsoever are presented for other dates in the deep change period. A "small sample" drawn from the census of 1850 does not constitute a proof about the period in question, and findings of moderate bias toward youth in it are quite ambiguous.[25] Even if accurate, a bias toward youth in the first half of the nineteenth century would not be in conflict with modernization theory, since industrialization was well under way by 1850. It remains a much more reasonable hypothesis to view decline in the status of the aged as fairly steady, underwritten across the nineteenth century by the relative decline of the agricultural economy. Nonetheless, this is but hypothesis, for we remain quite in the dark for solid evidence about the crucial transition period of the nineteenth century.[26]

Rather more light has been shed on the nineteenth century by Andrew Achenbaum's *Old Age in the New Land*, the second major history of old age in America and the second to stress attitudinal change as the driving force. Again, industrialization, urbanization, and demographic change cannot explain declines in status, because in this case they occur both before and after the onset of ageism.[27] Achenbaum commands a great range of evidence and he uses his sources with care and sensitivity. In an exhaustive survey of middle-class literature since 1790, he found ambiguity toward the aged at all times, but a relatively favorable climate before the Civil War. In the late nineteenth century, a decisive break occurred—a broad denial of age and a cult of youth—with hostility to age manifest in medical views and in perceptions of the aged worker.[28] Achenbaum was the first to identify this as a critical period (in a 1974 article), and most scholars now accept this periodization. His argument that the attitudinal shift at this time occurred independently of structural change (the aged's occupational and demographic status) depends on an analysis of labor force participation rates, to which we will return.

Carole Haber agrees with Achenbaum that the late nineteenth century brought forth a new order that oppressed the aged.[29] Her most intriguing work touches on the equation of old age with sickness. In *Beyond Sixty-Five*, Haber has inaugurated the critical history of geriatrics, pointing to its simultaneous reliance on advances in scientific medicine and cultural prejudices. The late nineteenth-century result was the segregation of the aged in a "postclimacteric" medical category that labeled old age as illness but offered no cure. Haber finds the same bureaucratic emphasis on classifications and segregation of the aged as dependents in studies of the labor market, institutionalization, and charity work. In a clear split from the attitudinal school,[30] she connects new discriminatory practices directly to structural change in economic and familial relations. Although such connections are strained for medical advances first realized in France, her recognition of the reciprocal relationship between increasing structural poverty among older people and the particularistic bureaucratic response to it among the "helping professionals" greatly enhances our understanding of the origins of ageism. Haber argues that a new concept of the work cycle, terminated by the "innovation" of retirement, developed at this time, motivated first by an excessive labor supply and second by the tendency of various elites to highlight the incapacity of the aged. Her labor supply argument does not fit well with employers' favorable attitudes toward immigration at the turn of the century, nor with the logic of capitalists' need for large labor markets; and her treatment of retirement, while sensitive to the negative effects of pensions as a substitute for work, fails to address the most obvious question: What proportion of workers was actually affected by these ideas? Pension plans and mandatory retirement applied to very few workers as late as 1930. It is debatable whether mandatory retirement has ever affected a large proportion of American workers, yet most of the new historians use any instance of it as proof of the general disfranchisement of the aged.[31] Still, Haber, along with William Graebner, has provided the best insight yet into the development of an idea—retirement—whose eventual implementation in the Social Security Act was to rewrite all age relations.

Thomas Cole has looked to religion as an index to the nineteenth-century history of the aged; he joins James Farrell in arguing that changes in religious expression had important repercussions for the elderly,[32] and Cole and Farrell show the pernicious effects of Evangelism on the integration of the aged with other generations. In emphasizing self-discipline and self-control, a "rigid form of moral self government," the evangelical ministers connected age with decay and dependency; and "old age emerged as the most poignant—and loathsome—symbol of the decline of bourgeois self-reliance."[33] Cole paraphrases Achenbaum in his identification of the causal pattern in the history of old age: "Values, ideas, feelings, perceptions, and attitudes toward aging, old age, and the aged clearly changed prior to changes in longevity, age-composition of the population, employment, and living arrangements."[34]

However, little concrete evidence is provided to prove this contention—most of Cole's sources are men from a bourgeois stratum most likely to reflect the impact of industrialization. Cole actually relies quite consistently on the links between religious forces and the capitalistic social order that they supported. His most stimulating observation is to see the connection between "the transformation of the Protestant theology of aging" and "the ideology and structure of an emerging liberal capitalist order."[35] In sometimes neglecting structural effects, Cole turns away from this insight. It is not necessary to make religion a function of capitalism to see that changes in economic life (e.g., the separation of work from the household) encouraged a religious climate more hostile to aging.

Family historians have focused attention on the composition of households and the timing of life events. Tamara Hareven and her colleagues have given their attention to the life course, or stages of the life cycle for various cohorts (calculating the timing of "transitions," such as marriage).[36] This research has given us a new understanding of the typical experience of the aged, has emphasized the absence of sharp discontinuities from life at younger ages, and has shown that such life events as a long "empty nest" period for older couples is a phenomenon that has become prevalent only in our own time.

Potentially the most important undertaking in the field of family research is the Newberry Library project, funded by the National Institute on Aging and headed by Daniel Scott Smith. Smith and his colleagues have taken national samples of the aged American population from the 1880 and 1900 manuscript censuses,[37] have recorded the somewhat limited information provided for individuals, and have also recorded data regarding the family and neighborhood of these aged persons. This additional material will permit much more sensitive analysis of kinship, occupation, and ethnicity. The samples taken are not probability samples, and Smith has anticipated criticisms of the sampling procedures chosen.[38]

Historians are more likely to object to conceptual than to sampling features. Only in 1900 was a large sample of the aged population taken; attention in the 1880 census was given to a special sample of the aged black population. What is lost is the opportunity to test differences between the two dates and to estimate what variables were significant in causing change. In this cross-sectional design, age, period, and cohort effects are confounded.

Smith acknowledges that the design limits analysis of change over time but justifies this decision by arguing that "change in the *family* status of the older population has been low historically, with most of the change occurring only in recent decades" (emphasis mine).[39] In essence, Smith rejects modernization theory's contention that industrialization and urbanization undermined the status of the aged. This assumption will come as a surprise to some of his colleagues. Its consequence, in terms of Smith's research design, is that we do not have two points in the period of rapid industrialization and urbanization for measurement.

Although confined on measurement of change, the studies that have issued from this project have given us an informative description of old age at the turn of the century: Older people were relatively independent, they tended to head or be spouses of heads of households, and the men among them had high labor force participation rates.

Findings also support the continuity of life that Hareven has emphasized. The sampling procedure allowed interesting examination of the
aged's neighborhood and kinship: 15 percent of the 1900 elderly sample had kin of the same surname living no more than five households
away.[40] Preliminary analysis of household composition shows little in-
stability by reason of age; thus marital status is a much better predictor
than age of an older man's chances of heading his household.[41] (It may
be objected that age is highly correlated with the significant variables,
and its indirect effects, such as increasing the likelihood of a change
in marital status, are not measured.) The Smith group has shown that
the three-generation household was a rare experience for the turn-of-
the-century American, because of the aged's household independence
and because the three-generation family was relatively uncommon. But
in 1880, 35 to 40 percent of those over sixty-five lived in extended
households.[42] When an older person was not the head or spouse of the
head, he or, more often, she coresided with a child. Thus the family
was "the welfare institution for old people"; the investigators do not
believe this was a product of "economic necessity," despite the fact
that the coresidents were generally aged women.[43]

In his most recent examination of these data, Smith concludes that
the area of change in the family history of the elderly is the twentieth
century, especially the period since 1940. But he is skeptical of structural interpretations that view such change as a product of the welfare
state or shifts in the composition of the aged population. Smith's most
striking assertion is that rising income cannot explain recent declines
in coresidence of children and aged parents. Using four proxies for income in 1900, he finds the lowest level of coresidence in poorer families and high coresidence levels in the middle classes. He concludes
that some change of values must have occurred. While the income effect is not really tested (since even the middle classes of 1900 may
have low incomes by 1970 standards), the distribution of coresidence
runs against what is to be expected and should prompt continued inquiry.[44]

Other quantitative studies provide valuable assessments of contemporary gerontological theory. Although social gerontologists sometimes conceive of residential segregation of the aged as a very recent
phenomenon,[45] Susan Kleinberg has found pronounced segregation in
nineteenth-century Pittsburgh, as has Gratton in twentieth-century
Boston.[46] Kleinberg's study of occupations in a city dominated by heavy

industry and undergoing rapid technological change leads her to support a basic tenet of modernization theory: "extreme age variation in occupations [was] rooted in the nature of the occupations themselves." However, any cross-sectional data will show such uneven distribution. Gratton's study of Boston reveals that variation in occupational distribution by age was in part a product of cohort effect.[47] All measurements of age discrimination must consider cohort effect.

THE PROBLEMS OF THE TWENTIETH CENTURY

Until quite recently, twentieth-century histories of the elderly have focused on and been influenced by the welfare reform movements that sprang up around the poverty of old people.[48] Fischer's twentieth-century section is largely derivative and prone to error because of that.[49] Christopher Lasch ties the degradation of the elderly in contemporary America to the rise of the narcissistic personality, which dreads age; since Lasch believes that the "helping professions"—from medical experts to social reformers—have encouraged this personality, he has little faith in their capacity to address the needs of older people. Lasch concedes that the objective conditions of the aged have declined in a society that finds the old useless and "forces them to retire," but what lies at the heart of negative views of aging is really an "irrational panic."[50] As in all Lasch's recent work, the nineteenth-century bourgeois emerge as knights of a better moral order; yet the work of Cole and Farrell suggests that it was this retinue's moral code that first devalued age.

Historians like Fischer, Haber, and Achenbaum tend to see twentieth-century developments as an inevitable working-out of a key deterioration they place at some point in the nineteenth century. Achenbaum's twentieth-century material is rewarding, especially in summarizing social security policy, but it is marred by a failure to address the negative effects of New Deal legislation on the labor force participation of the elderly.[51] His optimistic view of the mid-nineteenth-century aged worker leads to the judgment that decline in status came all in a rush in the twentieth century, propelled by "negative attitudes" toward the aged. Since "ideas . . . have a life of their own," the rise of ageism after the Civil War was not directly connected to "*actual* demographic, occupational, and economic" conditions.[52] Instead, like Fischer's "deep change" but a hundred years later, an attitudinal shift sets in motion a general decline in the status of the elderly. Insofar as social security changes the periodization in Achenbaum's account, it does so in the most traditional way, as a legislative "solution" to the problems of the aged: "something had to be done to help older Americans in need."[53] In *Shades of Gray*, Achenbaum gives his readers a Whiggish history of the Social Security Act (SSA), inventing a set of dichotomized American values that influence and are influenced by legislation showing "an unprecedented concern for the elderly by the federal government."[54] He rejects as deterministic the (measurable) hypotheses offered by other scholars, and argues that ideas and values must be taken "seriously" in explaining the evolution of old age policies.[55]

INDUSTRIAL CAPITALISM AND THE OLDER WORKER

The core of Achenbaum's ideational argument lies in its treatment of the aged labor force and returns us to the debate between structure and attitude. Achenbaum draws two labor force conclusions: (1) nineteenth-century industrialization did not undermine the status of the aged worker;[56] while (2) late nineteenth-century concepts of the "obsolescence" of the aged did, and led to steady declines in their labor force participation in the twentieth century.[57] The significance of these conclusions is patent. They form the foundation for an ideological explanation founded on ageism rather than a structural interpretation based on the economy. And they are views congenial to other scholars who locate a great shift of opinion in the late nineteenth century. Graebner, whose argument is utterly opposed to Achenbaum's for the twentieth century, accepts without question his contentions about the aged labor force in the nineteenth century.

Achenbaum's two conclusions rest on his analysis of the labor force activity of older workers. For the nineteenth century, he asserts that "the percentage of elderly white persons who were working declined only slightly, if at all, between 1840 and 1890."[58] But after 1890, the rates fall steadily. This treatment of the twentieth-century aged labor force is like that of most writers,[59] except that Achenbaum rejects industrialization as the culprit. In reviewing occupational and labor force statistics from 1890 to 1970, Achenbaum adopts a periodization centered on the late nineteenth century, which is certainly misleading since the world of the aged worker was shattered by the New Deal.[60] Achenbaum presents evidence that supports this very point, using a "drop-off ratio" for each census year from 1890 to 1970.[61] The drop-off ratios provide a measure of the falling participation of older workers in comparison to other workers. Examining this evidence, Achenbaum argues that his data

> reveal that the ratio of men over sixty-five years old in all occupations was 77% as large as that of men working between the ages of forty-five and sixty-four in 1890. It dropped fifteen percentage points over the next forty years and has plummeted thirty-four additional points during the past forty years. Significantly, this long-term trend exists in both the agricultural and nonagrarian sectors of the economy.[62]

There are long-term trends here, but they are not what Achenbaum makes of them.

Let us examine the period 1890–1930 in particular (See Table 1.1). Achenbaum notes without further comment that the forty years after 1930 show much more dramatic losses. But his attention to a 15 percent drop in the previous forty-year period obscures its cause. In agricultural occupations there is *no* drop-off, only variations, in the entire period 1890–1930. Older men maintain their position relative to men forty-five to sixty-four. In nonagricultural fields, older male percentages drop from 58 to 52 percent. During this period of rapid industrialization, the proportion of men in agriculture dropped equally for men forty-five to sixty-four and sixty-five and over. The proportion employed in nonagricultural fields rose, slightly more rapidly for men forty-five to sixty-four than for older men.

Turning to the combination of the stable agricultural area and the slightly declining agricultural fields—"all occupations"—we find the surprisingly steep 15 percent decline between 1890 and 1930. As we have seen, this collapse cannot be explained by declines in either of its component categories. Indeed, its explanation lies in the relationship *between* them, for across time the aged labor force is moving from an advantageous-to-the-aged agricultural area to the lower participation nonagricultural fields. It is this movement that explains the overall drop, not a change in participation rates themselves.

The labor force effects on New Deal legislation radically transformed this pattern of stable participation rates with population move-

Table 1.1
Drop-off ratio (percent), men 65 and over to men 45–64

Census	Agriculture, Fishing, or Mining	Nonagricultural Fields	All Occupations
	%	%	%
1890	89	58	77
1900	93	59	74
1920	82	53	64
1930	90	52	62
1940	87	44	55
1950	84	38	46
1960	68	30	34
1970	56	26	28

Note: Drop-off ratio = $\dfrac{\dfrac{\text{males 65 \& over in occupational category}}{\text{all males 65 \& over}}}{\dfrac{\text{males 45-64 in occupational category}}{\text{all males 45-64}}}$ X 100%

Source: Achenbaum, *Old Age in the New Land,* Table 5.6, p. 102, from Census
data; the author does not indicate whether figures were adjusted for changes
from gainful worker to labor force concepts.

ment from a higher to a lower field (simply, the shift from an agricultural to an industrial labor force.) Quite suddenly the drop-off ratio in
nonagricultural fields plummets, and, when social security is extended
to farm work in the 1950s, the ratio drops in agricultural fields as well.
"All occupations" follows suit; a trump card against the aged worker.
It is quite clear that we have viewed two distinct periods in the history
of older workers, and the dividing point lies in the midst of the twentieth century.

Indeed, the nineteenth century probably witnessed no single critical period. Achenbaum's belief that the elderly's labor force activity did not decline before 1890 rests on a technical defect in calculation,[63] and future research should show that labor force activity in the nineteenth century exhibited the same slowly declining pattern found in the early twentieth century, as the shift from an agricultural economy proceeded. Farms and the small-scale enterprises that evolved from skilled trades favored the aged, who often controlled access to skill and capital.[64] But the development of large-scale industry undermined their status.[65] It diminished their capacity to control their own employment as well as that of the sons and daughters on whom they depended in old age. It reduced, although it did not eliminate, the value of their bequests.[66] Even for those who farmed, industrial cities drew away from their influence the children they hoped would honor and work for them in the traditional way.[67] The *fin du siècle* witnessed a great transition in the industrial work force, the destruction of the skill base in primary industries like steel, and the proliferation of scientific management: conscious acts on the part of employers that stripped away the advantages of older workers.[68]

Even so, there is little proof that the aged's position within the industrial sector declined more dramatically during the early twentieth century. Scattered findings from the mid-nineteenth through the early twentieth centuries show a fairly consistent and stable pattern of high labor force participation and some accumulation of wealth for the majority, and downward mobility, poverty, and dependency on children for a minority.[69] Since the debate among economists is not whether, but how much, social security reduces labor force activity, historians would be well advised to consider carefully what kind of labor force was emerging before such welfare measures. The slight *increase* in labor force participation among men aged fifty-five to sixty-four between 1900 and 1930 should give pause to those who rely on ageism to explain changes in the work lives of the elderly.[70] Perhaps most important is the relatively *moderate* decline in participation in the nonagricultural sector *per se* between 1890 and 1930. Gratton's Boston study shows nearly flat labor force rates for older men between 1890 and 1930 (59.4 percent to 54.6 percent, adjusted for gainful worker concept).[71] Older women increased their work rates. In general, the labor force of this period was aging, and the proportion of aged men in it was increasing. The transfer from agricultural to industrial occupations continued to lower labor force participation, but notwithstanding the cultural interpretation, the rate of this process may have declined. Therefore, an explanation for continued deterioration requires attention to twentieth-century developments.

And here, fortunately, we have a fine recent study in Graebner's *History of Retirement*. Although the early twentieth-century phase of his argument is weak, Graebner's treatment of the SSA is brilliant. His revisionist view of the New Deal leads to a powerful critique of conventional interpretations of the history of old age. Graebner's argument is in one sense attitudinal: like Haber, he locates the rise of a retirement concept pernicious to the aged in the late nineteenth century, and, like Haber, he provides little evidence of its extent or impact. His discussion of unions (too often confused with the working class), government bureaucrats, educators, and management eventually loses coherence; it is never clear who is formulating the new view, who is resisting, and why. Other than a brief appeal to "corporate capitalism" and an underriding implication that older workers were inefficient in periods of technological change, Graebner provides no explanation of why the idea of retirement occurred at this time. By the fourth chapter, retirement has taken on so many "functions" that the reader must suspect that a functional view is not reasonable here.

But Graebner does demonstrate that a series of experiments in retirement, stimulated first by concern for efficiency and subsequently by fear of unemployment, led directly to the Social Security Act. Exploring the history of railroad retirement in the early thirties and the inner workings of the Committee on Economic Security, which drafted social security legislation, Graebner concludes that the 1935 act was a "piece of unemployment legislation,"[72] "designed within a labor market context" to make room for younger workers.[73] This has been said before, but never with such penetrating malice.

Some reservations about this account are necessary. The SSA and the state pensions that preceded it were popular measures, opposed by powerful elites, elites that receive little attention in *A History of Retirement*. Graebner virtually ignores the state old age pension movement, and he misreads it to think that it was, until the mid-twenties, motivated by a desire for efficiency. It was the working class, not the efficiency experts, who carried the pension campaigns. Yet it is clear that the evidence sustains his argument that the architects of policy in the Committee on Economic Security were moved by the idea of making room for younger workers as were those popular persuaders of congressmen, the leaders of the Townsendite movement.[74] What Graebner has provided historians (and social gerontologists) is this critical insight: that the SSA created dependency as much as it redressed it, and that it was "the fate of the elderly to serve the economic and social needs of other age groups."[75]

This revisionist interpretation of the SSA opens up the meaning of retirement in contemporary America. In a *tour de force* review of the postwar period, Graebner illustrates the uses to which the elderly were put by business, government, their own advocacy groups, and by academia.[76] Serious charges are raised against the critical integrity of social gerontology,[77] and Graebner exposes the cynicism at the heart of recent "reformist" attacks on retirement. Graebner's argument uses both the political economy of advanced capitalism and negative attitudes toward the aged as explanations for this course of events; his analysis is devastating to modernization theory's account of the twentieth century, which folds social security legislation into a natural, immanent process of change.[78]

Graebner's work should lead historians to play their part in the debate among social scientists over the political economy of the welfare state. In fact, the most interesting historical analysis of the fate of the elderly has recently been conducted by sociologists, who have provided both theoretical and empirical studies of the origins, growth, and current crisis of the Western welfare state. In some of these works, the "state" takes an independence of action that historians may find mystical as well as mystifying. But the insight in this literature—that the capitalist state uses welfare systems to balance the demands of the monopoly sector against the demands of political constituencies—delivers the *coup de grace* to modernization theory, in which welfare legislation is a depoliticized response to need. In particular, John Myles's stimulating discussion of the retirement wage is crucial to the history of old age, since his interpretation reveals the connections among the structural effects of industrialization, the deliberate building of the welfare state, and the satisfaction of working-class demands for a wage free from market criteria.[79]

Having exposed the weakness of modernization theory, the new historians have generally rejected structural factors in favor of culture: change in values, the rise of ageism. But their premise that industrialization did not undermine the advantages of the aged in an agricultural economy remains unproved, and the first task facing future researchers is to assess the consequences for older men and women of the loss of control of the means of production with the rise of a wage-labor system.

The next task, a critical history of the origins of the welfare state, goes beyond the structural effects of industrialization. We need to consider the SSA as both a democratic measure and one which served specific economic interests, and we should hesitate to assign this act any final meaning without considering the history and function of social security in other nations. That these questions are abstruse goes without saying: they are the difficult projects that an energetic and productive new history has given us.

NOTES

1. A. Epstein, *The Challenge of the Aged* (New York, 1928), pp. 1–13.

2. Raymond Grew, "Modernization and Its Discontents," *American Behavioral Scientist* 21 (1977): 298–312.

3. D. Cowgill and L. D. Holmes, eds., *Aging and Modernization* (New York, 1972).

4. A critical scholar can find every conceivable excess in modernization literature; another scholar could reproduce the theory with no flaws. My purpose is to recapitulate its consistent theses about aging in history. The sources from which my summary is drawn are E. W. Burgess, "Aging in Western Culture," in E. W. Burgess, ed., *Aging in Western Societies* (Chicago, 1960); E. W. Burgess, "Résumé and Implications," in Burgess *Aging*; M. Clark, "The Anthropology of Aging: A New Area for Studies of Culture and Personality," *Gerontologist* 7 (1967): 55–64; M. Clark, "Cultural Values and Dependency in Later Life," in Cowgill and Holmes, *Aging and Modernization*; M. Clark and B. G. Anderson, *Culture and Aging: An Anthropological Study of Older Americans* (Springfield, Ill., 1967); F. Cottrell, "The Technological and Societal Basis of Aging," in C. Tibbitts, ed., *Handbook of Social Gerontology* (Chicago, 1960); D. Cowgill, "A Theory of Aging in Cross-Cultural Perspective," in Cowgill and Holmes, *Aging and Modernization*; D. Cowgill, "The Aging of Populations and Societies," in F. R. Eksele, ed., *Political Consequences of Aging: Annals of the American Academy of Political and Social Science* (Philadelphia, 1974); Cowgill and Holmes, *Aging and Modernization*; J. Goody, "Aging in Non-Industrial Societies," in R. H. Binstock and E. Shanas, eds., *Handbook of Aging and the Social Sciences* (New York, 1976); L. D. Holmes, "Trends in Anthropological Gerontology: From Simmons to the Seventies," *International Journal of Aging and Human Development* 7

(1976): 211–220; R. A. Kalish, "Of Children and Grandfathers: A Speculative Essay on Dependency," *Gerontologist* 7 (1967): 65–69; R. J. Maxwell and P. Silverman, "Information and Esteem: Cultural Considerations in the Treatment of the Aged," *Aging and Human Development* 1 (1970): 361–392; Margaret Mead, "Review of *Culture and Aging* by M. Clark and B. G. Anderson," *Journal of Gerontology* 23 (1968): 232–233; E. B. Palmore, "Sociological Aspects of Aging," in E. W. Busse and E. Pfeiffer, eds , *Behavior and Modification in Late Life* (Boston, 1969); E. Palmore and K. Manton, "Modernization and the Status of the Aged: International Correlations," *Journal of Gerontology* 29 (1974): 205–210; Talcott Parsons, "Age and Sex in the Social Structure of the United States," *American Sociological Review* 7 (1942): 604–616; Talcott Parsons, "The Kinship System of the Contemporary United States," *American Anthropologist* 45 (1943): 22–38; Talcott Parsons and R. F. Bales, *Family, Socialization and Interaction Process* (London, 1956); Talcott Parsons and G. M. Platt, "Higher Education and Changing Socialization," in M. W. Riley and A. Foner, *Aging and Society*, vol. III, *A Sociology of Age Stratification* (New York, 1972); Michel A. Philibert, "The Emergence of Social Gerontology," *Journal of Social Issues* 21 (1965): 4–12; I. Rosow, *Socialization of Old Age* (Berkeley, 1974); L. Simmons, "Aging in Preindustrial Societies," in Tibbitts, *Handbook*; L. Simmons, *The Role of the Aged in Primitive Society* (Hamden, Conn., 1970; originally published 1945); Keith Thomas, "Age and Authority in Early Modern England," *Proceedings of the British Academy* 62 (1976): 205–248; C. Tibbitts, "Origin, Scope, and Fields of Social Gerontology," in Tibbitts, *Handbook.*

5. W. Andrew Achenbaum, "Humanistic Perspectives on Modernization Theory," paper presented at annual scientific meeting of the Gerontological Society, San Diego, November 1980; Peter Laslett, "Societal Development and Aging," in Binstock and Shanas, eds., *Handbook*; Dean C. Tipps, "Modernization Theory and the Comparative Study of Societies: A Critical Perspective," *Comparative Studies in Society and History* 15 (1973): 199–226.

6. E. B. Palmore, *The Honorable Elders: A Cross-Cultural Analysis of Aging in Japan* (Durham, N.C., 1975); but see T. Kii, "Recent Extension of Retirement Age in Japan," *Gerontologist* 19 (1979): 481–486; Brian Gratton, *Boston's Elderly, 1890–1950: Work, Family and Dependency* (Ph.D. dissertation, Boston University, 1980), p. 20.

7. W. Andrew Achenbaum, *Old Age in the New Land: The American Experience since 1790* (Baltimore, 1978); W. Andrew Achenbaum and Peter N. Stearns, "Essay: Old Age and Modernization," *Gerontologist* 18 (1978): 307–312; Philippe Ariès, "Review of *Growing Old in America* by D. H. Fischer," *New Republic* 2 (1977); 32–33; John Demos, "Old Age in Early New England," in David D. Van Tassel, ed., *Aging, Death and the Completion of Being* (Philadelphia, 1979); David Hackett Fischer, *Growing Old in America* (rev. ed.) (New York, 1978); David Hackett Fischer and Lawrence Stone,

"Growing Old: An Exchange," *New York Review of Books*, 15 September 1977; E. Friedmann, "The Impact of Aging on the Social Structure," in Tibbitts, *Handbook*; Jon Hendricks and C. D. Hendricks, "The Age Old Question of Old Age: Was It Really So Much Better Back When?" *International Journal of Aging and Human Development* 8 (1977–78): 130–154; R. Kastenbaum and B. Ross, "Historical Perspectives on Care," in J. G. Howells, ed., *Modern Perspectives in the Psychology of Old Age* (New York, Brunner/Mazel, 1975); H. M. Stahmer, "The Aged in Two Ancient Oral Cultures: The Ancient Hebrews and Homeric Greece," in Stuart Spicker, Kathleen Woodward, and David D. Van Tassel, eds., *Aging and the Elderly: Humanistic Perspectives in Gerontology* (Atlantic Highlands, N.J., 1978); Peter N. Stearns, *Old Age in European Society: The Case of France* (New York, 1976); Lawrence Stone, "Walking over Grandma," *New York Review of Books*, 12 May 1977; Thomas, "Age and Authority"; and for a review of the literature on attitudes, D. G. McTavish, "Perceptions of Old People: A Review of Research Methodologies and Findings," *Gerontologist* 11 (1971): 90–101.

8. Carl N. Degler, *At Odds: Women and Family in America from the Revolution to the Present* (New York, 1980); Laslett, "Societal Development and Aging"; Peter Laslett, "The History of Aging and the Aged," in Laslett, *Family Life and Illicit Love in Earlier Generations: Essays in Historical Sociology* (Cambridge, England, 1977); Robert V. Wells, "Family History and Demographic Transition," *Journal of Social History* 9 (1975): 1–19.

9. Achenbaum, *Old Age in the New Land*; Fischer, *Growing Old*.

10. P. T. Amoss and S. Harrell, "Introduction: An Anthropological Perspective on Aging," in P. T. Amoss and S. Harrell, eds., *Other Ways of Growing Old* (Stanford, 1981); also see David Gutmann, "Observations on Culture and Mental Health in Later Life," in J. E. Birren and R. N. Sloane, eds., *Handbook of Mental Health and Aging* (Englewood Cliffs, N.J., 1980); J. Keith, "The Ethnography of Old Age: Introduction," *Anthropological Quarterly* 52 (1979): 1–6; R. J. Maxwell and P. Silverman, "Cross-Cultural Variation in the Status of Old People," in Peter N. Stearns, ed., *Old Age in Preindustrial Society* (New York, 1982); T. Sheehan, "Senior Esteem as a Factor of Socioeconomic Complexity," *Gerontologist* 16 (1976): 33–40.

11. E.g., C. N. Nydegger, "Family Ties of the Aged in Cross-Cultural Perspective," *Gerontologist* 23 (1983): 26–31; Stearns, *Old Age in Preindustrial Society*.

12. Lutz K. Berkner, "The Stem Family and the Developmental Cycle of the Peasant Household: An Eighteenth-Century Austrian Example," *American Historical Review* 77 (1972): 398–418; Demos, "Old Age in Early New England"; Goody, "Aging in Non-Industrial Societies"; Hermann Rebel, "Peasant Stem Families in Early Modern Austria: Life Plans, Status Tactics, and the Grid of Inheritance," *Social Science History* 2 (1978): 255–291; Daniel Scott Smith, "Old Age and the 'Great Transformation': A New England Case Study,"

in Spicker, Woodward, and Van Tassel, eds., *Aging and the Elderly*; Thomas, "Age and Authority"; compare Stearns, *Old Age in Preindustrial Society*.

13. Fischer, *Growing Old*, pp. 76–78, 101–102, 109–113, 231; the periodization is summarized on pp. 198 and 220–231; his critique of modernization theory on pp. 20–25; in response to this assessment of his work as based on ideological change, Fischer notes the weight given to material determinants in his analysis, citing pp. 110–111 and 225; cf. pp. 76–78, 101–102, 108–110, 112, 231 in the 1978 edition; David Hackett Fischer, personal communication to Brian Gratton, 19 April 1983.

14. C. Vann Woodward, "The Aging of America," *American Historical Review* 82 (1977): 583, for approval; but see W. Andrew Achenbaum, "From Womb through Bloom to Tomb: The Birth of a New Area of Historical Research," (review of Fischer, *Growing Old*, and Paula Fass, *The Damned and the Beautiful*) *Reviews in American History* 6 (1978): 178–183; Michel Dahlin, "Review of *Growing Old in America*," *Journal of Social History* 11 (1978): 449–452; Stone, "Walking over Grandma"; M. S. Hindus, "Review of *Growing Old in America*," *William and Mary Quarterly* 35 (1978): 564–566.

15. James A. Henretta, "Families and Farms: *Mentalité* in Preindustrial America," *William and Mary Quarterly* 35 (1978): 7.

16. Fischer, *Growing Old*, pp. 26–76.

17. Ibid., p. 52.

18. Ibid., pp. 82–86.

19. The power of property-owning elders in colonial America, a power that extended to the control of sexuality, can be reviewed in a rapidly growing literature: J. W. Dean, Jr., "Patterns of Testation: Four Tidewater Counties in Colonial Virginia," *American Journal of Legal History* 16 (1972): 154–176; Philip J. Greven, Jr., "Family Structure in Seventeenth–Century Andover, Massachusetts," *William and Mary Quarterly* 23 (1966): 234–256; Philip J. Greven, Jr., *Four Generations: Population, Land and Family in Colonial Andover, Massachusetts* (Ithaca, 1970); R. A. Gross, *The Minutemen and Their World* (New York, 1976); A. Keyssar, "Widowhood in Eighteenth-Century Massachusetts: A Problem in the History of the Family," *Perspectives in American History* 8 (1974): 83–122; B. Levy, " 'Tender Plants': Quaker Farmers and Children in the Delaware Valley, 1681–1735," *Journal of Family History* 3 (1978): 136–149; D. B. Smith, "Mortality and Family in the Colonial Chesapeake," *Journal of Interdisciplinary History* 8 (1978): 403–427; Daniel Scott Smith, "Parental Power and Marriage Patterns: An Analysis of Historical Trends in Hingham, Massachusetts," *Journal of Marriage and the Family* 35 (1973): 419–428; Daniel Scott Smith, "Old Age and the 'Great Transformation' "; Daniel Scott Smith and M. S. Hindus, "Premarital Pregnancy in America, 1640–1971: An Overview and Interpretation," *Journal of Interdisciplinary History* 5 (1975): 537–570; D. O. Souden, "The Elderly in Seventeenth-Century New England: Personal and Institutional Care in Old Age,"

paper presented at the annual meeting of the Society for the Study of Social Problems, New York, August 1976. Smith, "Old Age and the 'Great Transformation' " comes to rather different conclusions from those I imply, but I agree with Fischer that Smith's evidence for middle-age dominance demonstrates the power of the aged rather than the reverse. (Fischer, *Growing Old*, pp. 242–244). As John Demos has pointed out, there was no concept of middle age in early America: "Historical Perspectives on Aging with Particular Reference to Mid Life," paper presented in the Humanistic Perspectives in Aging (lecture) Series, Boston University, December 1978; without a general retirement system, older people gave up land and office, but gradually and without prejudice.

Works that have stressed the traditional nature of early New England include Henretta, "Families and Farms"; Kenneth Lockridge, *A New England Town: The First Hundred Years, Dedham, Massachusetts, 1636–1736* (New York, 1970); John J. Waters, "The Traditional World of New England Peasants: A View from Seventeenth-Century Barnstable," *New England Historical and Genealogical Register* 130 (1976): 3–23; Wells, "Family History and Demographic Transition."

20. Dean, "Patterns of Testation," p. 170.

21. Smith, "Old Age and the 'Great Transformation'," pp. 290, 296; citing John J. Waters, "Hingham, Massachusetts, 1631–1661: An East Anglian Oligarchy in the New World," *Journal of Social History* 2 (1968): 351–370; see also Demos, "Old Age in Early New England"; J. Faragher, "Old Women and Old Men in Seventeenth-Century Wethersfield, Connecticut," *Women's Studies* 4 (1976): 11–31.

22. Smith, "Old Age and the 'Great Transformation'," p. 296; and see Gross, *Minutemen and their World*.

23. Henretta, "Families and Farms."

24. Achenbaum, "From Womb through Bloom to Tomb"; Fischer and Stone, "Growing Old"; Stone, "Walking over Grandma."

25. Fischer, *Growing Old*, pp. 84–85 n. 11; 225.

26. Fischer himself relies on an "impressionistic reading of high literature" (*Growing Old*, p. 256), which he criticizes in Achenbaum's work, to prove steady trends against the aged after 1800. His use of Walt Whitman's poetry is highly selective and inaccurate, and his review of a number of literary works proves only that one can find negative references to the elderly in a survey of American literature and popular culture between 1800 and 1970.

Thus, on Whitman: Fischer argued that Whitman showed nothing but contempt for old age, but he does not review Whitman's complete works; those pieces he does cite are not accurately dated or quoted and their interpretation misrepresents Whitman's view of old age. For example, Fischer believes Whitman became progressively gerontophobic, but the poems cited were not written in an extended series but in a single period of ill health. In addition he does not discuss Whitman's poems that celebrate old age, such as "To Old Age," and "My 71st Year." See Fischer, *Growing Old*, pp. 66–68, 119–120, 127 n. 13. Walt Whitman, *Daybooks and Notebooks* (vol. 2, *Daybooks, December 1881–1891*), W. White, ed. (New York, 1978), p. 453; and Walt Whitman, *Collected Writings*, G. W. Allen and E. S. Bradley, eds. (New York, 1961); G. W. Allen, *The Solitary Singer* (New York, 1967), pp. 527, 530–531; J. Kaplan, *Walt Whitman, A Life* (New York, 1980), pp. 12, 15, 31, 52–53, 345–349, 371–372; for a complete textual analysis, see Gratton, *Boston's Elderly*.

27. Achenbaum, *Old Age in the New Land*, pp. 57–86.

28. Ibid., pp. 3, 9–37, 39–54.

29. Carole Haber, "The Old Folks at Home: The Development of Institutionalized Care for the Aged in Nineteenth-Century Philadelphia," *Pennsylvania Magazine of History and Biography* 51 (1977): 240–257; Carole Haber, "Mandatory Retirement in 19th-Century America: The Conceptual Basis for a New Work Cycle," *Journal of Social History* 12 (1978): 77–96; Carole Haber, *Beyond Sixty-Five: The Dilemma of Old Age in America's Past* (Cambridge, England, 1983).

30. Haber, *Beyond Sixty-Five*, pp. 34–35 n. 23.

31. Thomas Cole, *Past Meridian: Aging and the Northern Middle Class*, Ph.D. dissertation, University of Rochester, 1980; Fischer, *Growing Old*; William Graebner, *A History of Retirement: The Meaning and Function of an American Institution, 1885–1978* (New Haven, 1980).

32. Cole, *Past Meridian*; J. J. Farrell, *Inventing the American Way of Death, 1830–1920* (Philadelphia, 1980).

33. Cole, *Past Meridian*, p. 12.

34. Ibid., pp. 9–10.

35. Ibid., p. 167.

36. Howard P. Chudacoff and Tamara K. Hareven, "From the Empty Nest to Family Dissolution: Life Course Transitions into Old Age," *Journal of Family History* 4 (1979): 69–83; Tamara Hareven, "The Last Stage: Historical Adulthood and Old Age," *Daedalus* 105 (1976): 13–27; Tamara Hareven, "Family Time and Historical Time," *Daedalus* 106 (1977): 57–70.

37. Michel Dahlin, "Perspectives on the Family Life of the Elderly in 1900," *Gerontologist* 20 (1980): 99–107; Daniel Scott Smith, "A Community-Based Sample of the Older Population from the 1880 and 1900 United States Manuscript Censuses," *Historical Methods* 11 (1978): 67–74; Daniel Scott Smith, "Life Course, Norms, and the Family System of Older Americans in 1900," *Journal of Family History* 4 (1979): 285–298; Daniel Scott Smith, "Historical Change in the Household Structure of the Elderly," paper presented at Workshop on the Elderly of the Future, Committee on Aging, National Research Council, Annapolis, Md., May 1979.

38. Smith, "Community-Based Sample," pp. 67–74.

39. Ibid., p. 67; and see Smith, "Historical Change in the Household Structure of the Elderly."

40. Dahlin, "Perspectives."

41. Smith, "Life Course," pp. 288–289.

42. Dahlin, "Perspectives"; Smith, "Community-Based Sample."

43. Smith, "Life Course," pp. 296–297.

44. See Daniel Scott Smith, chapter 5 in this volume, "Accounting for Change in the Families of the Elderly in the United States, 1900–Present."

45. M. Clark, "Patterns of Aging among the Elderly Poor of the Inner City," *Gerontologist* 7 (1971): 58–66.

46. Susan Kleinberg, "Aging and the Aged in Nineteenth Century Pittsburgh," manuscript, Western College, Miami University, Miami, Ohio, 1977; Gratton, *Boston's Elderly*.

47. Gratton, *Boston's Elderly*, pp. 122–151.

48. Thomas Cole, "An Essay on the Shaping of Old Age in America," M.A. thesis, Wesleyan University, Middletown, Conn., 1975; A. Holtzman, *The Townsend Movement: A Political Study* (New York, 1963); Roy Lubove, *The Struggle for Social Security, 1900–1935* (Cambridge, Mass., 1968); J. K. Putnam, *Old-Age Politics in California* (Stanford, 1970).

49. The most conspicuous error attends Fischer's attempt to set a fresh date for the "dawn of . . . discovery" of the aged as a social problem. Fischer believes that the recession of 1908 suddenly "dramatized" the issue and provoked an "extraordinary surge of social concern for the problem of old age." A substantial part of the evidence advanced for this view is that the year 1909 saw "the first public commission on aging" appointed. But this Massachusetts commission was established by the legislature in *1907* (Fischer, *Growing Old*, pp. 157, 159–160 n. 3, 238); for the establishment of the commission and for evidence of interest in the problems of old age before 1908, see A. A. Linford, *Old Age Assistance in Massachusetts* (Chicago, 1949).

50. Christopher Lasch, *The Culture of Narcissism: American Life in an Age of Diminishing Expectations* (New York, 1978), pp. 209–210.

51. Achenbaum, *Old Age in the New Land*.

52. Ibid., pp. 57–86; quotations, pp. 57, 86.

53. Ibid., p. 127; W. Andrew Achenbaum and P. A. Kusnerz, *Images of Old Age in America: 1790 to the Present* (Washington, D.C. and Ann Arbor, n.d.); W. Andrew Achenbaum, "Did Social Security Attempt to Regulate the Poor?" *Research on Aging* 2 (1980): 470–488.

54. W. Andrew Achenbaum, *Shades of Gray: Old Age, American Values, and Federal Policies since 1920* (Boston, 1983), p. 47.

55. Ibid., pp. 177–189.

56. Achenbaum, *Old Age in the New Land*, pp. 66–75, 183–184.

57. Ibid., pp. 95–106.

58. Ibid., p. 69.

59. G. Bancroft, *The American Labor Force: Its Growth and Changing Composition* (New York, 1958); J. Durand, *The Labor Force in the United States, 1890–1960* (New York, 1948); C. D. Long, *The Labor Force under Changing Income and Employment* (Princeton, 1958).

60. Howard Chudacoff and Tamara Hareven, "Family Transitions into Old Age," in Hareven, ed., *Transitions: The Family and the Life Course in Historical Perspective* (New York, 1978); Dahlin, "Perspectives," pp. 99–107; Haber, "Mandatory Retirement," pp. 77–96.

61. Achenbaum, *Old Age*, p. 103.

62. Ibid., p. 102.

63. Ibid., pp. 183–184, technical note c. In his calculations, Achenbaum solves for the unknown twice. Since he knows the total number in an occupation, his ratio estimates solve the equations:

$$a + b = c \qquad\qquad r = \frac{a/d}{b/e}$$

Where: a = number of aged in an occupation
b = number of those 10–65 in an occupation
c = total number in an occupation (known)
d = number of aged in population (known)
e = number of those 10–65 in population (known)
r = ratio (estimated from recent r's)

When c, d, e, and r are known, a and b can be derived.

But in point 3 of the technical note, Achenbaum estimates b, regressing from recent censuses. If this second estimate of b differs from that solved for above, we have a serious bias; since all other figures are fixed, only a, the number of aged, can vary. Since the *proportionate* place of the aged in occupations increased as their proportion in the population increased (despite relatively low participation rates), it may be that twentieth-century figures for the proportions 10–65 are relatively low by nineteenth-century standards. If this is the case, a is artificially reduced by the second estimate of b.

That this is probably the case is suggested by a consistency check. Using the known and estimated figures given in Achenbaum's technical note for 1840, the difference between the minuend of all gainfully employed people sixty-five and over and the subtrahend of all gainfully employed males sixty-five and over is sometimes negative, i.e., there were negative numbers of aged women in the labor force. Correction for this error raises the 1840 labor force activity of older men considerably.

64. Alan Dawley, *Class and Community: The Industrial Revolution in Lynn*

(Cambridge, Mass., 1976); L. Soltow, *Men and Wealth in the United States, 1850–1870* (New Haven, 1975).

65. Graebner, *History of Retirement*, pp. 10–16.

66. Stephan Thernstrom, *Poverty and Progress: Social Mobility in a Nineteenth-Century City* (Cambridge, Mass., 1964).

67. See M. C. Goldstein and C. M. Beall, "Indirect Modernization and the Status of the Elderly in a Rural Third World Setting," *Journal of Gerontology* 6 (1982): 743–748. David Gutmann's insightful discussion of the aged in contemporary traditional societies also provides a sense of the losses nineteenth-century American elderly incurred when their children left the farm: "Observations on Culture and Mental Health in Later Life," in J. E. Birren and R. B. Sloane, eds., *Handbook of Mental Health and Aging* (Englewood Cliffs, N.J., 1980).

68. K. Stone, "The Origins of Job Structure in the Steel Industry," *Review of Radical Political Economics* 6 (1974): 61–97; H. Braverman, *Labor and Monopoly Capital: The Degradation of Work in the Twentieth Century* (New York, 1975).

69. Chudacoff and Hareven, "From the Empty Nest," pp. 69–83; Dahlin, "Perspectives," pp. 99 107; Gratton, *Boston's Elderly*; Michael B. Katz, *The People of Hamilton, Canada West* (Cambridge, Mass., 1976); D. S. Smith, "Life Course," pp. 285–293; Soltow, *Men and Wealth*.

70. Durand, *Labor Force*, p. 34.

71. Gratton, *Boston's Elderly*, table III-1, pp. 111–112.

72. William Graebner, "Retirement and the Corporate State, 1885–1935: A New Context for Social Security," paper presented at the annual meeting of the Organization of American Historians, New York, April 1978.

73. Graebner, *History of Retirement*, p. 189.

74. Brian Gratton, "The Virtues of Insecurity," *Reviews in American History* 10 (1982): 17–23.

75. William Graebner, "Social Engineering through Social Security: The Retirement Act of 1935," manuscript, State College at Fredonia, New York, 1981.

76. Graebner, *History of Retirement*, pp. 215–262.

77. The reader might compare Graebner, *History of Retirement*; Richard Calhoun, *In Search of the New Old* (New York, 1978); Lasch, *Culture of Narcissism*; and Cole, *Past Meridian*. J. T. Freeman, *Aging: Its History and Literature* (New York, 1979), provides sources on this issue.

78. E.g., H. L. Wilensky, *The Welfare State and Equality: Structural and Ideological Roots of Public Expenditure* (Berkeley, 1975) and H. L. Wilensky, *The "New Corporatism," Centralization and the Welfare State* (Beverly Hills, 1976).

79. J. O'Connor, *The Fiscal Crisis of the State* (New York, 1973); L. J. Griffin, J. A. Devine and M. Wallace, "Accumulation, Legitimation and Pol-

itics: The Growth of Welfare Expenditures in the United States since the Second World War," paper presented at the annual meeting of the American Sociological Association, Toronto, August 1981; Theda Skocpol, "Explaining the Belated Origins of the U.S. Welfare State," paper presented at the conference Researching the Welfare State, Indiana University, Bloomington, March 1983; John F. Myles, *Old Age in the Welfare State: The Political Economy of Public Pensions* (Boston, 1983); Jill S. Quadagno, "Welfare Capitalism and the Social Security Act of 1935," *American Sociological Review* 49 (1984): 632–647: Ann Shola Orloff and Theda Skocpol, "Why Not Equal Protection? Explaining the Politics of Public Social Spending in Britain, 1900–1911, and the United States, 1880–1920," *American Sociological Review* 49 (1984): 726–750.

Explaining Old Age History: The Need for Empiricism

Since the 1960s, the writing of history has been transformed by a new generation of scholars. Political, intellectual, military, and traditional diplomatic history have been eclipsed by the "new" social history. In their efforts to study social structure and the inarticulate masses, historians have turned their attention to such novel topics as family structure, youth, adolescence, sex roles, working-class culture, and even death and dying. Concern with the stages of life inevitably has led to an interest in aging and, more particularly, to a preoccupation with perceptions of old age and dependency. The demographic reality—the gradual aging of the American population—has only reinforced scholarly interest in this topic.

In chapter 1 of this volume, Brian Gratton reveals how rapidly interest in aging and the aged has grown. As late as 1975 even social historians were all but oblivious to the subject; at present the history of the aged is becoming a major subdivision within the broader field of social history. Gratton's major point—that much of the work of historians has focused on attitudinal rather than structural change—is well taken, as is his call for a new history of aging based on the conse-

The research for this paper was supported by a grant from the National Institute of Mental Health (MH39030), Public Health Service, U.S. Department of Health and Human Services.

quences of the rise of industrial capitalism. Yet his critique does give rise to some general remarks.

Gratton is obviously discontented with a history that places primary emphasis on attitudes, perceptions, and culture, and he is critical of scholars who ignore the structural changes associated with industrial capitalism and its consequent impact upon the position of the aged. In his eyes, it is "much more reasonable . . . to view decline in the status of the aged as fairly steady, underwritten across the nineteenth century by the relative decline of the agricultural economy." The key element in the declining status of the aged involved the rise of large-scale industry, which diminished the capacity of the elderly "to control their own employment." In arguing against a cultural and attitudinal explanation, Gratton relies on Karl Marx's classic observation that it is not the consciousness of human beings "that determines their being, but, on the contrary, their social being that determines their consciousness."

The debate over consciousness, of course, involves views of human behavior that rest on certain kinds of assumptions (which, by definition, are unprovable). Gratton follows a line of analysis that places primary emphasis upon the social and structural context of behavior; the actions of human beings are largely a function of broad social and economic structures. Such an interpretation is at base deterministic in nature, for it denies the capacity of individuals to choose between alternatives irrespective of the social context in which they live. Thus Gratton obviously dislikes some of the recent works on aging that imply a discontinuity between attitudes and perceptions on the one hand, and social structures on the other.

Clearly, a scholarship that assumes a causal relationship between structure and behavior is highly attractive, if only because it provides a rationalistic and plausible model to explain behavior. However, such explanations are incompatible with a belief in the ability of human beings to make certain behavioral choices that are, at least in part, not culturally or structurally determined. For a variety of reasons, I am not enamored of explanations that at base involve a kind of implied overarching determinism (which cannot in any case be established, since as human beings we cannot assume an objective position outside of reality). Such explanatory mechanisms are in a certain sense ahistorical; they reduce the study of the past to a series of generalizations that operate independently of time and place. Finally, acceptance of such a hypothesis may lead us to ignore or to misinterpret data from the past. Admittedly, empiricism by itself has as many logical and philosophical difficulties as determinism. Yet data ought to precede generalization. And we know at present too little about the history of the aged to permit validation of any sweeping interpretation.

In much of the historical and social science literature, the aged are treated as though they constituted a single, unitary social group. A system of classification based on age is arbitrary (as are all classification systems) and excludes other categories that may be equally relevant. Is age, for example, more significant than sex, class, ethnicity, and race? Indeed, it may very well be inappropriate to speak of the "aged." The aged, after all, are as diverse a group as are other segments of the population. The experiences of aged men and women, white and black, rural and urban, well-to-do and poor, Protestant and Catholic, were by no means similar. When David Hackett Fischer argued that the authority of the elderly in the eighteenth century was of major importance, he clearly was not referring to blacks or females, but to elderly white and probably affluent males. Similarly, the withdrawal of the aged from the work force in the twentieth century was not equal across the board for all groups, suggesting once again that the experiences of the aged were by no means identical.

In disagreeing with Gratton's emphasis on the primary role of industrialization, I am not denying the importance of economic factors. But I am suspicious of all-embracing generalizations involving the relationship between broad economic change (industrial capitalism) and the lives of human beings. Not all individuals were affected equally by such changes; there were even differential responses within the same group. Individuals from similar environments, for example, responded quite differently to economic change, and these differential responses in turn shaped the economic environment. Nor should we assume that the lives of individuals are completely interrelated; there may be fundamental discontinuities between economic change on the one hand, and culture and attitudes on the other. To put the issue more bluntly, I am unwilling to accept an approach that *assumes* interrelatedness of all phenomena, as Gratton surely implies. This is not in any sense to suggest the irrelevance of economic change; it is merely to insist that the effects of such change must be demonstrated. Certainly Gratton is right when he calls for historians to study the impact of economic change upon the status and position of the aged; that an analysis of economic change will answer all questions is dubious.

The alternative to strictly economic analysis is not necessarily the focus on attitudes toward the elderly that Gratton has so well described as characteristic of the recent literature. Attitudes and perceptions tell us little about the experiences and conditions of aged persons of all varieties, and it is precisely those varieties that require a great deal of new research. Note that I am addressing two different categories: the first is the elderly; the second is the varieties of individuals found within specific age groups. For to study "the aged" is far too simplistic; we must understand how sex, class, race, and ethnicity—to cite only the most obvious—influence the condition of the aged.

Curiously enough, the lives of the elderly, despite interest in the history of the family and the publication of a number of excellent community studies, remain shrouded in mystery. Perhaps their relatively small numbers before the end of the nineteenth century caused them to be overlooked; perhaps the preoccupation of historians with other social groups led to the neglect of the history of the aged. Whatever the reasons, it is time to begin exploring old and new sources to shed light on the problem. Certainly the rise of industrial capitalism is not the starting point, for we run the risk of assuming that economic changes were the paramount determinant of change. We need only recall the familiar allegation that the nuclear family followed the industrial revolution to recognize the dangers of making logical (but ahistorical) linkages.

Nor can the history of the aged be understood in social isolation. The condition of elderly persons was often shaped by external events and elements, some of which initially had little or nothing to do with age *per se*, as the history of mental health policy, to take one example, suggests.

Before the end of the nineteenth century, relatively few aged persons were found in state mental hospitals. In 1854, Edward Jarvis, a significant figure in mid-nineteenth-century American psychiatry, conducted a comprehensive survey of all insane persons in Massachusetts hospitals, local welfare institutions, and the community at large. Working from his manuscript returns, Barbara G. Rosenkrantz and Maris A. Vinovskis found that slightly less than 10 percent of the institutionalized insane in the Bay State were aged sixty or more. The relatively low rate of hospitalization of older individuals, however, did not necessarily reflect a low incidence of mental illness. On the contrary, the highest rate of mental illness by age was found among the elderly (table 2.1). For a variety of reasons, younger persons were far more apt

Table 2.1
Number of insane in Massachusetts in 1854 (per 100,000 population)

Age Group	Number of Insane Per 100,000 Persons
0–19	24
20–29	189
30–39	360
40–49	569
50–59	579
60–69	735
70 and over	664

to be institutionalized than older individuals. Those in their twenties and thirties had the highest rate of hospitalization (67.1 and 72.3 percent, respectively), but only 36 percent of those in their sixties and 28.7 percent of those aged seventy and over were in institutions.[1]

The situation in mid-nineteenth-century Massachusetts was probably not unique. In most states, aged persons requiring aid were generally sent not to hospitals but to local and county almshouses, which provided assistance for a variety of groups. These institutions—about which relatively little is known despite their significance—were under local jurisdiction.[2] Although we have scanty information about the kinds of individuals and the circumstances that led to confinement in almshouses, it is clear that these institutions served as the equivalent of contemporary old age and chronic-care nursing homes. Among the varied groups in these institutions were the aged senile, a group not yet identified as requiring specific medical or psychiatric care.

Between 1880 and 1920, the almshouses declined in significance as a public institution. Admissions fell from 81,412 in 1904 to 63,807 in 1922 (a drop from 99.5 to 58.4 persons per 100,000). At the same time that admissions declined, the number of indigent aged individuals in almshouses rose sharply. In 1880, 33.2 percent of the almshouse

population was aged sixty and over; in 1904 and 1923, this group accounted for 53.1 and 66.6 percent of the total, respectively. During
this same period, the number of mentally ill in these institutions declined precipitously, from 24.3 percent in 1880 to 5.6 percent in 1923
(see table 2.2). The decline, however, was more apparent than real,
for the number of aged mentally ill persons committed to hospitals was
rising steadily. What occurred, in effect, was not a deinstitutionaliza-
tion movement, but rather a transfer of patients between different types
of institutions.[3]

Table 2.2
Mentally ill paupers in almshouses, 1880–1923

Year	Total Population	Total Almshouse Population	Mentally Ill Paupers Admitted During Year	Mentally Ill Paupers Enumerated on a Given Date	Percentage of Mentally Ill Persons in Almshouses Population
1880	50,155,783	66,203	----	16,078	24.3
1890	62,222,250	73,044	----	16,440	22.5
1904	81,792,387	81,764	3,375	8,432	10.3
1910	91,972,266	84,198	1,847	3,518	4.2
1923	109,248,393	78,090	2,091*	2,052	5.6

*During 1922. Unfortunately, the census provided no data on the
age distribution of mentally ill paupers in almshouses.

Sources: U.S. Bureau of the Census, *Paupers in Almshouses
1904* (Washington, D.C., 1906), pp. 182, 184; idem,
Paupers in Almshouses 1910 (Washington, D.C.,
1915), pp. 42–43; idem, *Paupers in Almshouses 1923*
(Washington, D.C., 1925), pp. 5, 8, 33; idem, *Insane and Feeble-Minded in Hospitals and Institutions 1904* (Washington, D.C., 1906), p. 29; idem,
Patients in Hospitals for Mental Diseases 1923
(Washington, D.C., 1926), p. 27.

The proportion of aged persons in mental hospitals continued to mount rapidly, especially in the twentieth century. Although reliable national data are not available, statistics from individual states and hospitals reveal the magnitude of the change. In many states, including Alabama, Kansas, Massachusetts, and Washington, the percentage of patients aged sixty and over rose 300–400 percent.[4] In New York, 18 percent of all first admissions to state mental hospitals in 1920 were diagnosed as psychotic because of either senility or arteriosclerosis. By 1940, this category accounted for nearly 31 percent of all first admissions. During this same period, the average age of first admissions rose from 42.69 to 48.47. The trend toward an older population continued even after the end of World War II (see table 2.3).[5] Nor was New York unique in this respect. Between 1916 and 1925, 16.3 percent of all first admissions to Warren State Hospital in Pennsylvania were sixty-five and older; the comparable figure for 1936–1945 was 23 percent. (Including aged fifty-five and over, the respective figures would be 29.3 and 36.2 percent.) The data for Illinois and Massachusetts reveal a similar pattern.[6]

Such statistics show that mental hospitals were to some extent serving as old age homes for elderly people suffering from some sort of physical and mental impairment. A breakdown of the 800 patients aged sixty-five and over in Massachusetts in 1900 (who represented 13 percent of the total hospital population) revealed that 127 of these 800 (15.9 percent) were confined to their beds; 211 (26.4 percent) were unable to maintain minimum personal hygiene; 215 (26.9 percent) were helpless and had to be cared for like infants; and 272 (34 percent) had no friends or acquaintances.[7]

The number of aged persons in state hospitals obviously varied over time and by geographical location. The increase in the aged population in the two Wisconsin state hospitals between 1875 and 1920 was relatively modest (from 11.9 to 15.1 percent); the county care system in that state, however, provided an alternative institution for the aged insane. Within a single state, wide variations among institutions were not uncommon. In Massachusetts in 1932, the average age of first admissions committed by the courts was 48.6 years. But individual hospitals showed widely diverging patterns: the highest average age was 54.4 years (Boston State Hospital); the figures for Taunton State Hospital, Grafton State Hospital, and Boston Psychopathic Hospital were 50.1, 41.7, and 39.1, respectively.[8] Despite institutional variations

Table 2.3
**First admissions to New York State hospitals, 1919–1921 and 1949–1951
(classified according to age)**

	1919–1921		1920 Percent Age Distribution of Population for N.Y.S.	1949–1951		1950 Percent Age Distribution of Population for N.Y.S.
Age(years)	Number	Percent		Number	Percent	
Under 15	72	0.4	29.7	689	1.4	22.6
15–19	963	4.7	7.9	1,871	4.0	6.1
20–24	1,812	8.9	8.9	3,187	6.8	7.3
25–29	2,386	11.8	9.4	3,612	7.7	8.1
30–34	2,336	11.5	8.6	3,314	7.1	7.9
35–39	2,388	11.8	8.1	3,367	7.2	8.0
40–44	2,003	9.9	6.7	3,158	6.7	7.6
45–49	1,771	8.7	5.9	2,998	6.4	7.0
50–54	1,513	7.4	5.1	2,989	6.4	6.6
55–59	1,190	5.9	3.7	2,935	6.3	5.6
60–64	1,085	5.3	3.0	3,155	6.7	4.6
65–69	907	4.4	4.7	3,350	7.1	3.6
70 and over	1,877	9.2		12,227	26.2	5.0

Sources: Benjamin Malzberg, "A Comparison of First Admissions to the New York Civil State Hospitals during 1919–1921 and 1949–1951," *Psychiatric Quarterly* 28 (1954): 314; U.S. Bureau of the Census, *Fourteenth Census of the United States,* vol. II, *Population 1920* (Washington, D.C., 1922), p. 248; idem, *Census of Population: 1950,* vol. II, *Characteristics of the Population,* part 32 (Washington, D.C., 1952), p. 58.

(which were related to varying rates for death, discharge, and retention), it is clear that the aged constituted a substantial proportion of the total hospital population. By the late nineteenth century, age-specific admission rates of older persons began to rise markedly as compared with admission rates for younger persons. In their classic study of rates of institutionalization covering more than a century, Herbert Goldhamer and Andrew W. Marshall found that the greatest increase occurred in the category of sixty-year-olds and over. In 1885, age-specific first admission rates in Massachusetts for men aged sixty and over was 70.4, for women, 65.5 (per 100,000). By the beginning of World War II, the corresponding figures were 279.5 and 223.0 (see table 2.4).[9] A study of Warren State Hospital in Pennsylvania covering 1916–1950 showed a similar pattern (see table 2.5).

Why were aged persons confined to mental hospitals? Communities could hardly perceive them as threats to personal security. Nor could it be said that the function of institutionalization was to alter their behavior or to provide them with restorative therapy. "The question of

Table 2.4
Male and female age-specific first-admission rates, Massachusetts, 1885 and 1939–1941 (per 100,000 population)

| | 1885 | | 1939/1941 | |
Age	Male	Female	Male	Female
10–19	22.0	15.0	57.2	42.8
20–29	96.4	75.0	124.2	91.1
30–39	111.0	107.9	159.9	108.2
40–49	110.0	108.1	164.0	106.0
50–59	102.9	78.8	174.5	117.3
60–	70.4	65.5	279.5	223.0

Source: Herbert Goldhamer and Andrew W. Marshall, *Psychosis and Civilization: Two Studies in the Frequency of Mental Disease* (Glencoe, Ill., 1953), pp. 54, 91.

Table 2.5
Average annual rate of first admissions, Warren State Hospital, Penn., 1916–1950 (per 100,000 population)

	1916–25	1926–35	1936–45	1946–50
Total Age Adjusted	51.6	57.9	68.2	76.5
Total Crude	43.7	54.1	68.3	79.1
Under 15 Years*	1.5	5.3	6.4	3.0
15–24	28.8	39.8	47.5	49.7
25–34	80.0	71.4	78.6	84.1
35–44	73.0	84.7	92.1	102.0
45–54	68.5	88.5	98.6	104.6
55–64	81.7	88.9	103.1	117.4
65–74	106.4	116.0	149.5	177.7
75–	176.2	185.7	289.2	398.7

*Using as a base the population 10–14 years of age

Source: Morton Kramer, et al., *A Historical Study of the Disposition of First Admissions to a State Mental Hospital: Experiences of the Warren State Hospital during the Period 1916–50* (U.S. Public Health Service, Publication No. 445, Washington, D.C., 1955), p. 10.

the care of the aged is one that will confront us always," noted one hospital superintendent who conceded that no effective treatment was available.[10] Mental hospitals, in fact, assumed the function of old age homes partly because of the lack of alternatives. The decline in birth and mortality rates, in addition, led to a relative and absolute increase in the number of the aged, thus giving rise to the social problems associated with an aging population.

Older persons ended up in mental hospitals for a variety of reasons. Some had no family to care for them; in other instances, families lacked sufficient means to offer care. Other aged individuals, especially those who exhibited strikingly abnormal forms of behavior, were institutionalized because relatives were unwilling or unable to assume responsibility for them. For some indigent aged persons, the mental hospital provided the only means of survival.

The use of mental hospitals as homes for aged senile persons did not go unnoticed. The New York State Commission on Lunacy in 1900 called attention to the increasing numbers of such cases in mental hospitals—a development in part associated with the passage of the State Care Act of 1890. Its members noted that only almshouses provided care for dependent aged persons who exhibited aberrant behavior. Mental hospitals, on the other hand, were in a position to provide an environment that included food, shelter, and personal care. Members of the commission, however, refused to endorse any legislation that precluded the admission of "dotards" to mental hospitals.[11]

Generally speaking, public officials saw no obvious solution to the dilemmas presented by aged senile persons. Some proposed that counties or families assume fiscal responsibility; others urged the construction of separate buildings at mental hospitals; and yet others insisted that sons and daughters be forced by law to meet their responsibilities toward parents. Admittedly, most state welfare officials never addressed the problem apart from the larger issue of dependency, and therefore they were often criticized for their passive acceptance of the status quo. A study of Illinois state hospitals in the early 1930s emphasized in disapproving tones the degree to which mental hospitals were serving as old age homes. A major problem, the report noted,

is the presence of increasingly large numbers of old people—primarily not mental cases—but described in medical parlance as "senile." Social revolutions, radical changes in housing and living problems, the growth of urban life, and countless other factors have tended to force the old man and woman from their homes. Simultaneously there has been a failure in the State of Illinois on the part of counties to adequately meet this problem, which under our political and statutory law is their responsibility.

The state mental hospital, organized for quite other purposes, has become their only haven. The state hospital, organized to provide more than mere shelter, offers a more expensive form of care than would otherwise be the case were such cases concentrated on the same scale. An illustration of the enormity of this difficulty is found in the Chicago State Hospital, which today is being converted into a huge infirmary, with nearly seventy percent of its 4,000 patients aged or infirm, suffering from no psychoses which would be beyond the capacity of the old-fashioned detached city cottage or rural home or of a well-managed county home.

Whether or not senility should be defined in psychiatric terms was largely beside the point; the necessity for caring for such persons was obvious to all. The structure of public financing and the fact that hospitals for the most part provided better care than almshouses combined to thrust upon mental institutions an increasing responsibility for the welfare of aged and senile persons.[12]

Why did the proportion of aged patients in mental hospitals rise so rapidly? Obviously the change in the age structure of the population accounts in part for the increase in absolute numbers, but not the relative increase in the proportion of first admissions aged sixty and over. It is possible to argue that the commitment of aged senile persons to hospitals reflected their increasingly marginal status, or the expansion of psychiatric categories that was associated with the rise of medical specialization. It may even be possible to argue—as Michael B. Katz and Andrew Scull have done[13]—that patients in mental hospitals were the discards of industrial capitalism and served as an example of the penalty for being nonproductive. This argument might in turn be congruent with a larger economic-structural approach to the modern history of the elderly. Yet these kinds of explanations are more often than not ideologically based; they are not for the most part grounded in deep research in primary sources.

The answer to the puzzling problem of the rise of aged patients in mental hospitals is not difficult to find. At the turn of the century, many states—led by New York's State Care Act in 1890 and a similar Massachusetts law a decade later—enacted legislation that mandated state responsibility for all mentally ill persons. These acts ended a system that had divided fiscal responsibility for the care of the mentally ill between the state and local communities. One of the inadvertent consequences of these laws was a dramatic change in both the character of the patient population and the size of hospitals. The source of funding, as a matter of fact, was probably the single most important element in determining the kind of institution in which mentally ill persons were placed. Throughout much of the nineteenth century, local officials found that it was less expensive to maintain mentally ill persons in almshouses than to send them to state hospitals (which required communities to pay a higher weekly maintenance charge and often lacked space for all patients). But when the state assumed the burden of supporting mentally ill residents, officials in effect reclassified many aged senile persons as mentally ill. Such a move facilitated their admission to mental hospitals, thus shifting the burden of support to the state. Psychiatrists themselves were cognizant of the problem but could do little to alter the pattern of admissions.[14] As Dr. Charles G. Wagner, superintendent of the Binghamton State Hospital and a future president of what is today the American Psychiatric Association, remarked in 1900:

We are receiving every year a large number of old people, some of them very old, who are simply suffering from the mental decay incident to extreme old age. A little mental confusion, forgetfulness and garrulity are sometimes the only symptoms exhibited, but the patient is duly certified to us as insane and has no one at home capable or possessed of means to care for him. We are unable to refuse these patients without creating ill-feeling in the community where they reside, nor are we able to assert that they are not insane within the meaning of the statute, for many of them, judged by the ordinary standards of sanity, cannot be regarded as entirely sane.[15]

The increase in the number of aged patients in mental hospitals and the subsequent redefinition of senility in psychiatric terms is but one example of the complexity of the subject. Indeed, the most pressing need at present is to uncover a body of data relating to the history of the aged that will lessen our ignorance. To argue such a position may not be especially popular. The traditional role of the historian—to examine as many primary sources as possible and to make critical distinctions—seems curiously old fashioned and obsolete alongside the social and behavioral science goal of articulating broad and all-encompassing generalizations. Perhaps historians ought not even address directly the question as to whether the aged have lost or gained status over several centuries; the question itself may not be susceptible to historical analysis. Clearly, comprehensive and symmetrical theories have an irresistible attraction; they provide clear answers and exclude the intrusion of a reality that is downright untidy and messy. Indeed, a comprehensive history of aging will in all probability remain incomplete, if only because the data of human history may be incapable of being encompassed within broad social theories. It would be a pity if historians, in their quest for unity, were seduced and abandoned those qualities that defined and differentiated their discipline.

NOTES

1. Barbara G. Rosenkrantz and Maris A. Vinovskis, "The Invisible Lunatics: Old Age and Insanity in Mid-Nineteenth-Century Massachusetts," in Stuart Spicker, Kathleen M. Woodward, and David D. Van Tassel, eds., *Aging and the Elderly: Humanistic Perspectives and Gerontology* (Atlantic Highlands, N.J., 1978), pp. 97–100. The manuscript returns can be found in the "Report of the Physicians of Massachusetts, Superintendents of Hospitals . . . and Others Describing the Insane and Idiotic Persons in the State of Massachusetts in 1855. Made to the Commissioners on Lunacy," Countway Library of Medicine, Harvard Medical School, Boston, Mass. The history of Jarvis's study can be followed in Gerald N. Grob, *Edward Jarvis and the Medical World of Nineteenth-Century America* (Knoxville, Tenn., 1978); the original report to the legislature was reprinted as Gerald N. Grob, ed., *Insanity and Idiocy in Massachusetts: Report of the Commission on Lunacy, 1855 by Edward Jarvis* (Cambridge, Mass., 1971).

2. For examples of what can be gleaned from the institutional records of nineteenth-century welfare institutions, see Elizabeth Gaspar Brown, "Poor Relief in a Wisconsin County, 1846–1866: Administration and Recipients," *American Journal of Legal History* 20 (1976): 79–117; and Michael B. Katz, *Poverty and Policy in American History* (New York, 1983), pp. 57–89.

3. My discussion of aged senile mentally ill persons is drawn from Gerald N. Grob, *Mental Illness and American Society 1875–1940* (Princeton, 1983); a fuller discussion and more extensive citations can be found in this volume.

4. Alabama Insane Hospital, *Biennial Report* (1891–1892): 56; Trustees of the Alabama Insane Hospital, *Report* (1925): 34, (1926): 73, (1940): 52, 97; California State Commission in Lunacy, *Biennial Report* 1 (1896–1898): 161, 2 (1900–1902): 85; California Department of Institutions, *Biennial Report* 6 (1930–1932): 174; California Department of Institutions, *Statistical Report* (1939–1940): 50; Iowa Board of Control of State Institutions, *Biennial Report* 2 (1898–1899): 338, 9 (1912–1914): 268–269; Kansas Board of Trustees of State Charitable Institutions, *Biennial Report* 3 (1880–1882): 61, 13 (1900–1902): 84; Topeka State Hospital, *Biennial Report* 23 (1920–1922): 17, 31 (1936–1938): 22; Massachusetts State Board of Lunacy and Charity, *Annual Report* 9 (1887): 166; Massachusetts Commission on Mental Diseases, *Annual Report* 1 (1920): 218–219; Massachusetts Commissioner of Mental Health, *Annual Report* 21 (1940): 307–308; Oregon State Board of Control, *Biennial Report* 4 (1919–1920): 56, 14 (1938–1940): 47; Washington State

Board of Audit and Control, *Biennial Report* 10 (1919–1920): 152–153, 208–209; Washington Department of Finance, Budget and Business, *Biennial Report* 3 (1939–1940): 72, 113.

5. New York State Department of Mental Hygiene, *Annual Report* 52 (1939–1940): 174–175; Benjamin Malzberg, "A Statistical Analysis of the Ages of First Admissions to Hospitals for Mental Disease in New York State," *Psychiatric Quarterly* 23 (1949): 346.

6. Morton Kramer, et al., *A Historical Study of the Disposition of First Admissions to a State Mental Hospital: Experiences of the Warren State Hospital during the Period 1916–50* (U.S. Public Health Service, Publication No. 445, Washington, D.C., 1955), p. 10; Carney Landis and Jane E. Farwell, "A Trend Analysis of Age at First-Admission, Age at Death, and Years of Residence for State Mental Hospitals: 1913–1941," *Journal of Abnormal and Social Psychology* 39 (1944): 3–23.

7. Massachusetts State Board of Insanity, *Annual Report* 2 (1900): 32.

8. Wisconsin State Board of Charities and Reform, *Annual Report* 5 (1875): 135, 150; Wisconsin State Board of Control, *Biennial Report* 15 (1918–1920): 106–107, 160; Neil A. Dayton, "A New Statistical System for the Study of Mental Diseases and Some of the Attained Results," *Bulletin of the Massachusetts Department of Mental Diseases* 18 (1934): 179–180.

9. Herbert Goldhamer and Andrew W. Marshall, *Psychosis and Civilization: Two Studies in the Frequency of Mental Disease* (Glencoe, Ill., 1953), pp. 54, 91.

10. Ohio Department of Public Welfare, *Annual Report* 15 (1936): 303–304.

11. New York State Commission on Lunacy, *Annual Report* 12 (1900): 26–29.

12. "The Care of the Mentally Disordered in Illinois: The State Hospitals" (c. 1931), pp. 7–8, typescript copy in American Foundation for Mental Hygiene Papers, Archives of Psychiatry, New York Hospital-Cornell Medical Center, New York, N.Y. For examples of other discussions by state officials, see Minnesota State Board of Control, *Biennial Report* 5 (1908–1910): 8–9; Kentucky Department of Public Welfare, *Biennial Report* (1931–1933): 36; Texas State Board of Control, *Biennial Report* 8 (1935–1936): 59.

13. Michael B. Katz, "Origins of the Institutional State," *Marxist Perspectives* 1 (1979): 6–22; Andrew Scull, *Decarceration: Community Treatment and the Deviant: A Radical View* (Englewood Cliffs, N.J., 1977).

14. For a discussion of public policy, see Grob, *Mental Illness and American Society*, pp. 88–92.

15. New York State Commission on Lunacy, *Annual Report* 12 (1900): 22–36.

Interestingly enough, the pattern between 1890 and 1940 was replicated in recent decades. Because of a shift toward federal funding for welfare, states tended to discharge patients from mental hospitals in order to make them eligible for federal programs. For data on this point, see Richard W. Reddick, "Patterns in Use of Nursing Homes by the Aged Mentally Ill," National Institute of Mental Health *Statistical Note 107* (1974). Between 1962 and 1975, the number of first admissions to state and county mental hospitals fell from 163.7 per 100,000 to 36.7 per 100,000, but the number of such persons in nursing homes rose by nearly an equivalent number. Laura Milazzo-Sayre, "Changes in the Age and Sex Composition of First Admissions to State and County Mental Hospitals, United States 1962–1975," National Institute of Mental Health *Statistical Note 145* (1978): 9.

PART II

ATTITUDES TOWARD THE ELDERLY

"Putting Off the Old": Middle-Class Morality, Antebellum Protestantism, and the Origins of Ageism

> The day of earth's redemption can never come, til the traditions of the elders are done away. . . . These traditions of the elders are the grand sources of most of the fatal errors of the present day.
>
> —Charles G. Finney

> The conversion of an aged sinner is an event that justly strikes the mind with astonishment.
>
> —Nathaniel Taylor

> The time of youth compared with old age has about the same relation to salvation, which spring-time and summer, compared with winter, have with reference to a harvest. The chills and frosts of age are about as unfavorable to conversion to God as the frosts and snows of December are to the cultivation of the earth.
>
> —Albert Barnes

Over the past decade, gerontologists, humanists, social activists and others have launched a concerted attack on restrictive age norms and roles, and on negative stereotypes of aging and old age.[1] The champions of the new old seek to liberate older people from popular myths of weakness, disease, passivity, decline, uselessness, and other images of loss commonly associated with aging. We have yet, however, to locate these ideas in their historical context—a context that illuminates their origins and enduring social functions. Prejudice against old people, or ageism, is no mere epiphenomenon, no simple set of misperceptions that can be "corrected" by image makers or social engineers.[2] On the contrary, ageism is historically rooted in a broader ideological system, parts of which are now stronger than ever.

The ideas and attitudes toward aging and old age that are currently under attack emerged within a middle-class system of values that took shape in the northern United States after 1800. This system of values, here referred to as "civilized" or Victorian morality,[3] arose in the first quarter of the nineteenth century—ushered in by health, sex, and temperance reformers, revivalists, ministers, and educators who opted for an especially rigid form of moral self-government following the erosion of hierarchical and communal authority. Coinciding with the decline of household production, the growth of a market economy, the cult of true womanhood, and a new emphasis on domesticity, civilized morality relied heavily on female child-rearing and voluntary church organizations to instill its ideal of conduct in young people, especially males, who would soon face the dangers and opportunities of the marketplace.

Civilized morality was the secular value system of the modern bourgeois man, free to pursue the main chance unfettered by tradition. This ideal required tight inner control over "the passions" in order to harness the body for work and restrain the excesses of individual competition. To discipline his desire for material wealth, calm the persistent anxieties of his lonely struggle for advancement, and anchor his identity, the would-be self-made man was to follow a strict regimen of industry, self-denial, and restraint. Observers have long associated rigid sex roles and a repressive style of sexuality with civilized or Victorian morality. And scholars have recently revealed this morality's intimate relationship with the rise of liberal capitalism.[4] Yet it has not been generally realized that restrictive norms of aging and negative stereotypes of old age assumed their most virulent form in the same cultural matrix.[5]

Antebellum northern Protestantism played a key role in shaping and legitimizing civilized morality as a system of values and a style of social discipline—with important consequences for American attitudes toward aging and old age. This chapter demonstrates this using evidence primarily taken from the published works of revivalists of the

Second Great Awakening: Albert Barnes, Lyman Beecher, Peter Cartwright, Charles Finney, Herman Humphrey, Jacob Knapp, and Nathaniel Taylor. Sermons from nonrevivalists William Ellery Channing, Theodore Parker, Charles Porter, and Cortlandt Van Rensselaer have also been used. Despite important variations between perfectionist revivalists, theological conservatives, and Unitarian ministers, northern Protestantism's overwhelming commitment to middle-class morality led ineluctably to ideas about aging and old age that have only recently been called into question.[6]

For nineteenth-century evangelicals, the purpose of religion was not to glorify God, but to make individuals virtuous. Post-Calvinist piety consisted of proper behavior—obedience to the laws of God and morality for the attainment of happiness. Jonathan Edwards, on the other hand, had acknowledged the importance of social morality—the virtues of honesty, sobriety, industry, faithfulness, thrift—yet he described these as "secondary virtues," necessary for self-interest and self-preservation. These instrumental virtues, he argued, should not be confused with "true virtue," or absolute love of God and "benevolence to Being in general." Edwardean piety demanded respect for God-given reality ("Being in general"), for man's connection to and dependence on a world often indifferent to personal welfare. Post-Edwardean evangelicals, arguing that obedience to God would make men happy, gradually suppressed the inherent tragedy of human life. Transforming piety into moralism, they raised bourgeois virtues to the status of religious truths and reduced love of God and His creation to one of several essential virtues required for happiness.[7]

When early nineteenth-century evangelicals transformed the content of their religious devotion, they also revised their conception of the devout. As self-reliance and self-control achieved religious stature, the image of the aged saint, whose faith supported him through physical decay, lost much of its cultural resonance. The traditional association of salvation with maturity gave way to a preoccupation with youth, a tendency particularly marked among revivalists.

After 1800, the major evangelical instrument for sweeping large numbers into the church and anchoring the internal restraints of civilized morality was the revival. Antebellum revivalists revised the Puritan orientation to the past and its living symbols, the aged, to accord with the decline of communalism and the altered character of generational relations.[8] While many ministers adapted slowly and reluctantly to the disestablishment of religion and the rise of party politics,[9] revivalists often led the way into reform efforts to shape the emerging market society.[10]

Post-Puritan clergymen located authority not in an organic community but in the morally instructed individual. Identifying social order with individual piety, men like Albert Barnes and Charles Finney freely attacked intemperance or godlessness among elders or betters. Revivalists conceived the aged not as standard-bearers of authority and morality, but as obstacles to religious perfection and national progress. Whereas Puritans drew inspiration by looking back to a covenant of the fathers, revivalists looked ahead to a millennial future cut loose from the imperfections of the past.[11] Mirroring the expansive optimism of bourgeois culture, they emphasized the individual's ability to shape both earthly and eternal fate, unencumbered by what Finney called the "traditions of the elders."

Such evangelism focused on youth. Puritanism had not encouraged conversion in childhood or adolescence, in part because young people remained dependents in patriarchal households during the seventeenth and most of the eighteenth centuries. Daily supervision and control, and a future of well-defined roles, permitted the slow absorption of religious tradition. In mid-eighteenth-century Andover, Massachusetts, for example, conversion extended over a four-year period and was completed at roughly the time of marriage and economic independence (twenty-six for men and twenty-four for women).[12] Nineteenth-century revivalists, on the other hand, emphasized teenage conversion, reflecting a new evangelical preoccupation with both the liberation and control of young people. Evidence from five New England Congregational churches between 1730 and 1835 suggests that not until the Second Great Awakening did a significant number of fifteen- to nineteen-year-olds achieve church membership.[13]

Rather than gradual conversion, which required reflection, doctrinal education, and patience (virtues associated with age), revivalists called for immediate repentance and conversion. As Donald Scott notes, the new evangelical style of conversion was "less the careful construction of a mature Christian personality than a concrete experience of 'rebirth.' In this abrupt, cataclysmic, and deeply transforming event, [the new converts] felt themselves to have in fact died in sin and been born again into righteousness, to have broken abruptly, immediately, and utterly with their sinful past."[14] Just as laissez-faire capitalism aspired to remove all restraints on individual accumulation of wealth, the new revivalism aspired to sweep away all hindrances to the pietistic perfection that would usher in the millennium. Old age, it seems, was either irrelevant or antithetical to these aspirations.

Antebellum Americans recognized four loosely distinguished stages of life: infancy (or childhood), youth, adulthood, and old age.[15] Of these stages, nineteenth-century evangelicals universally agreed with Albert Barnes that "youth is the most favorable time always for becoming a Christian . . . the time of youth compared with old age has about the same relation to salvation, which spring-time and summer, compared with winter, have with reference to a harvest. The chills and frosts of age are about as unfavorable to conversion to God as the frosts and snows of December are to the cultivation of the earth."[16]

Revivalists Barnes, Finney, and Taylor all explicitly argued that youth was the time when character was formed for eternity. Those who failed to embrace religion before they entered the "schemes of business, the cares of life, the countless perplexities and pursuits of manhood," would almost surely be lost. Expressing a common preference for the virtues of youth, Barnes argued: "All that there is in the character and circumstances of man to awaken hope is to be found in this period of life. All that follows is cause for fear and anxiety, and in the case of multitudes, as God sees it, for despair."[17]

Rather than risk the "hardening of the heart" that might overtake a person waiting for God's grace, revivalists compressed the old Puritan morphology of conversion,[18] eliminated the value of doubt, and demanded active transformation of the heart.[19] In 1868, aging revivalist Jacob Knapp recalled the more gradual methods of nonrevivalist ministers:

Thirty-five or forty years ago, Baptists, Presbyterians, and Congregationalists would tell their inquirers to go home, read their Bibles, reflect upon their condition, look within, dig deep, and be not deceived. They enforced a process of introspection rather than . . . looking out from themselves unto Jesus. The Methodists would tell them to put their names on the "class" paper, and become probationers for six months . . . but before the allotted period had expired their interest would die out, and they would find themselves where they started, with this difference, that they were more hardened, and less likely to make another effort.

Knapp, who traveled throughout the north and stopped counting after converting over 100,000 souls, insisted on "speedy admission" of young converts.[20]

Revivalists argued that each additional day of waiting threatened to turn probation into reprobation. "How long, sinner, have you lived?" pressed Finney. Using the traditional metaphor of life as a spiritual voyage, Finney described the "fearful rocks of damnation" and the "darkness of the tempest" that threatened one's journey through manhood.[21] Both Taylor and Finney agreed that every year over twenty "fearfully" diminished the probability of conversion; they often cited conversion lists that appeared to confirm this view, by revealing an inverse relation between age and conversion. Since revivalists designed their preaching specifically to bring young men into the church (women of all ages generally constituted the majority of communicants), this argument was obviously self-serving. Like later "scientific" findings about the relations between age and productivity, physical strength, mental functioning, and reaction time, these conversion lists strengthened the ideological bias that informed them.

Revivalists, then, claimed that conversion for young people was essential preparation for adult life. Complete regeneration would insulate an individual from the moral blandishments of the world and point the way to perfection on earth. "Only make it your invariable rule to do right, and do business upon principle, and you control the market," claimed Finney.[22] Linking piety to the legitimacy of capitalist social relations, revival sermons claimed that God would be present in the marketplace if future farmers, shopkeepers, and wage earners experienced the rebirth of conversion.[23]

Clergymen, however, did not rely on thoughts of God alone to guarantee a moral life. The act of surrendering oneself to God simultaneously opened the heart to incorporating the norms of civilized behavior. Instructions to young converts invariably linked piety with self-denial and obedience to God with control over "the passions," thereby weaving together qualifications for salvation and bourgeois ideals of conduct. Charles Finney, for example, advocated Sylvester Graham's dietary reforms while attacking luxury, idleness, novel-reading, theatergoing, card-playing, dancing, gluttony, and sexual indulgence.[24] "The time to teach these things with effect," he wrote in his *Lectures on Revivals of Religion* (1835), "is when they are young converts." Dismayed by the lustful indulgence of many "old professors" (i.e., those

professing religion), Finney insisted that the church would not progress toward the millennium until young converts were "faithfully taught
in the outset of their religious course to be temperate in all things."[25]

For all their prescriptions, the revivalists studied here never instructed young people on proper conduct toward old people. This suggests that, unlike the Puritan ideal of veneration,[26] prescribed attitudes
and conduct toward old people played no essential role in the ideology
of civilized morality. The collapse of the ideal of veneration did not
challenge the universal assumption that adult children would attend to
the needs of old, infirm parents. A pious Christian, "temperate in all
things," did not have to be told to care for his aged parents. Rather
than altering the structure of intergenerational family life, civilized
morality loosened the ideological and psychological constraints of deference to the hierarchical authority of the aged, marking a step toward
the transfer of responsibility for the infirm aged from the family to the
state.

Revivalists not only abandoned the ancient practice of advising the
young to venerate the old, they also withheld the traditional gestures
of consolation for the aged. Revivalists never addressed the trials of
aging; they simply demanded immediate conversion of all sinners before it was too late. Older believers who attended church faithfully but
showed little interest in revivals often experienced pressure for recon-
version.[27]

If revival sermons neither prescribe proper conduct toward the aged
nor contain comforting advice for old people, they nevertheless radiate
a wealth of imagery about aging and old age—primarily as antipodes
to youthful qualities of vigor, immediacy, action, self-control. These
sermons often bristle with hostility toward old age, that unwelcome
reminder both of the oppressive weight of the past and of man's inevitable weakness and dependence. Antebellum revivalists commonly
attacked the "prudent old professors" who denied Finney's claim that
"religion is something to do, not something to wait for."[28] They encouraged young people to rise before the congregation and exhort it to
greater spiritual efforts—a principle objection of those who opposed
revivals.

Jacob Knapp, recalling his efforts in Jefferson County, New York,
in the autumn of 1833, criticized the Congregationalists there who barred
revivalists from the pulpit and refused to allow young converts to speak
or pray: "The 'old fogies' went poking along . . . like an old lazy

yoke of oxen, keeping a little ahead of the converts, and hooking them back lest they should go too fast."[29] Finney charged that the elders of many Presbyterian churches had a "blighting influence" in prayer meetings. He rejected the custom of teaching young converts to "file in behind the old, stiff, dry, cold members and elders." Unless young converts were encouraged to take an "active part in religion," they would grow "cold and backward." Against the formal and dignified approach to prayer meetings, Finney even urged rebellion against church officers in the name of pious zeal.[30]

Methodist preacher Peter Cartwright, who was converted at fifteen and soon began riding circuits in Kentucky, Tennessee, Indiana, Ohio, and Illinois, exemplifies the muscular approach to revivalism. Though he was appointed a "presiding elder" at age twenty-one, this title scarcely inhibited his physical approach to opposition. When describing those who opposed the intensely emotional, rollicking camp meetings of his revivals, Cartwright noted the "old dry professors" and "old starched Presbyterian preachers." Like the corpulent "old lady" he knocked over onto her backside in Knox County, Kentucky, in 1834, the opposition of the old failed to restrain the great revival in which "our country seemed all coming home to God."[31]

Despite Cartwright's physical prowess, revivalist hostility to old age was largely symbolic. In one of his most famous sermons, Finney combined most heresies under the heading "Traditions of the Elders." "The day of earth's redemption can never come, til the traditions of the elders are done away," he insisted. "These traditions of the elders are the grand sources of most of the fatal errors of the present day."[32] If Finney directed his attack more at "tradition" than at "the elders," he made no effort to separate the two.

Old age suffered another important symbolic setback at the hands of revivalists. Their perfectionist view gave new prominence and meaning to the biblical metaphor for regeneration: putting "off the old man,"[33] and putting "on the new man" (Ephesians 4:22–25; Romans 6:6; Colossians 3:9–10). Perfectionism revised the old Calvinist view that the Adamic nature of sin could never be fully transformed by even the most pious convert. The "old man" of human sinfulness and the "new man" of God's grace existed side by side in all Christians. Revivalists, on the other hand, argued that born-again Christians could remove sin from their lives entirely; that is, they would completely "put off the old man." Emerson Andrews, for example, described the "Great

Change'' of conversion: ''There is no patchwork, no sewing new cloth into the old garments. . . . Not dry leaves and old branches of a barren tree, but all is green and fruitful, growing up from the divine root of a hundred-fold. The old man is put off and the new put on.''[34] In a culture devoted to the future and preoccupied with youth, the growing hostility toward old age found ample resonance in the revivalist attempt to ''put off the old man.''

Although nonrevivalists and theologically conservative ministers did not aspire to ''put off the old man,'' they came to a similar position via a different route. Revivalists devoted all their energy to gaining converts; they held out little hope for the old. Nonrevivalists, on the other hand, had pastoral obligations requiring them to address the spiritual and emotional needs of their older parishioners. Nonrevivalists showed none of the revivalists' rhetorical hostility to old age; they took a more positive approach to conversion in later life; and they specifically discussed the duties and comforts of old age. Nevertheless, if nonrevivalists mourned rather than welcomed the decline of patriarchal authority, they too accepted the verdict of civilized morality—old age was closer to death than to life.

Prior to the sentimentalism of the Romantic Evangelicals (1850–1880), advice and consolation for the aged persisted mainly in the late Calvinist style of Nathaniel Emmons, Joseph Lathrop, and John Stanford.[35] Ministers portrayed old age as a time of ''peculiar'' care and sorrow, a succession of irreparable losses. Friends, senses, memory, health, and sociability all departed—evoking, as one old-school Presbyterian put it, ''an inexpressible loneliness and desolation of the soul.'' Nonperfectionist ministers made little attempt to disguise the ravages of time; indeed, they often belabored the infirmities of age to underscore the saving qualities of faith. With the Puritans, antebellum ministers believed that old age was insupportable without the fruits and consolations of religion.

Preaching to settled congregations, nonrevivalists (or mellowing revivalists like Albert Barnes) showed leniency toward unregenerate old age. ''Aged friend! Stop! There is mercy in heaven!'' implored Cortlandt Van Rensselaer. ''Relatives, friends, pray for him! The star of Bethlehem yet shines, though on the very edge of his horizon! . . . Pray that even in old age, his youth may be renewed by the strength of an immortal hope!''[36] Ministers argued that faith in old age transformed darkness into light in two basic ways: it endowed life on earth with individual security and broader social purpose; and it secured safe passage through death to eternal life. Just when existence seemed an "intolerable burden," when "nature bends under the weight of years and seems to ask imploringly for the undisturbed rest and quiet of the grave," the aged Christian could turn confidently to God and the fulfillment of divine promise: "Even to good old age I am He, and even to hoar hairs will I carry you. I have made and I will bear, even will I carry you and deliver you."[37]

These two promises—of renewed social purpose and of life after death—constituted the evangelical defense against uselessness and hopelessness in old age. Even after his days of public service were over, the aged saint's existence continued to have social purpose; an "impressive spectacle to men," he revealed both the progress of sanctification—control of the passions—and the efficacy of God's grace in renewing depraved human nature. Consistent, mature piety and gentleness of spirit served to show the next generation that "even amid the infirmities of age, there is enough to make a man calm, cheerful, and happy."[38]

The usefulness of old age depended in part on fulfillment of "solemn responsibilities." Most prominent among these was the life review, rooted in the Puritan tradition of introspection and revived in the 1960s in secular form by the psychiatrist Robert Butler.[39] Ministers advised old people to seek confirmed assurance of their regeneration and reconciliation with God through solemn reflections on the past. "The aged should diligently and prayerfully look for evidence of their soul's renovation and sanctification," asserted Charles Porter, minister of the First Presbyterian Church in Utica, New York.[40]

Along with prayer and reflection, the duties of the aged included the moral exercises detailed in Galatians 5:22–23: "love, joy, peace, long-suffering, gentleness, goodness, faith, meekness, temperance." Here again, socially useful conduct overlapped with qualifications for salvation. The aged provided essential lessons for others. "The patient, cheerful, active piety of the aged, may and does, speak impressively to the hearts of the young," noted Porter. "Age has its advantages for moral purposes; and gray hairs may sow seed that shall spring and bear fruit into everlasting life, longer after they themselves have been hid in the grave."[41]

More important, however, than the assurance of divine strength or social usefulness in old age, was the promise of life after death. Ministers encouraged older people to release their worldly interests to the next generation and recognize that their real interests lay beyond the grave. "The older a Christian grows, the more does he desire to enter Heaven, the more does he pant for the enjoyments of its endless service," claimed Van Rensselaer. "The aged saint is, as it were, a mediator between life and death, interceding through his decaying frame for his speedy departure to glory. He would rather be in Heaven than on earth, yet the breath of his prayer is, 'Not my will, but thine be done.' "[42]

Antebellum Protestant ministers, irrespective of denominational differences or their view of revivalism, tightened the conceptual links between old age and death. Long before demographic changes in the age distribution of death had significantly reduced the high frequency of death in childhood (in 1850, roughly 50 percent of all deaths occurred under the age of fifteen), ministers revised the old Puritan view, epitomized by Nathaniel Emmons. In his sermon "Death Without Order," Emmons, the last of the Great Puritan Divines, emphasized that God called men out of the world without respect to age or station of life.[43] Those who survived to old age had been spared as "monuments to sovereign grace," symbols of life rather than death.

Belief in immortality encouraged aged believers to view their old age not as a period of terminal decline but as a final stage of earthly probation leading to eternal glory. Unlike the aged Puritan, who might express hope and faith but not absolute assurance, the aged Protestant of the mid-nineteenth century might quiet his fears with the belief that God granted life after death freely to all believers. The most difficult and dangerous part of life lay behind; a future of endless peace and joy lay ahead.[44]

Although nonrevivalist clergymen rarely showed the outright hostility toward old age displayed by revivalists, their commitment to civilized morality ineluctably led them to the depreciation of old age. The decaying body in old age, the "old man," came to signify precisely what bourgeois culture hoped to avoid—dependency, disease, and death. Listen to Cortlandt Van Rensselaer, delivering the funeral service for old Joseph Nourse in 1841:

If old age be the utmost boundary of life, how forcibly are we reminded by it of the certainty of death. Though we may attain to manhood without a perceptible diminution of strength, yet gray hairs, feeble steps and failing sense be at last the monitors of our decay. From death old age brings no deliverance, but is on the contrary a delayed assurance of its final doom. As the limit of life, old age likewise reminds us of sin, which thus consigns the body to degradation. "Death by sin," is the explanation of all our miseries. Our return to dust is a sentence incurred by Adam's transgression. Every symptom of disease we feel, every pang we suffer, every infirmity we bear, is an expression of our depravity. In Paradise, infirmity was no element in our constitution. The decay of age, as of death, is the sinner's accomplishment. Every old man, therefore, presents in his body the testimony of nature to SIN and DEATH. Two dread realities![45]

This remarkable passage illustrates the frightening character of the aging male body in a culture where control of that body formed the linchpin of secular morality and its mortification the condition of salvation. Although Van Rensselaer here equates old age and death as equal forms of punishment for sin, this sermon actually represents an early stage in the gradual substitution of old age for death as the wages of sin. After the mid-eighteenth century, the ambivalence inherent in the Puritan view of death (as simultaneously heavenly reunion and punishment for the sin of Adam)[46] slowly gave way to a domesticated, superficial, optimistic view that guaranteed sweet salvation to all believers. This transition was not fully accomplished until the mid-nineteenth century; by then, ministers had broken apart and suppressed the old Puritan ambivalence, transferring it in a dualistic form onto aging and old age. Having abandoned death as punishment of a sovereign God, northern Protestants seized on the threatening aspects of masculine decay in place of death.

New England Calvinists had offered an integrated view of old age, emphasizing *both* inevitable loss and hope of redemption.[47] Their Arminian successors created a dualistic vision, splitting old age into sin, decay, and dependence on the one hand, and virtue, self-reliance, and health on the other. According to the Victorian consensus constructed by revivalists, Romantic Evangelicals, and popular health reformers,[48] anyone who lived a life of hard work, faith, and self-discipline could preserve health and independence to a ripe old age; the shiftless, faithless, and promiscuous, however, were doomed to premature death or a miserable old age.

The decline of patriarchial authority also nurtured the identification of masculine old age with death. "Society is now a quick-shifting pageant," remarked William Ellery Channing in 1837. "The authority which gathered around the aged has declined. The young seize impatiently the prizes of life . . . he who retires from active pursuits is as little known to the rising generation as if he were dead."[49] Charles Porter made the same point in 1842. "Our fathers, where are they?" he asks. "One by one we carry them forth from our dwellings to the place of sepulchre; nor are they missed, except by the surviving few who have grown old with them, or have been the companions of their declining years."[50]

For the aged, increasingly receding from social honor and prominence, death was all that remained of life. "I take it that old age is the only natural death for mankind," asserted Unitarian Theodore Parker, "the only one that is unavoidable, and must remain so. As virtue is the ideal life of man, so old age is the ideal death."[51] Whether they viewed death primarily as punishment, as heavenly reunion, or as a natural end to life, northern Protestants gradually tightened the conceptual links between old age and death. In so doing, they not only performed the last rites for patriarchal authority, they also added old age to the Victorian legacy of repression, denial, and fear.

The origins of ageism, then, lie *both* in the revolt against hierarchical authority and in the rise of bourgeois morality. If old age in America had only suffered the usual misfortune of being identified with an old order, the impact might have been short-lived. But old age not only symbolized the eighteenth-century world of patriarchy and hierarchical authority, it also respresented an embarrassment to the new morality of self-control. The primary virtues of civilized morality—independence, health, success—required constant control over one's body and physical energies. The decaying body in old age, a constant reminder of the limits of physical self-control, came to signify dependence, disease, failure, and sin.

When antebellum ministers identified old age with death, they meant to defend it against these implications. Old age could still have vital significance because death was a goal—the passageway to eternal life. But in the twentieth century this strategy backfired. Death lost its spiritual significance and gradually replaced sexuality as the taboo subject of modern culture. Old age, too, succumbed to the vacuum of meaning surrounding the end of life.

The contemporary attack on ageism has yet to confront the existential and spiritual impact of this legacy, inherited from the marriage of

Protestant perfectionism and bourgeois preoccupation with the body. The currently fashionable activity orientation to aging (which encourages older people to remain active, healthy, and independent) is not so much a repudiation of civilized morality as an updated version of it. Older people today are encouraged to strive for the physical health and self-control previously attributed only to the young and middle-aged. Underneath this vision of ceaseless activity, spurred on by the illusory promise of scientifically abolishing biological aging, lies a profound failure of meaning.

As we join the search for more satisfying meanings of aging,[52] we would do well to remember the existential wisdom once signified in Calvinist terms. Human beings are flawed and mortal; we live in a universe that is ultimately uncontrollable and indifferent to personal welfare. Spiritual growth emerges from our confrontation with physical limitation and decline. One goal of such growth might be what Edwards called "true virtue"—renewed love and respect for "being in general."

NOTES

The author gratefully acknowledges the comments and suggestions of David Hackett Fischer, Brian Gratton, Thomas Olsen, Richard Shields, Amy Stanley, and Leonard Sweet.

1. See, for example, Robert Butler, *Why Survive?* (New York, 1975); Sharon Curtin, *Nobody Ever Died of Old Age* (Boston, 1972); Ronald Gross, Beatrice Gross, and Sylvia Seidman, *The New Old* (New York, 1978); Alex Comfort, *A Good Age* (New York, 1976); Stuart F. Spicker, Kathleen M. Woodward, and David D. Van Tassel, eds., *Aging and the Elderly* (Atlantic Highlands, N.J., 1978).

2. See Richard B. Calhoun, *In Search of the New Old* (New York, 1978), for the opposite view.

3. My use of the term "civilized" morality derives from the work of Sigmund Freud, Nathan G. Hale, Jr., and Norbert Elias. In 1908, Freud's essay " 'Civilized' Sexual Morality and Modern Nervousness" (*Complete Psychological Works, S.E.*, vol. IX [London, 1959], pp. 181–204) voiced a limited protest against the dominant moral code, which restricted the expression of sexuality to procreation within marriage through rigidly internalized control of sexual behavior and impulse. Discussing the early reception of Freud's thought in America, Nathan Hale, Jr., (*Freud and the Americans* (New York, 1971), ch. 2, rightly points out that "civilized" morality operated as a coherent set

of social, economic, and religious norms, regulating not only sexuality but virtually the entire routine of daily life. Although we do not yet have a definitive study of the subject, Victorian culture seems to embody the high-water mark of the "civilizing" process described by Norbert Elias in *The Civilizing Process*, Edmund Jephcott, trans. (New York, 1978)—the gradual, postmedieval shift of social controls from the community to the individual.

4. See Stephen Nissenbaum, *Sex, Diet, and Debility in Jacksonian America* (Westport, Conn., 1980); and Martin C. Van Buren, "The Indispensable God of Health," Ph.D. dissertation, UCLA, 1977.

5. My position differs from those of other historians who have addressed this question. According to David Hackett Fischer, *Growing Old in America* (New York, 1977), the Revolutionary Era ushered in a "cult of youth" between 1780 and 1820. W. Andrew Achenbaum, on the other hand, argues in *Old Age in the New Land* (Baltimore, 1978) that the "obsolescence of old age" did not replace appreciation of its usefulness until after 1865, with the rise of modern science and industry. And Gerald J. Gruman, "Cultural Origins of Present-Day Age-ism," in Spicker, Woodward, and Van Tassel, eds., *Aging and the Elderly*, pp. 359–378, argues that a modernist cultural transformation created an ideology of generational replacement at the end of the nineteenth century.

6. I have not here undertaken the fascinating and difficult task of charting variations in conceptions of aging based on differences in theology, geography (both urban/rural and north/south), social class, and ethnicity. I expect that such research will modify, but not vitiate, my central claim that religious ideas about aging and old age both shaped and were profoundly shaped by bourgeois ideology.

7. For a penetrating critique of New England theology after Edwards, see Joseph Haroutunian, *Piety Versus Moralism* (New York, 1983). Recent interpretations have considerably modified Haroutunian's influential view of New Divinity theology; see Joseph A. Conforti, *Samuel Hopkins and the New Divinity Movement* (Grand Rapids, Mich., 1981), and William Breitenbach, "Unregenerate Doings: Selflessness and Selfishness in New Divinity Theology," *American Quarterly* 34 (1982): 479–502. Nevertheless, Haroutunian's basic insights apply with unaltered force to the later perfectionist phase of the Second Great Awakening and to the broad evangelical Protestantism that characterized the middle class in the mid–nineteenth century.

8. On the declining power of the older generation in the early nineteenth century, see Joseph Kett, *Rites of Passage* (New York, 1977).

9. See Ronald P. Formisano, *The Transformation of Political Culture* (New York, 1983), pp. 93–106.

10. Ronald G. Walters, *American Reformers* (New York, 1978), ch. 1.

11. Perry Miller, "From Covenant to Revival," *The Life of the Mind in America* (New York, 1965).

12. Philip J. Greven, Jr., "Youth, Maturity, and Religious Conversion: A Note on the Ages of Converts in Andover, Massachusetts, 1711–1749," *Essex Institute Historical Collection* 108 (1972): 119–134.

13. I am grateful to Richard D. Shields for sharing this data with me. See "Revivals of Religion among New England Congregationalists, 1730–1835: The Evidence in Church Records," manuscript, Department of History, Ohio State University at Newark, 1979.

14. Donald M. Scott, *From Office to Profession* (Philadelphia, 1978), p. 77.

15. See Kett, *Rites of Passage*; Thomas Cole's series of paintings, "The Voyage of Life"; and Nathaniel Taylor, "The Goodness of God Designed to Reclaim," in Taylor, *Practical Sermons* (New York, 1848).

16. Albert Barnes, "The Harvest Past," in Barnes, *Practical Sermons: Designed for Vacant Congregations and Families* (Philadelphia, 1841), pp. 349–350.

17. Barnes, "The Harvest Past," pp. 442–443.

18. On the Puritan morphology of conversion, see Edmund S. Morgan, *Visible Saints* (New York, 1963), ch. 3.

19. See Charles Finney, "Instructions to Converts," *Lectures on Revivals of Religion* (New York, 1960; originally published 1835), pp. 386–387.

20. Jacob Knapp, *The Autobiography of Elder Jacob Knapp* (New York, 1858), p. 217.

21. Finney, "All Things Conspire for Evil to the Sinner," *Sermons on the Way of Salvation* (Oberlin, Ohio, 1891), p. 237.

22. Finney, "Means to Be Used with Sinners," *Lectures on Revivals of Religion*, pp. 149–150.

23. Taylor, "The Habitual Recognition of God," *Practical Sermons*, pp. 65–66. See Paul Johnson, *A Shopkeeper's Millennium* (New York, 1978).

24. William McLoughlin, ed., "Introduction" to Finney, *Lectures on Revivals of Religion*, p. XIX.

25. Finney, "Instructions to Young Converts," *Lectures on Revivals of Religion*, p. 418.

26. On veneration, see Fischer, *Growing Old*, ch. 2; and Thomas R. Cole, "The Ideology of Old Age and Death in American History," *American Quarterly* 31 (1979): 223–231.

27. See, for example, Herman Humphrey, *Revival Sketches and Manual* (New York, 1859), p. 460.

28. Cited in McLoughlin, ed., "Introduction."

29. Knapp, *Autobiography*, p. 88.

30. McLoughlin, "Introduction," n. 130.

31. Peter Cartwright, *The Autobiography of Peter Cartwright* (New York, 1956; originally published 1834), p. 43.

32. Finney, "Traditions of the Elders," *Lectures on Revivals of Religion*, p. 88.

33. For a reference to this metaphor in seventeenth-century French religious literature, see David G. Troyansky, "Old Age in the Rural Family of Enlightened Provence," in Peter N. Stearns, ed., *Old Age in Preindustrial Society* (New York, 1982), p. 209.

34. See, for example, Emerson Andrews, "The New Birth," *Revival Sermons Preached in Protracted Meetings* (Boston, 1870), p. 37.

35. For a description of the late Calvinist and Romantic Evangelical approaches to aging, see Thomas R. Cole, "Past Meridian: Aging and the Northern Middle Class, 1830–1930," Ph.D. dissertation, University of Rochester, 1980, chs. 2, 4.

36. Cortlandt Van Rensselaer, *Old Age: A Funeral Sermon* (Washington, D.C., 1841), p. 21.

37. Charles S. Porter, *Abandonment of God Deprecated by the Aged* (Utica, N.Y., 1842), pp. 9–10.

38. Albert Barnes, *Life at Three-Score and Ten*, 2d ed. (Philadelphia, 1869), pp. 51–52.

39. Robert N. Butler, "The Life Review: An Interpretation of Reminiscence in the Aged," *Psychiatry* 26 (1963): 65–76.

40. Porter, *Abandonment of God*, p. 11.

41. Ibid., pp. 11, 13.

42. Van Rensselaer, *Old Age*, p. 5.

43. Nathaniel Emmons, "Death without Order," *Works*, vol. III (Boston, 1842), pp. 36ff.

44. See Porter, *Abandonment of God*, pp. 13–14.

45. Van Rensselaer, *Old Age*, p. 7.

46. See David Stannard, *The Puritan Way of Death* (New York, 1977); and Gordon E. Geddes, *Welcome Joy: Death in Puritan New England* (Ann Arbor, Mich., 1981).

47. See, for example, Nathaniel Emmons, "Piety: A Peculiar Ornament to the Aged," *Works*, vol. II, pp. 492–505; Cotton Mather, *The Angel of Bethesda*, Gordon W. Jones, ed. (Waltham, Mass., 1972), pp. 317ff.

48. See Cole, "Past Meridian," chs. 3, 4, 5.

49. William Ellery Channing, "The Philanthropist," *Complete Works* (Boston, 1893), p. 602.

50. Porter, *Abandonment of God*, p. 5.

51. Theodore Parker, "The Nature of Man," *The Works of Theodore Parker*, vol. V (Boston, 1913), pp. 65–66.

52. See, for example, Sally Gadow, "Frailty and Strength: The Dialectic in Aging," *Gerontologist* 23 (1983): 144–147; Henri Nouwen and Walter Gaffney, *Aging* (New York, 1974); and Eugene Bianchi, *Aging as a Spiritual Journey* (New York, 1982).

Geriatrics: A Specialty in Search of Specialists

In his Pulitzer Prize–winning book *Why Survive? Being Old in America*, Robert Butler noted the persistent reluctance of young doctors to specialize in the diseases of old age. Despite the fact that the elderly account for one-quarter of the nation's health expenditures, consume 25 percent of the country's drugs, and spend twice as long in hospitals and long-term health facilities as other groups, geriatrics attracts few specialists.[1] The reasons for this are not hard to discern. As Butler and other prominent gerontologists have pointed out, the specialty by its very nature remains somewhat ambiguous. Theorists have yet to define precisely the parameters of the field or to distinguish clearly between normal and pathological aging. Moreover, doctors often bring a well-established set of prejudices to the treatment of the old. Early in their medical studies, they are led to belittle the aged "crock" with a multiplicity of complaints. There appears little reason to dedicate great care to those whose demise seems both irrevisible and imminent.[2]

This attitude is hardly novel. In 1909, I. L. Nascher coined the word *geriatrics* and pleaded with his fellow physicians to devote themselves to the study of old age. He envisioned a new field that would parallel pediatrics; the doctor would dedicate himself to every aspect of the elderly person's care.[3] Although numerous physicians wrote an article or two on the diseases of senescence, the response was hardly overwhelming. No medical school offered courses on the aged, nor did prestigious journals fill their pages with extensive studies on old age care. Most physicians simply ignored Nascher's plea and continued to concentrate on more lucrative and popular specialties. In contrast to surgery or gynecology, geriatrics remained a field of few avid practitioners.

The fact that medical attitudes toward geriatrics have changed little since the late nineteenth and early twentieth centuries is hardly surprising. The present-day reluctance to specialize in this field can be linked to the original model on which it was based. From the start, physicians who saw a need to treat the old as a separate group characterized their prospective patients as highly undesirable and incurable. They gave their fellow professionals little reason to think that extensive research would alter the nature of senescence. These gerontologists portrayed the aging process in such a way as to all but eliminate the notion of a healthy old age. Viewing senescence from a pathological perspective, they described the entire stage of life as one long progressive disease. Furthermore, the early experts left the scope of the new field rather ill defined. Economically, as well as theoretically, the rationale for the field's existence often seemed unclear. As a result, geriatrics became—and to a degree remains—a specialty of little definition and less appeal.

Early nineteenth-century physicians did not set out to portray the study and treatment of the old in such negative terms. Rarely, in fact, did they consider the elderly as a separate group requiring distinctive age-based treatment. Prior to the nineteenth century, no unified body of literature instructed practitioners on how to care for the particular needs of the elderly.[4] Most physicians prescribed for the old—if they prescribed at all—much as they would for younger persons. As conventionally described in *materia medica* texts, traditional therapeutics did not consider differences in age. Instead, treatment centered on the effects of specific drugs on the individual's system as a whole. Certain compounds stimulated, others calmed, and still others were noted for their ability to produce vomiting, sweating, or a purge.[5] Once an individual had survived childhood, however, his age had little effect on the theoretical operations of the chemical. A large dose of calomel was likely to produce the desired—and highly visible—result whether the patient was twenty or seventy.

Similarly, medical texts that classified diseases, either as specific entities or as general states, rarely considered the age of the adult. There were, to be sure, diseases that were routinely associated with senescence. Physicians believed that gout and rheumatism, for example, were particularly prevalent in the elderly. Yet neither the diagnosis nor the treatment of these illnesses altered with the advancing years. Once the appropriate symptoms appeared, a well-defined treatment was sure to follow, regardless of the patient's age. Other, more general, disease states, such as fevers or catarrhs, were classified by their external appearance, course, and cure, or by their seat and cause. These nosologies, though, took little notice of the life stage.

In addition, age played only a small part in those systems that explained disease in terms of a single factor. Since antiquity, scores of medical experts had attempted to find a single cause of all maladies. Depending on their chosen philosophy, they pinpointed the way to cure any disease. The practitioner need only relieve the pressure on the blood vessels, balance the humors, control the electric field around the body, or do whatever else might be called for in the logic of his explanatory system. Here again, life stages played but a small part. If all diseases had a single cause, there could hardly be one set of ailments for the old and another for the young.[6]

Yet pre-nineteenth-century physicians were not oblivious to the changes that came with age, nor did they expect all patients to react in precisely the same fashion. The scarcity of medical texts containing information on the care of the elderly was due to an unquestioning acceptance of their disabilities rather than to a failure to recognize them. The weakness of the old was not considered a state amenable to cure. Instead, physicians believed that this was the essential, irremediable quality of growing old. In describing senescence, writers consistently called upon the centuries-old metaphor in which the body was conceived of as a limited fund of vitality. At birth, the organism was endowed with a supply of energy that it used for growth and activity. As that supply diminished, the body was by adulthood merely able to maintain itself. Finally, its energy spent, it slowly decayed. Here, then, were the primary and highly visible stages of life: childhood, maturity, and old age. Loss of vitality explained this basic transformation and the obvious changes that came with the passage of years.

This hypothetical model also served to explain the numerous and often incurable illnesses that afflicted the elderly. Viewing the body in holistic terms, physicians believed that a change in any part of the system would affect the entire constitution. Thus, the organism's loss of vitality quickly led to a "predisposing debility,"[7] which might cause either systemic or specific diseases. In this sense, it mattered little whether a physician adhered to the belief that illness was an entity that entered the body from without, an imbalance among the humors, or the result of improper stimulation. Drained of energy, the elderly individual was unable to sustain the vital balance between the body and the environment. Disease was, then, an inevitable and predictable aspect of this stage of existence.

This model of aging did not require physicians to create a distinct senile therapeutics. Although the weakened condition of the old allowed the disease to "take over" the system, the manifestations of illness did not alter with age. The lack of vital energy, though, did have a systemic effect. Not only did it lead to a variety of ailments, but it also caused the dimming sense perceptions and weakening motor skills of the aged. The physician, however, had few remedies for this condition. Usually, he simply attempted to increase tonics. This was neither a revolutionary nor an age-distinctive treatment. Traditional therapeutics had long been based on the notion that the body was a product of the dynamic interactions between its own internal functions and the outside environment. By introducing stimulants into the bloodstream, medical authorities believed that they could revitalize the entire system, giving power to the senses and agility to the muscles, and thus making the body less susceptible to disease. In addition, they might hope to monitor and "adjust" the primary organs of the body in order to create a harmonious relationship among all the parts. In the early nineteenth century, for example, Sir Anthony Carlisle recommended regular bloodletting for the aged patient with a debilitated heart.[8] Again, the prescription followed the logic of rational therapeutics: the enervated organ, unable to pump at full capacity, would be greatly relieved if less blood flowed through the system. Once a new equilibrium was established, the body would operate at a lower, though presumably more efficient, level.

Such prescriptions were not abundant, however. Few physicians devoted themselves to the development of novel treatments of the aged. The debilitated state of such patients discouraged the application of experimental procedures—both for the sake of the patient and the reputation of the physician. Because he could not hope to restore completely the vitality of the old, the doctor's active intervention might only raise public doubt about the power and efficacy of his practice. "The prudent physician," advised one such medical man,

will not interfere, or if at all, with care and limitation, in cases where changes irresistible in their actions have occurred in any organ or function of the body. To urge medical treatment in the face of distinct proof to this effect is to sacrifice at once the good faith and usefulness of the physician.[9]

The doctor would not, in any case, have to face harsh criticism if his aged patient died without his therapeutic intervention. The same model that justified the numerous infirmities of the old also explained their demise. It was hardly the physician's fault. Each person, after all, had been allocated only a limited amount of energy and time. "The last calamity . . . in old people," concluded Richard Mead in 1762,

is that the whole body is afflicted. The very course of the blood is interrupted; hence the wretched man is seized with difficulty of breathing, apoplexies, or lethargies. The heart also, the principle and fountain of life, sinks through want of its usual force, and "the broken chariot falls into the pit."[10]

There was little that could be done for such aged persons. They had died natural deaths, the consequence of living long, and thus necessarily debilitating, lives.

In the first half of the nineteenth century, a small group of French clinicians began to challenge this traditional view of old age. These physicians did not suddenly see great hope for extending the life of the elderly. Their studies, in fact, only further convinced them there was little they could do to eradicate the ills of great age. They did, however, propose a new way of understanding and thus treating the aged patient. Using the latest medical theories and techniques, these elite clinicians began to characterize old age not merely in terms of advanced years or lack of energy but according to its unique physiological, anatomical, and psychological conditions. By midcentury, at least fifteen doctors had published monographs based on this new perception.[11] In their texts, these experts formulated a definition of old age that separated it medically from all other age groups and demanded the doctors' complete attention. They had, they believed, defined a clinical basis for senescence.

Initially, these physicians had not attempted to explain the aging process as such. Their conception of old age was only one of the many novel ideas produced by the Paris school of medicine. Under the leadership of physicians such as M. F. X. Bichat, F. J. V. Broussais, and P. C. A. Louis, elite French doctors began to question classic assumptions about the nature of disease. Redefining the direction of medical inquiry, they first became clinicians and pathologists; the hospitals of France evolved into centers for empirical study. As a result of this new approach, these physicians discarded traditional systems of nosology. Fits, fevers, and inflammations, they declared, were only symptoms of disease, not actual illness. Instead, they attempted to correlate these external ailments with subsequent pathological findings. Disease, they believed, left unmistakable traces in the tissues of the body. Postmortem findings, such as sclerosis, fibrosis, and degeneration, were keys to the classification of disease. Viewed in these terms, illness could no longer be thought of as a general systemic condition. Instead, these clinicians and pathologists began to devise nosologies based on specific localized disease entities.[12]

In the course of this work, clinicians came to draw medical implications about the effects of aging. At the outset, much of the research had been conducted on elderly individuals. Two of the large Paris hospitals in which they worked, the Bicêtre and Salpatrière, housed not only the sick and dying but a sizable population of aged paupers as well. At the start, these elderly persons had been of particular interest to physicians because of their accessibility. Institutionalized as a consequence of destitution and illness, the aged poor became captive subjects of long-term scientific inquiry. Research into the pathological effects of disease convinced clinicians of the distinctive nature of the ailments that vexed these elderly patients. Aging, like many disease entities, appeared to cause numerous pathological transformations. In the autopsies performed on elderly persons, physicians repeatedly discovered evidence of general degeneration, ossification, calcification. Similarly, in both the noticeably ailing and seemingly well, they discovered unmistakable signs of arteriosclerosis. Bichat stated that this was the case in seven out of ten elderly persons, regardless of the apparent state of their health.[13] Other physicians placed the percentage close to one hundred. Hardening of the arteries, they declared, was the universal condition of the senescent.[14] If this were true, those who survived to extreme old age had little hope of escaping debilitating illness. According to the laws of nature, the productive years of life were sharply and irreversibly limited.

The pathological findings cited by the French clinicians were not entirely novel. Even before the nineteenth century, a limited number of autopsies on extremely aged individuals had revealed anatomical alterations. In 1706, for example, an English physician, Dr. James Keill, performed an autopsy on John Boyles, a button-maker who died allegedly at age 130. Keill noted the same hardening of the arteries, the deterioration of various organs, and the addition of fibrous material cited by French clinicians more than a century later. The English physician, however, believed that his findings were inconclusive; too few dissections had been (or, at the time, could be) performed to justify any definitive statement about the nature of aging.[15] Most eighteenth-century physicians, however, strongly believed that the arteries played an essential role in the aging process. This theory, along with an emphasis on the importance of the bloodstream, neatly coincided with their systemic view of the body. The statement "a man is as old as his arteries" had allegedly been coined by Thomas Sydenham in the late seventeenth century. Two hundred years later, it had achieved the status of maxim. Physicians repeated it with the frequency and authority of a classic verity.[16] In addition, doctors were hardly surprised to discover fatty deposits or fibrous material in the organism. In the writings of both solidists and humoralists, the increasing substance and dryness of the elderly body had long been cited as proof of the validity of their conceptual systems.

French clinicians, however, placed these findings into a new framework. When doctors defined and classified disease by changes in the tissues, the visible transformation of the organism acquired new meaning. The pathological aspects of the anatomy were not secondary to life processes generally but constituted a primary deterioration of the fundamental elements of existence. Merely by growing old, the individual had developed the exterior symptoms and internal lesions that were the signs of specific debilitating illnesses. This degeneration of the body had not occurred merely because the patient lacked the vitality to resist. Even in the seemingly healthy and active, fibrosis, ossification, and other lesions were found to exist. In old age, disease seemed to be a discrete condition. As revealed by the deterioration of tissues, it was an inherent, progressive part of senescence.

On the basis of these findings, Paris clinicians viewed old age as a distinctive and irreversible segment of the life cycle.[17] The changes that came with advanced age were almost always degenerative. There was little hope that the body would ever return to its original condition. To these physicians, senescence had its own distinctive physiological nature; it differed from youth in ways that the untrained observer could not begin to comprehend. A new professional tone characterized their descriptions of the elderly organism. The body was no longer portrayed as a united system, slowly disintegrating in every part. Instead, citing the findings of postmortem studies, clinicans attempted to reduce the operations and malfunctions of the old to "hard" pathological mechanism and lesions. The sight of the aged, for example, could hardly regain its power of perception. The internal structure of the eye was radically different from that found in most young persons. The physiologist François Magendie traced its internal changes through three distinct phases:

1st, the diminution of the quantity of the humours of the eye, which diminishing the refractive power of the organ, prevents the old man from distinguishing with precision surrounding objects; and in order to see them distinctly he is obliged to remove them to a distance, because the light which proceeds from them is less divergent, or he is obliged to employ convex glasses, which diminish the divergence of the rays.

2nd, the opacity beginning in the crystalline, which dims the sight, and tends by its increase to bring on blindness, in producing that malady known by the name of cataract.

3rd, the diminution of the sensibility of the retina, or otherwise of the brain, which prevents the perceptions of the impression produced on the eye, and which leads to total and incurable blindness.[18]

Similar anatomical malfunctions were cited for all parts of the body. These changes had important implications for the practicing physician. He could no longer assume that a single disease would have the same symptoms in all his patients, nor could he rely upon a unified therapeutic regimen. Disease categorization, based on the pathological transformation of tissues, necessitated a clear understanding of the normal and abnormal conditions for each stage of existence. The doctor who attempted to return senile tissue to its adolescent state would be truly foolhardy if not indeed destructive.[19] The elderly needed to be treated by standards that conformed to their own stage of life.

Here lay the basis for a specialization in the diseases of old age. The physician was required to know what ailments plagued the elderly, the physiological and anatomical basis, and the best—if any—method of treatment. By mid-nineteenth century, these points were being raised by German and English, as well as French, clinicians. They urged their fellow physicians to understand the importance of gerontological studies and to further work in the field. The declaration of one of the most important forerunners of geriatric medicine, Jean Charcot, was typical of the sentiment that would be repeated for decades. "The importance of a special study of the diseases of old age," he wrote in 1861, "cannot be contested at this day. We have come to recognize in reality that the pathology presents its difficulties, which cannot be surmounted except by long experience and a profound acquaintance with its peculiar characteristics." [20]

Despite such pleas, the concerns of the gerontologist remained rather ambiguous. Physicians lacked a well-defined set of standards by which to evaluate the condition of the old. These criteria were not easy to devise. The ideal of the field was to treat the elderly patient by recognizing the problems of his age, rather than by the standards of the young adult. As in pediatrics, the individual's development or decline was to be related to his specific life stage. No one assumed that the child was feeble who had not yet developed adult teeth or muscle control. Why then, physicians were fond of asking, was the old person labeled debilitated when his body continued to undergo natural anatomical transformations?

Concerned doctors discovered, however, that the two stages were not precisely analogous. The child began from a position of weakness. His development marked a measurable increase in both strength and capabilities. The point of origin for old age, however, was maturity; physicians continually returned to this stage to chart the individual's decline. The advent of age was then marked by the same anatomical changes that were a basis for the classification of disease. Where then did old age and illness begin? And, perhaps even more perplexing, could the old ever be vigorous, or was the very notion of a healthy senescence a contradiction in terms?

Most European clinicians seemed to imply that illness and old age were inseparably intertwined, if not quite synonymous. At best, the division between the two was extremely subjective. A large proportion of the diseases of old age were attributed to natural, intractable changes in the organism. "We shall have to note," wrote Charcot in his lectures on senescence, ''that the textural changes which old age induces in the organism sometimes attain such a point that the physiological and pathological states seemed to mingle by an imperceptible transition, and to be no longer distinguishable.''[21] In addition, there were numerous senile diseases—diseases that might also appear in the young but which would have distinct, age-related symptoms due to the transformed state of the elderly anatomy. Yet Charcot's specificity in classifying disease was not equaled by an emphasis upon therapeutics. As clinician, he endorsed only a few remedies; along with exercise and diet, Charcot relied upon such widely used drugs as mercury and opium.[22] Once anatomical changes had begun, he confessed, there was little that could be done to return the individual to his former condition.

Part of the difficulty in devising age-related therapeutics lay in the physician's inability to define the cause of aging. French clinicians had rejected the vital energy model for one based on the degeneration of tissues. With the work of Theodor Schwann and Rudolf Virchow, the importance of the tissue was augmented by an emphasis on the cell. This was the basic unit of life, responsible for growth and thus for aging. Several physicians theorized that throughout a person's life, old cells were constantly dying, some to be replaced by new generations, others simply to be eliminated. In old age, the process seemed to work extremely inefficiently. The cells that were replaced appeared less able to receive and assimilate food. With the use of the microscope, the scientist became aware that the composition of the cells had changed: a larger proportion of the mass was protoplasm, a far smaller part nucleus. As a result, the old suffered from numerous ''gouty'' diseases in which their bodies were unable to digest proper nourishment.[23] In the course of this process, the aged organism became feeble and seemed to waste away. Moreover, some types of cells were never replaced. In the brain, this depletion was tragically apparent as the once intellectually active individual gradually lost the use of his mental facilities.

Physicians had little control over this process. They could not stop the cell from evolving into its senile state, nor were they able to isolate the mechanism that controlled aging. In effect, what the elite European clinician had done was to divide the cause of aging into smaller and smaller units: a general vital energy had, by midcentury, been replaced by a degeneration of tissues, and, finally, by an inexorable devolution of cells. In the process of this reformulation, aging had become defined as a progressive disease that caused a multitude of physiological and anatomical changes. Growing old was itself the source of the inevitable organic alterations known as old age.

This conception of aging—with both its lack of therapeutics and its ambiguous causality—became the basis for the medical specialty of geriatrics. The specialty was officially named by the American physician I. L. Nascher, whose numerous articles and whose book *Geriatrics: The Diseases of Old Age and Their Treatment* became the standard for the new field.[24]

Like the French and German physicians on whom he based his work, Nascher approached the study of old age from a clinical perspective. Linking the cause of aging to the evolution of the cell, he defined the process of growing old as one beset by pathological problems. "In senility," he explained, "the cells of most tissues are retrograding and are not well adapted to the available nutrition and surroundings."[25] As a result, elderly men and women could expect to experience a wide variety of anatomical alterations. According to Nascher, "degeneration, infiltrations, atrophy, hyperthrophy, ossification, calcification, sclerosis, ankylosis, contraction, compression, change of form or shape, and the formation of new tissue" were all a normal part of the aging process.[26]

Based on this belief, Nascher, like the French clinicians before him, argued that a separate medical practice for the old was imperative. Doctors who treated the elderly's "normal" debility as an illness or confused a senile kidney with Bright's disease might do real harm to their aged patients. With the study of geriatrics, however, Nascher contended, this would not occur. Physicians would then be able to differentiate between physiological and pathological change and treat the diseases, rather than the normal conditions, of old age.[27]

At least, that was the theory. Yet even Nascher had some difficulty distinguishing between the normal and diseased state of the elderly. The same lesions and other degenerations that physicians believed were an expected part of growing old also defined the elderly's illnesses. "It is impossible," Nascher wrote,

to draw a sharp line between health and disease in old age. With every organ and tissue undergoing a degenerative change which affects the physiological functions, it is a matter for personal opinion to determine at what point the changes in the anatomic features and physiologic functions depart from the normal changes of senility and to what degree.[28]

Despite his hopes, therefore, Nascher had to admit that geriatrics did not exactly parallel pediatrics. For children, the standards of health could be clearly charted as they gained strength and intelligence; for the old, the standards of health implied progressive and incurable ailments. The increasing debility of the elderly followed a course that led naturally to death.[29] Moreover, Nascher discovered that the field of geriatrics differed from pediatrics in another significant way. Physicians looked upon the young as worthy patients, likely to benefit from extensive research and treatment. The old, however, were generally perceived as being too decrepit and infirm to profit from great care. "While the dependence of the child arouses sympathy," he wrote, "in the aged the repugnance aroused by the disagreeable facial aspect and the idea of economic worthlessness destroys the sympathy we bestow upon the child and instills a spirit of irritability if not positive enmity against the helplessness of the aged."[30]

Nascher's own work did little to change this image of old age; his portrayal of the elderly repeated many of the most negative stereotypes of his day. In his text, the old were pictured as "selfish," "suspicious," "egotistical," and "out-of-date."[31] These characteristics, though, were more than the prejudices of one man; they seemed to be supported by the most scientific model of senescence. The brain, like any other organ composed of living cells, underwent physiological decay. With each passing year, it became less sensitive to stimulation and less able to process complicated information. As a result, the elderly grew set in their ways, unable to achieve intellectually or adapt to the modern world. "Owing to the weakened intellect in old age," Nascher wrote, "the individual loses control over the emotions, weakened memory, especially of recent events, makes him more conscious of the old order of things, he becomes 'old fashioned,' holding on to ancient ideas and methods and becomes irritated when these are displaced."[32] With the dying of brain cells and the onset of arteriosclerosis, the debility and unproductiveness of the elderly seemed inevitable. Senility, with its irreversible mental and physical demise, awaited all those who lived to advanced life.[33]

But the changes that came with senility did not stop with the loss in intellect or memory. Nascher, like most physicians of his era, also as-

sumed that a small but significant proportion of the aged would engage
in immoral activities. By senescence, he believed, the "normal" individual had lost both the ability and inclination for sexual relations.
With senility, however, the desire for sexual activities returned, without the corresponding capability. As a result, the cravings of the old
often led them to commit numerous sexual perversions. The individual
had little control over these desires; he was subject to his own abnormal physiology.[34] The dirty old man had become more than a repul-
sive stereotype. His portrayal was seemingly based on the findings of
clinical research.

With this view of old age, most physicians, Nascher realized, approached the treatment of the old with little hope and anticipation. The
elderly, after all, hardly qualified as ideal subjects for medical attention. Compared to the young or middle-aged, their diseases were extremely complicated. Normal senile degenerations made even the simplest diagnosis difficult. Outward physical appearances gave little clue
to inward condition; physiological alterations often masked serious illness.[35] And, even if the proper diagnosis was made, Nascher admitted
that he had few sure remedies to prescribe. Like Charcot, he focused
more on the pathology of old age than on its therapeutics. His cures
for senile diseases, he admitted, were severely limited. As long as researchers continued to ignore the problems of the aged, physicians would
be unsure of the effects of most drugs on senile tissue.[36] Thus, like
clinicians before him, Nascher relied upon a variety of traditional ther-
apies. Generally, he treated the debility of the elderly with tonics and
stimulants, while recommending changes in the patient's regimen. Along
with gardening, fishing, music, reading, and gossip, "the favorite pas-
time of the aged," he endorsed the companionship of a young person,
"preferably of the opposite sex."[37]

Such recommendations could hardly be considered the most modern
therapeutics. In contrast to the revolutionary advances being made in
surgery or epidemiology, they appeared strangely unscientific and old
fashioned. Even so, Nascher complained, doctors often had a difficult
time getting their aged patients to comply. Most old people, he contended, viewed medical prescriptions as impositions: retirement was
rejected, institutionalization dismissed.[38] Nor, Nascher warned, could
physicians expect great cooperation from the relatives of the elderly.
Family members were more apt to cater to their unwise whims than to
adhere to the practitioner's wise admonitions. Usually, the old neither

knew how to care for themselves nor could be dissuaded from following harmful routines.[39]

These were hardly words of encouragement to the young physician considering a specialty in the diseases of old age. The old seemed difficult to diagnose, impossible to cure, and rarely grateful for treatment. Not surprisingly, then, Nascher's publications convinced few doctors to devote themselves to geriatrics.[40] Yet the clinical model on which he based his work found a wide and ready audience. In the late nineteenth and early twentieth centuries, medical experts consistently portrayed old age as a pathological state. In case after case, they depicted the elderly as irreversibly ''senile'' despite varied and often conflicting symptoms.[41] Once so labeled, the infirm old were given little chance or consideration. Administrators of acute-care hospitals rejected them; superintendents of private mental asylums advised them to seek shelter in the wards of the county almshouse.[42] For the practical physician, there seemed, as even Nascher admitted, ''a natural reluctance to exert oneself for those who are economically worthless and must remain so, or to strive against the inevitable, though there be the possibility of momentary success.''[43]

With this prevailing belief, Nascher's call for a new field devoted to the old understandably met with little success. In the early twentieth century, geriatrics remained a specialty in name only. Its ambiguous causality and negative image of the patient population deterred extensive research and care. Moreover, the development of geriatrics was further inhibited by its continued lack of definition and scope. As new specialties such as cardiology developed, which dealt largely with the old, geriatrics appeared somewhat repetitious and general. Most aged persons, and even the medical profession as a whole, remained relatively unconvinced that the establishment of the specialty was a clear necessity.[44]

Beginning in the 1940s, there were some signs that this attitude was starting to change.[45] Two new organizations, the American Geriatrics Society (1942) and the Gerontology Society (1945), focused upon the needs and treatment of the aged. Publications such as *Geriatric Medicine* (1943), edited by Edward J. Stieglitz, attempted to define and encourage the study of senescent care.[46] Stieglitz approached geriatrics from a far more optimistic stance than had the pathologists of the past. Medical and technological advances meant that physicians finally had hope of eradicating many of the most troublesome ills of old age. Greater care for the elderly was also stimulated by the federal government, through the passage of Medicare legislation in 1965. For the first time, the treatment of the aged seemed both economically and medically justified.

Yet, even today, despite these changes, geriatrics is hardly well established; compared to other popular fields it is still in its infancy. Many medical schools fail to offer a single course on the care of the elderly, while few doctors choose to limit their practice to the old.[47] In 1977, in fact, only 317 physicians listed their primary interest as geriatrics; another 312 identified the specialty as their secondary or tertiary concern. These 629 practitioners made up a mere 0.2 percent of the American medical profession.[48] Advocates for the field explain such minute numbers by pointing to the unresolved issues that still deter the would-be specialist. Consistently they note the problems doctors face in defining illness in old age and call for research that would both make the definition of normal and abnormal senescence more explicit as well as identify the mechanism behind the aging process.[49] Moreover, they repeatedly note the antagonism that many young doctors feel toward treating the aged. Physicians, whether in hospitals or in their own offices, generally spend far less time with elderly persons than with their younger counterparts.[50] They continue to assume that extensive care for the old is economically unjustified and, ultimately, futile. Such beliefs, of course, are not new; the words echo those expressed by both Nascher and the French clinicians. In both theory and sentiment, in fact, they can be linked to the model of old age developed by the first nineteenth-century gerontologists.

NOTES

1. Robert Butler, *Why Survive? Being Old in America* (New York, 1975), p. 174. See also Leslie S. Libow and Frederick T. Sherman, *The Core of Geriatric Medicine* (St. Louis, 1981), p. 5.

2. Butler, *Why Survive?*, pp. 179–180.

3. I. L. Nascher, "Geriatrics," *New York Medical Journal* 90 (21 August 1909): 358–359.

4. This is not to say that before the nineteenth century individual physicians did not discuss senescence or describe the best regimen for attaining old age. See, for some examples, Gerald Gruman, *A History of Ideas about the Prolongation of Life* (Philadelphia, n.d.); Frederic D. Zeman, *Life's Later Years:*

Studies in the Medical History of Old Age, reprinted in Gerald J. Gruman, ed., *Roots of Modern Gerontology and Geriatrics* (New York, 1979). Yet, with a few exceptions, they rarely developed a specific senile therapeutics or theory of disease causality. For one notable American exception, see Benjamin Rush, *Medical Inquiries and Observations* (Philadelphia, 1797), pp. 308–310.

5. For a discussion of the theoretical system on which traditional therapeutics was based, see Charles E. Rosenberg, "The Therapeutic Revolution: Medicine, Meaning and Social Change in Nineteenth-Century America," *Perspectives on Medicine and Biology* 20 (1977): 485–506.

6. Richard Harrison Shryock, *The Development of Modern Medicine* (New York, 1947), p. 29.

7. This is Benjamin Rush's terminology. See Esmond Ray Long, *A History of American Pathology* (Springfield, Ill., 1962), p. 17.

8. "I am convinced," Anthony Carlisle wrote, "that the feebleness of age, when produced by sanguineous oppression, can only be removed by diminishing the quantity of blood, and that, on the promptitude of the patient will depend," Carlisle, *An Essay on the Disorders of Old Age and the Means of Prolonging Human Life* (Philadelphia, 1819), p. 14; see also Benjamin Rush, "An Account of the State of the Body and Mind in Old Age and Observations upon Its Diseases and Their Remedies," in Rush, *Medical Inquiries*, p. 320.

9. Henry Holland, *Medical Notes and Reflections* (Philadelphia, 1839), p. 154.

10. Richard Mead, *The Medical Works of Richard Mead* (London, 1762), p. 609.

11. In the first half of the nineteenth century, the French physicians who wrote on old age were Delseries (1802), Auchner (1804), Mauvid-Montergon (1804), Delphin-Lamothe (1806), Millot (1807), Junin (1813), Brossar-Ysabeau (1815), Vinache (1816), Belloir (1817), Secretain (1827), and Venus (1837). Erwin H. Ackerknecht, "Hygiene in France, 1815–1848," *Bulletin of the History of Medicine* 22 (1948): 122f.

12. Erwin H. Ackerknecht, *Medicine at the Paris Hospital, 1794–1848* (Baltimore, 1967), ch. 7, in which he discusses the philosophy of Corvisart, Bayle, and Laennec. See also Oswei Temkin, "Health and Disease," in Temkin, ed., *The Double Face of Janus and Other Essays in the History of Medicine* (Baltimore, 1977) pp. 429–430.

13. Ackerknecht, *Medicine at the Paris Hospital*, p. 56.

14. Emile Demange, cited in Elie Metchnikoff, *The Nature of Man: Studies in Optimistic Philosophy* (New York and London, 1903), p. 36; see also Julius Althaus, "Old Age and Rejuvenescence," *Lancet* 1 (21 January 1899): 150; Frederick N. Brown, "Some Observations upon Old Age and its Consequences," *Providence Medical Journal* 10 (January 1909): 58; J. Madison Taylor, "The Conservation of Energy in Those of Advancing Years," *Popular Science Monthly* 64 (March 1904): 406.

15. Sir John Sinclair, *Code of Health and Longevity* (Edinburgh, 1807), app. VI, pp. 21–22.

16. Reynold Webb Wilcox, "The Therapeutics of Old Age," *American Medicine* 4 (April 1909): 178.

17. The importance of the different life segments was also emphasized by the development in the nineteenth century of the study of embryology. Oswei Temkin, "German Concepts of Ontology and History around 1800," in *Double Face of Janus*, pp. 373–389.

18. François Magendie, *An Elementary Compendium of Physiology: For the Use of Students*, trans. W. Mulligan (Philadelphia, 1824), pp. 61–62.

19. Review of "On the Diseases of Old Age and Their Care," by Dr. C. Constatt, *British and Foreign Medical Review* 17 (1848): 111.

20. J. M. Charcot and Alfred Loomis, *Clinical Lectures on the Diseases of Old Age* (New York, 1881), p. 18. The parallel with pediatrics was continually stressed, despite the fact that, when Charcot first wrote this statement (1861), pediatrics, as a specialty, was still being debated. Yet the link between the two studies seemed natural: if children were not to be treated by "adult" therapeutics and standards, neither should the elderly. Thus, many of the physicians who defended the need for a study of children's diseases also called for the creation of geriatrics. The introduction to I. L. Nascher, *Geriatrics: The Diseases of Old Age and Their Treatment* (Philadelphia, 1914), was written by Abraham Jacobi, often credited as the father of pediatrics. See also Clarence Bartlett, "Clinical Lectures on Diseases in Old Age," *Hahnemannian Monthly* 41 (February 1906): 107; R. R. Hopkins, "Diseases and Conditions Peculiar to Old Age," *Cincinnati Medical Journal* 11 (1896): 393; S. Newton Leo, "A Consideration of the Senile State," *New York Medical Journal* 74 (22 December 1906); J. M. Taylor, "The Hygiene and Management of Old Age," *Journal of Orificial Surgery* 7 (1899–1900): 74.

21. Charcot and Loomis, *Clinical Lectures*, p. 20.

22. Ibid., pp. 74–75.

23. Althaus, "Old Age and Rejuvenescence," p. 151; J. Bandaline, "Struggle of Science with Old Age," *Medical Record* 64 (1903): 82–83; J. W. Bell, "A Plea for the Aged," *Journal of the American Medical Association* 33 (4 November 1899): 1137; Charcot and Loomis, *Clinical Lectures*, p. 21, on gouty diseases, pp. 38–92; John D. Covert, "The Pathology of Old Age: Can It Be Delayed?," *Texas State Journal of Medicine* 4 (1909): 277; W. M. Gibson, "Some Considerations of Senescence," *New York State Journal of Medicine* 9 (September 1909): 380–382; I. N. Love, "The Needs and Rights of Old Age," *Journal of the American Medical Association* 29 (1897): 1034; Joseph C. Martindale, *Human Anatomy, Physiology, and Hygiene* (Philadelphia, 1872), p. 213; Charles Sedgwick Minot, *The Problem of Age, Growth and Death* (New York, 1907), p. 487; Nascher, *Geriatrics*, pp. 1–4, 43–47; Rudolf Virchow, *Cellular Pathology* (New York, 1858), pp. v, 29, 84–85,

358–359; Ernst Wagner, *A Manual of General Pathology*, trans. John Van Drugen and E. C. Sequin (New York, 1876), p. 50; Wilcox, "Therapeutics of Old Age," p. 178.

24. I. L. Nascher, "Longevity and Rejuvenescence," *New York Medical Journal* 74 (1909): 795–800; idem, "Geriatrics," pp. 428–429; idem, "The Treatment of Diseases in Senility," *Medical Record* 76 (1909); 987–992; idem, "Anatomical Changes in Senility," *Medical Council* 15 (January 1910): 17–22; idem, "Physiological Change in Old Age," *Medical Council* 15 (February 1910): 52–56; idem, "Pathology of Old Age," *Medical Council* 15 (March 1910): 94–99; idem, "Hygiene and Regimen in Old Age," *Medical Council* 15 (May 1910); 166–169 and (June 1910): 200–201; idem, "The Treatment of Disease in Senility," *Medical Council* 15 (August 1910): 271–275; idem, *Geriatrics*.

25. Nascher, *Geriatrics*, pp. 46–47.

26. Nascher, "Anatomical Changes in Senility," p. 17.

27. Ibid., p. 7; idem, *Geriatrics*, p. 11; idem, "Treatment of Disease in Senility," p. 274.

28. Nascher, "Pathology of Old Age," p. 94.

29. Nascher, "Anatomical Changes in Senility," p. 17; "Treatment of Disease in Senility," p. 988.

30. Nascher, *Geriatrics*, pp. 12–13.

31. Ibid., pp. 15–16, 38, 477–478; Nascher, "Physiological Change in Old Age," p. 56.

32. Nascher, *Geriatrics*, p. 38.

33. The changes in connotation of the word *senile* reflected the impact of the fatalism of the clinical model of old age. Before the nineteenth century, the term had little to do with disease; anything "suited for or incidental to old age" could be considered senile. By the late nineteenth century, *senile* was strictly and monolithically applied to age-related ailments. In terms of usage, at least, the entire stage of life had acquired a medical connotation. Moreover, doctors now assumed that most people would suffer the debility associated with senility. As the cells of the body decayed, so too did those of the mind. The normal state of being old, it seemed, was that of debilitating illness. See *Oxford English Dictionary*, "senile"; Carole Haber, *Beyond Sixty-Five: The Dilemma of Old Age in America's Past* (Cambridge, Eng., 1983), pp. 73–76.

34. Nascher, *Geriatrics*, pp. 19, 38, 484. For some other physicians who agree with this point of view, see Allen McLane Hamilton, *A Manual of Medical Jurisprudence* (New York, 1883), pp. 27–28; J. H. Kellogg, *Plain Facts for Old and Young* (Burlington, Iowa, 1877), p. 385; Bernard Van Oven, *On the Decline of Life in Health and Disease* (London, 1853), pp. 99–100.

35. Nascher, "Anatomical Changes in Senility," p. 22; idem, "Treatment of Diseases in Senility," p. 274.

36. Nascher, *Geriatrics*, pp. 58–60.

37. Ibid., pp. 13–14, 489.

38. Ibid., pp. 477–478, 484–490.

39. Ibid., pp. 477–478; idem, "Hygiene and Regimen in Old Age," p. 166.

40. Joseph T. Freeman, "Nascher: Excerpts from His Life, Letters and Works," in Gruman, ed., *Roots of Modern Gerontology*, p. 17.

41. In 1903, for instance, in an investigation of the Boston Almshouse and Hospital at Long Island, Alderman Nolan asked Dr. F. P. Lord, "What are the symptoms of senility? It seems to me to cover every case here." Dr. Lord's reply, which brought laughter from the audience, was, "It is old age itself." *Majority and Minority Reports of an Investigation of Boston Alms House and Hospital at Long Island* (Boston Municipal Printing Office, 1904), p. 106. See also Haber, *Beyond Sixty-Five*, pp. 74–78, 90–91.

42. Haber, *Beyond Sixty-Five*, pp. 89–91.

43. Nascher, *Geriatrics*, pp. v, vi, 12–13.

44. Even as late as 1977, the American Geriatric Society opposed a separate specialty. Robert L. Kane, et al., *Geriatrics in the United States* (Lexington, Mass., 1981), p. 83.

45. Kane et al., *Geriatrics*, p. 83.

46. Edward J. Stieglitz, ed., *Geriatric Medicine. Diagnosis and Management of Disease in the Aging and the Aged* (Philadelphia, 1943).

47. In 1979, 63 out of 124 medical schools reported that they did not offer a course on geriatrics or gerontology. Kane et al., *Geriatrics*, p. 31.

48. Ibid., p. 18.

49. See, for example, Butler, *Why Survive?*, pp. 179–180; Rodney M. Coe, "The Geriatric Patient in the Community," in *Cowdry's The Care of the Geriatric Patient*, Franz U. Steinberg, ed. (St. Louis, 1976), pp. 493–503; Libow and Sherman, *Core of Geriatric Medicine*, pp. 3–5; Franz U. Steinberg, "The Evaluation and Treatment of the Geriatric Patient," in *Cowdry's Care of the Geriatric Patient*, pp. 3–10.

50. Kane et al., *Geriatrics*, pp. 21–29.

PART III

THE ELDERLY AS HISTORICAL ACTORS: FAMILY AND DEMOGRAPHY

Accounting for Change in the Families of the Elderly in the United States, 1900–Present

The twentieth century is the era of change in the social history of the elderly. Every quantitative indicator related to the older population points to this conclusion, with the more recent forty years encapsuling more change than the first four decades of this century. In the United States, the number of persons over age sixty-five has expanded from three million to over twenty-five million between 1900 and 1980; the share of this group in the total population has increased from 4 to 11 percent over the same interval. At the beginning of this century, two-thirds of men over age sixty-five were gainfully employed, but by 1980, only one older man in five remained in the labor force. Inasmuch as there is a "before and after" in the social history of the elderly, that transition has occurred in this century.[1]

To these well-known demographic and economic changes must be added evidence of substantial alteration in the family structure of the elderly. Under current census definitions, old people have shifted from living as relatives in family households to living alone or apart from related individuals.[2]

The dominant perspective in the history of aging has neglected or minimized the importance of this twentieth-century change in family structure. Resting on the works of both economists and historians, the reigning interpretation makes the present fit comfortably into the past. If not manifest in earlier periods, current preferences, particularly the

Relationship of elderly person to householder	1900	1980
Family householder or spouse	57.0%	55.4%
Other relative of householder	28.6%	8.9%
Nonfamily householder	6.4%	28.6%
Nonrelative, group quarters, or inmate of institution	8.0%	7.1%

Source: U.S. Bureau of the Census, *Census of Population, 1980: General Population Characteristics* (Washington, D.C., 1982), vols. 2–52, Table 21; Daniel Scott Smith, "A Community-Based Samples of the Older Population from the 1880 and 1900 United States Manuscript Censuses," *Historical Methods* 11 (1978): 67–74.

desirability of independent residence for the elderly and current institutional arrangements, especially the role of the welfare state, are not
radical innovations. Even if there is a significant element of truth in
this widely accepted viewpoint, its limits have not yet been carefully
explored.

The dominant interpretation emphasizes the continuity of the family
over the centuries; the name usually given to this persistence is the
northwest European family pattern.[3] While this pattern has demographic aspects, including late marriage, a narrow age gap between
spouses, and a high proportion never marrying, the key familial element is a stress on marriage instead of a larger kin network or lineage.
The fundamental principle of family identity, and as a consequence,
the normative and often prevailing rule of residence, appears in Gen-
esis 2:24: "Therefore a man leaves his mother and father and cleaves
to his wife."

This emphasis on the unit of husband and wife as the core of the
family was present from the beginnings of European settlement in
America. Prescriptive writings on the family, as, for example, by Puritan divines, stressed family relationships and roles rather than this
biblical or other rule of residence. The residential specification of the
family, usually called the household, was of lesser concern. Addition-
ally, some forms of multigenerational coresidence do not violate this
biblical precept; the passage leaves open, for example, the normative
living arrangement between a widowed parent and his or her married
child.[4]

Interpreting the history of the Western family in terms of its essential and perdurable nuclearity finds confirmation in current evidence.
Public opinion surveys now find strong support in all age groups for

independent residence of adult generations within the family. Those old people who live with their children today tend to be poorer or in poorer health than those who reside apart from their children. Economists who have examined recent time series, ecological units, and individual-level data all find a positive relationship between higher income and the likelihood of the old living alone or apart from children.[5]

Since the predictors of living arrangements among the elderly today are consistent with the historical distinctiveness of the northwest European family pattern, the dominant perspective must ignore or minimize the extent and significance of the transformation of the family structure of the elderly in this century. To explore the validity of this interpretation, four types of change—compositional, structural, processual, and categorical—must be examined. The dominant view is compatible with the first and last of these categories; to the extent that structural or processual change has occurred during the twentieth century, the accepted perspective requires modification. Although the distinctiveness of each type of change depends on matters of definition, this accounting approach can bring clarity to the study of change in the families of the elderly during this century.

Compositional change refers to alterations in the distribution of categories of the important independent variables (sex, age, marital status, and gainful employment) that influence family structure. Compositional change exists if the overall rate changes, but the coefficient relating dependent and independent variable remains unchanged. *Structural* change, on the other hand, involves a changing relationship between a dependent and independent variable. *Processual* change refers to a change in the dependent variable that is unrelated to compositional or structural changes. A residual category, processual change is usually captured in regression analysis by a time or "*Zeitgeist* dummy" variable, a nice bit of jargon that describes both the phenomenon and the historian left puzzling over it; that "times have changed" is not an explanation so much as a fact that needs explaining. *Categorical* change is also a perplexing category, particularly for quantitative analysis. If what is quantitatively measured is qualitatively different at two points in time, then a comparison is of limited value. Absence of gainful employment in 1900, for example, does not have the same implications for income of an elderly man as retirement from the labor force in 1980. Similarly, living *near* a child in 1980 may be qualitatively similar to living *with* a child in 1900.[6]

COMPOSITIONAL CHANGE

It is logically possible that the transformation in the family structure of the elderly in the twentieth century was driven by the other great shifts in the structure of the older population. If compositional change was crucial, then the dominant perspective needs no reconsideration. If such compositional changes were important in accounting for the transformation of the family structure of the elderly, then several of the characteristics shown in table 5.1 should be involved. First, major differences in type of living arrangement were connected to these characteristics in 1900. For example, only 10.1 percent of employed married men between ages sixty-five and seventy-four lived with a married child in 1900, compared to 57.6 percent of unmarried, unemployed men aged seventy-five and older. These differences are much larger than those associated with region, ethnicity, rural-urban residence, or occupational strata. Second, there have been marked shifts in the sizes of these demographic groups, as column two and three of table 5.1 indicate. The overall female share of the total elderly has increased from 50 to 59 percent; the proportion of employed males in the population aged sixty-five and older has plummeted from 36.3 to 8.2 percent over these eight decades. The share of the old-old (over age seventy-five) in the older population has risen from 27.5 to 37.1 percent. Because of declining mortality, the proportion of the older population that is not currently married has been relatively stable, declining from 49.0 percent in 1900 to 46.2 percent today.

Instead of census family categories, the classification scheme most frequently used by gerontologists is employed in table 5.1. The typology depends on a set of priorities in coding: living with a married child has precedence over all other arrangements; living with an unmarried child has priority over living with other kin, which in turn has priority over living apart from kin or, if married, living with a spouse.[7] The final columns of the table give the proportions who were household heads or heads' spouses and the proportion who were relatives of the household head; omitted from the table is the fraction who were non-kin of the household head.

Compositional changes fail miserably as explanations for changes in the distribution of the relationship-to-head categories and in the types of living arrangements of the elderly, as demonstrated in figures 1 and 2. The great change in the number of elderly residing with younger

Table 5.1
Distribution of living arrangements and relationship-to-head in 1900

Group	Proportion of older population 1900	1980	Type of living arrangement With married child	With unmarried Child	With other kin	Alone or with spouse	Relationship to head Head or spouse	Kin of head
Women:								
Married, 65-74	.1397	.1720	.171	.357	.089	.382	.878	.119
Unmarried, 65-74	.2200	.1840	.360	.294	.171	.172	.439	.500
Married, 75+	.0315	.0512	.255	.260	.060	.425	.745	.225
Unmarried, 75+	.1064	.1833	.423	.316	.068	.193	.315	.613
Men, 65-74:								
Married:								
Employed	.2117	.0618	.101	.504	.084	.312	.955	.032
Unemployed	.0453	.1581	.233	.352	.042	.373	.787	.206
Unmarried:								
Employed	.0753	.0116	.249	.224	.103	.425	.552	.226
Unemployed	.0327	.0412	.432	.165	.233	.170	.272	.612
Men: 75+								
Married:								
Employed	.0527	.0067	.144	.486	.063	.306	.943	.045
Unemployed	.0297	.0887	.353	.332	.032	.283	.647	.348
Unmarried:								
Employed	.0233	.0021	.347	.279	.136	.238	.605	.327
Unemployed	.0320	.0393	.576	.167	.064	.192	.182	.704

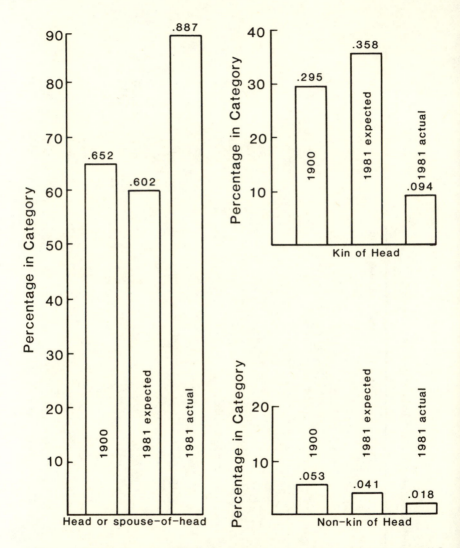

Figure 1. Distribution of relationship-to-head status of non-institutionalized U.S. population over age 65 in 1900, 1981, and that expected on the basis of change in age, sex marital status, and male employment status, and male employment status between 1900 and c. 1980.

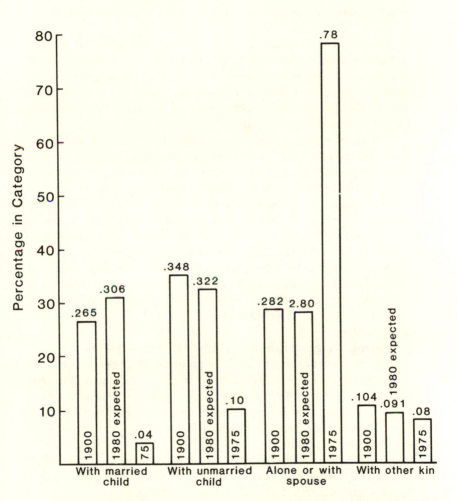

Figure 2. Distribution of living arrangements of the non-institutionalized U.S. population over age 65 in 1900, 1975, and that expected in c. 1980 on the basis of compositional changes in age, sex, marital status, and male employment status between 1900 and c. 1980.

kin is not accounted for by a decrease in the types of old people likely, in 1900 terms, to use such coresidence. In fact, the reverse is true, which means that further explanation of the residential shift is required.

Thus most of the compositional changes between 1900 and the present increased the type of older people most likely to reside with younger relatives. In 1900, older persons in the aged population, the unmarried, and the non–gainfully employed were more likely to live with married children than those—the young-old, the married, and the employed—in the alternative statuses.

With no change in the 1900 rates, only 60.2 percent of the population aged sixty-five and older would be household heads or spouses today compared to 65.2 percent in 1900; instead, the figure has jumped dramatically, to 88.7 percent. Instead of the 35.8 percent expected in 1980 to be relatives of the head if the propensities extant in 1900 had continued, a mere 9.4 percent actually held that household position in 1980. While an increase from 26.5 percent to 30.6 percent of old people living with a married child was to be expected, only 4 percent of the noninstitutionalized older population in 1975 lived with a married child. Although no change in the fraction who lived alone or with spouse was to be expected, a full half of the older population moved into this living arrangement, an increase from 28 to 78 percent of the total elderly population.

Thus the changes anticipated on the basis of the application of 1900 rates to the current share of each group in the older population were in the opposite direction to what actually occurred. These expected shifts toward more extended families in the older population would have been magnified in the total American population because of the change in the age distribution between 1900 and 1980. In 1900 there were three (2.99) people aged thirty-five to forty-four for each person aged sixty-five or older; in 1980 these age groups, roughly those of adult children and their aging parents, were in balance (1.06 persons aged thirty-five to forty-four per person aged sixty-five and older).[8]

The secular decline in American fertility has reduced the number of adult children with whom old people can live. Adjustments for compositional changes in figures 1 and 2 do not take account of change in the age distribution under age sixty-five. A rough calculation suggests the order of magnitude of this effect. If all of these householders aged sixty-five and older in March 1981 were redistributed into households with younger reference persons, some 25.8 percent of the remaining households in the United States would gain one or more old people. The identical hypothetical redistribution of the 1,568,161 households headed by a person aged sixty-five and older in 1900 would have affected only 10.9 percent of the remaining 14,341,003 households in the American population that year.[9]

Frances Kobrin has argued that the demographic pressure from the expanding ratio of aging parents to their middle-aged children indirectly altered the norms regarding the acceptibility of coresidence of adult generations within a family. Latent in this interpretation is the assumption that such coresidence is inherently unstable or undesirable. Thus norms supporting such complex family structures exist only for as long as only a small minority are forced to conform to them. Although the peculiar nuclearity of the northwest European family pattern gives this view special relevance to the American case, the validity of Kobrin's interpretation depends on these assumptions rather than on any direct evidence concerning changes in norms regarding household formation.[10]

SOCIOECONOMIC STATUS AND LIVING ARRANGEMENTS: COMPOSITIONAL OR STRUCTURAL CHANGE?

The key variable omitted from this compositional analysis is income, or other reliable indicator of economic status. The absence of gainful employment in 1900 differs sharply from retirement in 1980, since income from nonhousehold sources was probably unusual in the earlier year. In a sample of working-class families surveyed in 1889 and 1890, only 22 percent of those in which the head was aged sixty or older had income from sources other than the labor of household members or from boarders; income from nonhousehold sources made up only 5 percent of total household income. A minimum of 81.6 percent of total income in 1889 and 1890 came directly from the labor of family members. During the early 1970s, in contrast, income from employment of household members comprised only 31 percent of income of the elderly, while retirement income accounted for 40 percent of the total.[11]

The high proportion, more than 60 percent, of persons aged sixty-five and older in 1900 who lived with children may be explained by the fact that Americans simply were too poor to afford independent residence of adult generations within the family. Three economists have argued that the shift toward autonomous residence of the elderly required a "threshold level" of income that was not attained in the United States until the 1940s.[12] The movement away from extended families for the elderly accelerated after World War II. If the rate of decline in living as a relative of the head of household between 1900 and 1940 had continued, some 22 percent of women and 10 percent of men would have held this status in 1981; instead, only 10.3 percent of women and 3.3 percent of men were relatives (other than spouse) of the family householder in 1981. Although breakdowns by age are not available for Britain, the percentage of households with a relative present declined only slightly, from 20.2 percent to 15.0 percent, in the century before 1951. By 1961, this figure had dropped to 12.8 percent, and ten years later, to only 7.7 percent. In sum, there was more change in this aspect of the British family in the two decades after 1951 than in the previous century.[13]

The threshold income interpretation does not require the introduction of a change in the norms of household formation, as Kobrin postulated, or a shift in the taste for privacy, as Alice Rivlin and John Beresford theorized some years ago.[14] Yet it now has only the standing of the other two interpretations: consistent with the discontinuity in the living arrangements of the elderly after World War II, but lacking in direct evidence of its validity. If the argument about a threshold level of income is correct, and it is certainly consistent with the northwest European family pattern, then the impressive rate of economic growth during the nineteenth century may have allowed certain groups within the population to attain the ideal of autonomous residence for the elderly. On this basis, the notion that economics alone explains the residential shift can be treated.

Three socioeconomic indicators—the presence of a servant, homeownership, and occupation and residence—will be examined for their effect on the family structure of the elderly in 1900. The first indicator isolates a presumably quite wealthy group that comprised only 6 percent of the households in which the elderly lived in 1900; the second splits the population aged sixty-five and older in a ratio of seven owners to three renters; and the final indicator provides for a more detailed differentiation of the population, with the residential measure capturing a small strata at the bottom of the urban social structure.

The wealthy aged, those who had servants in their households, were more likely to be living in extended households (using the typology developed by Peter Laslett, the northwest European family pattern) or with a married child (employing the scheme of the gerontologists) than were the old in servantless households. The differences shown in table 5.2, however, are not large enough to be statistically significant, given the number of cases and an assumption of random sampling.[15] In census data, furthermore, the direction of causation is uncertain. A child

Table 5.2
Family structure of population aged 55 and older in 1900 by presence or absence of domestic servant

Family type	55–64 Servant		65 or older Servant	
	Absent	Present	Absent	Present
Laslett classification				
Solitary	3.8%	4.2%	6.6%	6.8%
Nuclear	64.5	59.7	46.7	38.9
Multiple, extended and no family	31.7	35.2	46.6	54.2
Sample size	1,775	119	**2,664**	177
Gerontologist classification				
Alone or with spouse	20.3%	17.8%	24.9%	21.9%
with married child	14.7	18.6	27.7	30.9
with unmarried child	56.0	56.8	36.6	34.8
with other kin	8.9	6.8	10.8	12.3

Note: Persons living as non-kin of head excluded from this comparison.

might, for example, simultaneously bring a gravely ill parent into his or her household and employ a servant to help provide care. Still, the pattern in table 5.2 hints at the existence of a relationship between wealth and family structure different from that characteristic of the era since World War II. Unlike traditional England, the use of servants was not an alternative to intergenerational coresidence of adults within a family.[16]

Homeownership would seem to supply a relevant indicator for assessing the relationship between socioeconomic status and family structure. Although the census does not report which family member owned the house, the steep positive relationship between age and ownership suggests that the older person who was a household head was also the owner. Since the house probably had been owned for some years, and since some of the children had departed, there was room to accommodate additional persons from the family of a married child. On the other hand, the old person or couple controlled a resource permitting the choice, if they desired, of greater privacy and more living space.

At first glance, the ownership index appears to confirm the current relationship between socioeconomic status and family structure. Some 52.4 percent of the aged living in rented dwellings had extended families present (see table 5.3), compared to only 45.4 percent in family owned homes.[17] Correspondingly, 40.7 percent of the old who rented lived in nuclear families, in contrast to 48.4 percent in family owned homes. Using the gerontologists' classification, renters similarly were slightly more likely than owners to be living with married children.

The contradictory inferences forthcoming from the examination of the servant and homeownership indicators can be resolved by introducing the concept of a "ladder of homeownership." Figures for the entire country reported in the published census show that some 70.8 percent of households headed by a person aged sixty-five and older were family owned; the percentages decrease in the younger age groups of heads: 62.5 percent (fifty-five to sixty-four); 53.0 percent (forty-five to fifty-four); 43.6 percent (thirty-five to forty-four); and 27.6 percent (twenty-five to thirty-four).[18] When the national figures for age-specific homeownership proportions of all household heads below age fifty-five are compared to those of households in which sampled old people were relatives of the head (see bottom panel of table 5.3), it is clear that homeowning younger families were more likely to have a coresi-

Table 5.3
Family structure of population aged 55 or older in the United States in 1900

Family Type	55-64 Heads or spouses Owner	Renter	55-64 All family residents Owner	Renter	65 or older Heads or spouses Owner	Renter	65 or older All family residents Owner	Renter
Laslett classification								
Solitary	3.8%	4.8%	3.4%	4.0%	8.6%	11.0%	6.1%	6.8%
Nuclear	73.4	69.9	67.2	59.6	63.9	61.1	48.4	40.7
Multiple, extended and no family	22.8	25.1	29.6	36.3	27.5	27.8	45.4	52.4
Sample size	1109	545	1215	649	1351	550	1891	891
Gerontologist classification								
Alone or with spouse	22.4%	22.7%	20.5%	19.1%	36.0%	33.6%	25.8%	20.8%
with married child	9.6	7.5	12.9	18.9	10.8	8.0	27.5	30.8
with unmarried child	63.1	61.4	58.2	52.6	43.0	50.0	35.8	37.9
with other kin	5.0	8.1	8.4	9.3	10.2	8.4	11.2	10.6

Age group of household head	Sample size	Total population of heads Owner	Renter	Unknown	Sample members, relatives-of-head Owner	Renter	Unknown
25-34	215	26.1%	68.4%	5.5%	35.4%	60.8%	4.0%
35-44	274	41.6	53.9	4.5	53.6	42.6	3.8
45-54	220	50.7	35.7	4.8	64.5	30.0	5.5

dent old person than were renter families with a same-age head. This differential between owners and renters in the younger age groups could arise if the home was currently or formerly owned by the old person, who used the asset to gain the security provided by living with his or her child. No strong or even consistent pattern exists among those old people who were heads or spouses of heads; children were not more likely to remain with homeowning parents than with parents who rented their dwellings.

The final indicator, occupational class and character of the residential neighborhood, provides the most compelling evidence for a structural change in the relationship between socioeconomic status and family structure between 1900 and the post–World War II period. Households characterized by a person with an unskilled occupation or those listed on a census page with a high percentage of unskilled occupations were more likely to be those with an old person living alone, or if married with the spouse only, than the households of people in other occupational groups. The family structure of persons in the low-status group and neighborhood resembled that of persons living in non-farm households in places under 25,000 in population. (See table 5.4.)

Urban middle-class and farm households were more prone to have married children present with a parent or parents than other households. Although these differences again are rather small, they suggest the motive of inheritance as an additional reason for the coresidence of old people with their adult children.

Welfare and inheritance motives are explored in table 5.5 from the perspective of both children and aging mothers who had one or more children still alive in 1900. That a larger fraction of children lived with a widowed than with a currently married mother (44 versus 34 percent), and especially that a widowed mother was more likely (84 versus 65 percent) to have at least one child present than were mothers with living husbands, testifies to the importance of the family welfare motive. This intention of providing assistance to an aging parent was also evident for fathers, as the higher percentages of unmarried, non–gainfully employed men in table 5.1 who had a child present in their households indicate.

Although children seemingly responded to the needs of their aging parents, they also were more likely to have departed from households that promised fewer future economic advantages. A larger percentage (63 percent) of children were no longer present with their mothers in

Table 5.4
Family structure of population aged 55 and older in 1900

Occupation or residential group	Alone or with spouse	With children			With other kin	Sample size
		Married	Single	Total		
Occupation						
Middle Class	23.1%	24.9%	43.5%	68.4%	8.4%	773
Skilled workers	28.1	22.8	42.4	65.2	6.7	817
Unskilled workers	31.5	18.8	41.0	59.8	8.6	914
Farmers	16.3	23.0	49.2	72.2	11.5	1928
Residence						
Urban middle-class neighborhood	24.4	22.8	44.8	67.6	8.2	329
Urban heterogeneous neighborhood	24.3	20.7	49.2	69.9	5.8	671
Urban working-class neighborhood	33.4	17.5	43.3	60.9	5.7	389
On Farm	18.9	22.7	46.9	69.6	11.5	2077
Non-farm, places under 25,000	35.1	15.8	40.1	55.9	9.0	1517

Note: Each group standardized to have overall fraction married and unmarried in 55–64 and 65 and older age groups.

Table 5.5

Analyses of percentage of children of mothers aged 55 and older who resided with their mother in 1900, and percentage of mothers who resided with one or more children

Variables	Percentage of sample	Percentage of children living with mother Unadjusted	Controlled	Percentage of mothers with one or more coresident children Unadjusted	Controlled
Residence (eta/beta)		(.19)	(.15)	(.16)	(.15)
Urban working-class	8.5	40%	37%	73%	72%
Urban heterogeneous	14.6	51	47	84	82
Urban middle-class	7.3	51	46	83	81
Farm residence	38.7	39	40	78	80
Non-farm under 25,000	30.9	32	32	65	66
Ethnicity(eta/beta)		(.08)	(.06)	(.11)	(.09)
Blacks	7.4%	32%	32%	62%	62%
Whites born in South	18.5	38	40	80	78
Whites born in North	37.8	38	38	73	75
Foreign-born whites	36.2	42	41	78	76
Homeownership(eta/beta)		(.06)	(.01)	(.04)	(.03)
Owner	64.5%	38%	39%	74%	74%
Other	35.5	42	40	78	77
Marital status(eta/beta)		(.14)	(.13)	(.16)	(.22)
Married, spouse-present	47.9	34%	34%	68%	65%
Other	52.1	44	44	82	84
Variance explained		5.5%	16.4%	6.4%	10.2%
Covariates(coefficient and contribution to R^2)					
Number of living children			−0.045(9.0%)		+0.033(3.3%)
Age of mother in 1900			−0.007(1.8%)		−0.004(0.5%)

Sample size: 1,939 mothers with one or more living children in 1900.

urban working-class neighborhoods, in rural farm households (60 percent), in rural non-farm households (68 percent), and in black families
(68 percent) than in other groups. Some 80 percent of mothers of living children in rural farm households, 81 percent in urban middle-class
neighborhoods, and 82 percent in urban heterogeneous neighborhoods
had at least one child in residence (see table 5.5).

The similarity between urban groups and the older rural farm population is misleading, and the introduction into the analysis of the gender of the children suggests that the term "inheritance motive" is an
imprecise designation of the reason for the high rate of intergenerational coresidence in urban middle-class and occupationally heterogeneous neighborhoods (see table 5.6).

The source of the high incidence of older people living with children, particularly in middle-class neighborhoods, is the frequency of
coresidence with daughters, both married and unmarried. Some 14.6
percent of those aged fifty-five and older in middle-class neighborhoods lived with a married daughter, and 17.0 percent resided with an
unmarried daughter or daughters; only 17.5 percent lived with a married or unmarried son. The respective figures for the total population
over age fifty-five were 9.4, 12.5, and 23.5 percent. Farm households,
on the other hand, were characterized by the presence of sons. Some
14.3 percent of older farm dwellers resided with a married son, and
an additional 14.8 percent lived with an unmarried son or sons; only
18.4 percent lived exclusively with daughters. The identical figures for
the total population aged fifty-five and older in 1900 were 10.2, 13.3,
and 21.8 percent.

Dorrian Sweetser developed the contrast between a rural inheritance
pattern of patrilineal succession and a modern industrial pattern based
on expressive relationships between mothers and daughters. In the United
States today, daughters typically are the primary relatives involved with
older people.[19]

An additional economic motive is suggested by the parallel figures
for coresidence with married and unmarried sons or with married and
unmarried daughters among the different types of residential areas. Those
environments in which it was more common for an old person to live
with a married son were areas in which living with an unmarried son
or sons was more frequent. Sons remained on farms first to work and
eventually to inherit. In urban middle-class and heterogeneous dis-
tricts, single daughters remained at home into the years of mature

Table 5.6
Characteristics of families of population age 55 and older in 1900 (in different residential areas)

| | | Type of Neighborhood | | | | |
| | | Cities over 25,000 | | | Places under 25,000 | |
Characteristic	Total	Working class	Hetero-geneous	Middle class	Farm households	Non-farm households
With children						
Total	64.8%	60.9%	70.0%	67.5%	69.6%	55.9%
Unmarried doughter(s) only	12.5%	13.0	15.4	17.0	10.0	13.3
Unmarried son(s) only	13.3	12.7	12.3	9.4	14.8	12.0
Unmarried children of each sex	19.5	17.6	21.5	18.4	22.0	14.8
Married daughter	9.4	10.0	12.8	14.6	8.4	7.8
Married son	10.2	7.4	7.8	8.1	14.3	8.0
Married children(total)	19.6	17.5	20.7	22.8	22.7	15.8
Difference between living with sons and with daughters	+1.6	-3.0	-8.0	-14.1	+10.7	-0.1
Sex ratio of children	107.4	96.3	78.7	69.1	139.1	95.1
Mothers of living children:						
Widows living with children	82%	77%	89%	87%	87%	73%
Total living with children	75%	73%	83%	83%	78%	65%
Sample size	4983	389	671	329	2077	1517

Note: Each group standardized to have same fraction married and unmarried in both 55-64 and 65 and older age groups as in total population.

adulthood. In this period, more educated daughters were less likely than others to marry, and less likely to marry at early ages. Working-class neighborhoods had a larger proportion of children who had left the parental households, and no distinctive sex ratio among those children who remained. Daughters in these neighborhoods may have married at higher rates or departed from the parental household to become domestic servants. Sons also had less incentive to remain in the parental household. For the same reasons, both sons and daughters left rural nonfarm households to find work in the city. Although the argument for a strong linkage between mothers and daughters has been made most forcefully for working-class families,[20] the tendency is not apparent in table 5.6. Instead, the incidence of coresidence by the gender of children is most remarkable in urban middle-class neighborhoods and on farms.

The relationship of occupational class to family structure within the older population changed between 1900 and the period after World War II. In 1962, some 32 percent of Americans aged sixty-five and older with blue-collar or service-worker backgrounds who had living children lived with one or more of them. Only 23.0 percent of older agricultural workers and 20.2 percent of older white-collar workers did so.[21] Although the definition of occupational categories differs in the 1900 and 1962 data, the reversal in the direction of the relationship must be counted as an important structural change.

Increases in per capita income between 1900 and 1980 would have augmented the proportion of old people who lived with married children, had the patterns of 1900 persisted. Income, however, probably is the wrong index of socioeconomic functioning. Two important influences on the family structure of the elderly in 1900—inheritance motives and relative employment opportunities—no longer are important. The size of the farm sector has withered, and the norms favor early succession even if tax laws delay actual inheritance until the death of both farm parents.[22] What is present in both eras is the family welfare motive, the willingness of children to assist a needy parent; today, however, such assistance only rarely involves coresidence.

PROCESSUAL AND CATEGORICAL CHANGE

The evidence for 1900 presented above does not support the notion of a hypothetical threshold income level necessary for the rise of independent households for adult generations within the family. A more complex story must be told, one involving the residual category of processual change. Even in the post–World War II era, the propensity to live alone has increased at a faster rate among old people than would be expected on the basis of rising incomes.[23]

Indeed, adult Americans of both sexes and all ages have moved out of family residential situations, especially in the last two decades; whether charted as increases in female-headed households, primary individuals, or nonfamily householders, the process has been pervasive and seemingly contagious. Although, for example, the economic outlook for young adults was comparatively bleak during the last decade, the young single population has not remained in the households of their parents. Although the return to the parental nest has been widely discussed in the mass media, the share of twenty- to thirty-four-year-old Americans living as children of family householders increased only from 17.1 to 18.7 percent between 1970 and March 1981. Excluding those married persons living with a spouse, only 40.9 percent of those aged twenty to thirty-four lived as a child of the family householder in 1981, compared to 54.7 percent of the same group in 1970.[24]

While it is not difficult to find documentation for changing American family norms in the recent past,[25] the decline in the coresidence of children with parents aged sixty-five and older involves a rather secondary attitudinal change. The psychological meaning of the family has changed less than its economic role for the older population. In 1900, the *Instructions to Enumerators* laid out this rule for census-takers in recording members of the household: "Enter the members of each family in the following order, namely: Head first, wife second, children (whether sons or daughters) in order of their ages, and all other persons *living with* each family, whether relatives, boarders, lodgers, or servants" (emphasis mine).[26] Under this definition of the normative family, relatives lived *with*, not *in*, the families of their kin. In 1947, the *Current Population Survey* introduced the terms "primary" and "secondary" individual to designate those "other persons" mentioned in the instructions to enumerators in 1900. After World War II, these persons were increasingly likely to live apart from kin. By 1980, they had become nonfamily householders in census terminology, a reform that eliminated the controversial authoritative connotations of the phrase "head-of-household."

What the census categories miss, both in 1900 and today, is the sense of joint headship or mutual responsibility in husband-wife families, the key element in American family organization. For example, the increase in divorce rates in the twentieth century has generated far more debate and concern than the revolution in living arrangements of the elderly. Similarly, few have noticed that social security payments to the old and Aid to Families with Dependent Children stipends to mothers have the same familial effect—supporting the establishment and maintenance of more than one family, or nonfamily households. The former program has assisted the fission of intergenerational household units, the latter the dissolution of marital or quasimarital relationships; the former program is nearly universally accepted, while the latter is controversial in a way completely apart from its cost to the taxpayer.

The historiography of old age is ready for complexity in interpretation. While the definition of the family has always favored independence for married couples, old and young, this preference did not preclude coresidence of older persons with their kin in the era before World War II. Older couples typically lived with unmarried children, the widowed old with married children, and the never married, especially spinsters, with their siblings. In 1900 and before, such coresidence was acceptable, unremarkable, and sometimes of economic benefit to the old, the young, or to both. Since 1945, a silent revolution has occurred in intergenerational living arrangements.

NOTES

Data from the 1900 census reported on in this chapter were gathered under Grant AG 00250–02 from the National Institute on Aging. The author wishes to thank Professor Barbara Laslett of the University of Minnesota for helpful comments on an earlier draft of this chapter.

1. For a critique of the before-and-after approach to the history of old age, see Peter Laslett, "Societal Development and Aging," in Robert H. Binstock and Ethel Shanas, eds., *Handbook of Aging and the Social Sciences* (New York, 1976), pp. 87–116. Peter Uhlenberg, "Changing Structure of the Older Population of the U.S.A. during the Twentieth Century," *Gerontologist* 17 (1977): 197–202, provides a useful summary of the characteristics of cohorts entering old age during this century.

2. Details of the national sample of 3,001 noninstitutionalized persons aged sixty-five and older from the 1900 census are given in Daniel Scott Smith, "A Community-Based Sample of the Older Population from the 1880 and 1900 United States Manuscript Censuses," *Historical Methods* 11 (1978): 67–74;

an estimate of 2.9 percent for the institutionalized population in 1900 was made on the basis of the 1910 census.

3. For this pattern, see Peter Laslett, "Characteristics of the Western Family Considered over Time," *Journal of Family History* 2 (1977): 89–115; and for its implications for the comparative history of the elderly, see Daniel Scott Smith, "Historical Change in the Household Structure of the Elderly in Economically Developed Societies," in Robert W. Fogel, et al., eds., *Aging: Stability and Change in the Family* (New York, 1981), pp. 91–114.

4. Walter J. Dickie, "Family and Polity in Atlantic England," (Ph.D. dissertation, Department of Anthropology, University of Chicago, 1978).

5. Robert T. Michael, Victor R. Fuchs, and Sharon R. Scott, "Changes in the Propensity to Live Alone, 1950–1976," *Demography* 17 (1980): 39–56. Fred C. Pampel, *Social Change and the Aged: Recent Trends in the United States* (Lexington, Mass., 1981).

6. This accounting framework draws on that proposed by Barbara Laslett, "Beyond Methodology: The Place of Theory in Quantitative Historical Research," *American Sociological Review* 45 (1980): 214–218; the term "processual" comes from Pampel, *Social Change and the Aged*, pp. 7–12.

7. Ethel Shanas, et al., *Old People in Three Industrial Societies* (New York, 1968).

8. For the intervening decades, the figures are 2.95 (1910), 2.86 (1920), 2.59 (1930), 2.03 (1940), 1.75 (1950), 1.45 (1960), and 1.15 (1970).

9. Since it is assumed that each younger householder absorbs only one older householder and his or her family, these are maximum figures.

10. Frances Kobrin, "The Fall in Household Size and the Rise of the Primary Individual in the United States," reprinted in Michael Gordon, ed., *The American Family in Social-Historical Perspective*, 2d ed. (New York, 1978), pp. 78–79.

11. Michael Haines, *Fertility and Occupation: Population Patterns in Industrialization* (New York, 1979), table VI–6, p. 227. Denis F. Johnston and Sally L. Hoover, "Social Indicators of Aging," in Matilda White Riley, et al., eds., *Aging from Birth to Death, Sociotemporal Perspectives* vol. II (Boulder, Colo., 1982), pp. 197–215. Because the 1889–1890 survey was taken of the families of employed workers, the importance of income from employment is overstated. Some 15 percent of the population aged sixty-five and older in 1900 lived in a household that did not include a gainfully employed person; most of these individuals, typically widows, received income from some other source.

12. Michael, Fuchs, and Scott, "Changes in the Propensity to Live Alone," pp. 39–56.

13. Richard Wall, "Regional and Temporal Variations in the Structure of the British Household since 1851," in Theo Barker and Michael Drake, eds., *Population and Society in Britain, 1850–1980* (New York, 1982), pp. 69–99.

14. John C. Beresford and Alice M. Rivlin, "Privacy, Poverty, and Old Age,"*Demography* 3 (1966): 247–258.

15. Smith, "Community-Based Sample of the Older Population."

16. Laslett, "Societal Development and Aging," p. 115.

17. Those who were reported as boarders, servants, or other non-kin of the head of household were excluded from the comparisons in tables 5.2 and 5.3.

18. U.S. Census Office, *Abstract of the Twelfth Census of the United States, 1900* (Washington, D.C., 1902), table 33, p. 30. Olivier Zunz, *The Changing Face of Inequality: Urbanization, Industrial Development, and Immigrants in Detroit, 1880–1920* (Chicago, 1982), pp. 152–161, discusses the correlates of homeownership in that city in 1900. See also table 5.3, above.

19. Dorrian Apple Sweetser, "The Effect of Industrialization on Intergenerational Solidarity," *Rural Sociology* 31 (1966): 156–170.

20. See Elizabeth Bott, *Family and Social Network: Roles, Norms, and External Relationships in Ordinary Urban Families*, 2d ed. (London, 1971).

21. Shanas et al., *Old People*, pp. 234–238.

22. Sonya Salamon and Shirley M. O'Reilly, "Family, Land and Developmental Cycles among Illinois Farmers," *Rural Sociology* 44 (1979): 525–542; Sonya Salamon and Vicki Lockhart, "Land Ownership and the Position of the Elderly in Farm Families," *Human Organization* 39 (1980): 324–331.

23. Pampel, *Social Change and the Aged*, pp. 192–198.

24. U.S. Bureau of the Census, *Current Population Reports* (hereafter cited as CPS) series P–20, no. 212, "Marital Status and Family Status: March 1970," (Washington, D.C., 1971), table 2, p. 13; *CPS*, series P–20, no. 372, "Marital Status and Living Arrangements: March 1981," (Washington, D.C., 1982), table 2, p. 13.

25. Joseph Veroff, et al., *The Inner American: A Self Portrait from 1957 to 1976* (New York, 1981).

26. Robert G. Barrows, "Instructions to Enumerators for Completing the 1900 Census Population Schedule," *Historical Methods Newsletter* 9 (1976): 201–212.

Life-Course Transitions and Kin Assistance in Old Age: A Cohort Comparison

The emergence of "old age" as a social and cultural phenomenon can be best understood in the context of the entire life course and the historical changes affecting it. Underlying a life-course approach is the assumption that the family status and position that people experience in later years of life is molded by their cumulative life history and by the specific historical conditions affecting their lives at earlier times. For that very reason, the differences in the experiences of various cohorts that result from their location in historical time is critical to our understanding of their respective adaptations to old age.[1]

Older people are not viewed simply as a homogeneous group but as age cohorts moving through history. The different life-history paths by which people reach their later years of life are contingent on the ways in which social and economic events have shaped their life history at earlier points of time as well. Particularly important in this respect are earlier life experiences, shaped by different cultural heritages in areas such as men's and women's views of family relations, expectations of support from kin and the ability to interact with public agencies and bureaucratic institutions, all of which are crucial to determining their ability to adapt to conditions they encounter in the later years.

An essential aspect of the life-course approach is timing—the synchronization of individual life transitions with the collective family unit as its members change over time and in their relation to external historical conditions.[2] Its essence is the interaction among "individual time," "family time," and "historical time." A life-course approach attempts to follow the movements of individuals through different family configurations and roles and is concerned with the determinants of timing patterns that affect these transitions.[3]

Three essential features of life-course analysis are particularly significant to an understanding of historical changes in the family: (1) timing, which entails the synchronization of different individual roles over a person's career; (2) interaction, which involves the relationship between individual life-course transitions and changing historical conditions; and (3) integration, which represents the cumulative impact of earlier life-course transitions on subsequent ones.

All these aspects are influenced by demographic, social, and economic factors as well as by one's cultural background. For example, cultural changes in norms of timing and economic changes in the opportunity structure affect entry into the labor force, job availability, and, ultimately, retirement. Institutional and legislative changes such as compulsory school attendance, child labor laws, and mandatory retirement affect the transitions of different age groups into and out of the labor force.

The life history of individuals is shaped by earlier life-course transitions, which in turn are affected by historical circumstances specific to their own time, all along the life course.[4] This complex pattern of cumulative life-course effects involves both the impact of earlier life-course experiences on subsequent ones and the effect of historical conditions encountered at each stage of the life course.

Thus the social experiences of cohorts are influenced not only by the historical conditions at the particular point in time when they reach old age but also by the historical conditions that shaped their earlier life experiences. The historical developments in the timing of life transitions as they affect the family status of older people in American society over the past century are discussed in this chapter. These patterns are exemplified through a comparison of two cohorts in Manchester, New Hampshire, and examination of the changes in their respective attitudes toward assistance to older people.[5]

HISTORICAL CHANGES IN THE TIMING OF LIFE TRANSITIONS

The emergence of old age as a distinct stage of life was shaped by a larger historical process involving the segmentation of the life course into societally acknowledged stages: childhood, adolescence, youth, middle age, and old age. In trying to understand this historical process, one must keep in mind that these various stages of life were integrated in an entire life-course continuum and in relation to familial obligations.

In the timing of transitions to adulthood, especially in leaving home, marriage, and setting up a separate household, John Modell, Frank Furstenberg, and Theodore Hershberg have shown that, during the past century, age uniformity in the timing of transitions to adulthood has been increasingly more marked. Transitions have become more rapidly timed and abrupt.[6]

In contrast to present times, nineteenth-century transitions from the parental home to marriage, to household headship, and to parenthood occurred more gradually and were less rigidly timed. In the late nineteenth century, the time range necessary for a cohort to accomplish such transitions was wider, and the sequence in which transitions followed one another was not rapidly established. In the twentieth century, on the other hand, transitions to adulthood have become more uniform for the age cohort undergoing them, more orderly in sequence, and not frequently revised.

The very notion of embarking on a new stage of the life course and the implications of movement from one stage to the next have become more firmly established in the society. The timing of life transitions has become more regulated according to specific age norms rather than in relation to the collective needs of the family. These changes in the timing of transitions to adulthood are significant for the later years of life as well, since the pace of young people's movement into their family of procreation also affects the status and needs of their families of orientation.

Transitions at different points in the life course are interlocked and interdependent in the life paths of individuals as well as in the family as a whole. Timing on one end of the life course affects timing on the other end, and vice versa. The postponement of the assumption of adult responsibilities for adolescents and the resulting prolonged residence of children in the household have affected the family's economy.

The recognition of old age as a distinct stage, and especially the imposition of mandatory retirement, has had a serious impact on the timing of later life transitions. It has also affected the family status of older people, leading to an increase in dependency or semidependency among certain groups in old age. As a result, tensions and demands on family obligations have increased. Since the turn of the century, important changes have occurred in the synchronization of individual life transitions with the collective timetables of the family unit.

Demographic, economic, and cultural factors have combined to account for differences in the timing of such transitions as leaving home, entry into and exit from the labor force, marriage, parenthood, the "empty nest," and widowhood.[7]

At the turn of the century, for example, later life transitions into the empty nest, into widowhood, and out of household headship were not closely synchronized, and they extended over a relatively long period of time. Most men surviving to old age continued their labor force participation and maintained the headship of their household. Only at very advanced ages, when their capabilities were impaired by infirmity, did men withdraw from the labor force and live in someone else's household. Since widowhood was such a common experience, older women experienced more marked transitions than did older men. The continuing presence of adult children in the household meant, however, that widowhood did not necessarily mark a dramatic transition into the empty nest, as it does today.[8]

In summary, the nineteenth-century pattern of transitions allowed for a wider age spread within the family and for greater opportunity for interaction among parents, adult children, and other kin. During the twentieth century, on the other hand, demographic changes combined with the increasing rapidity in the timing of transitions have converged to isolate and segregate age groups. At the same time, they have generated new stresses on familial needs and obligations.

The most marked discontinuity in the adult life course has been the emergence of the empty nest in a couple's middle age. Earlier marriage, earlier childbearing, and fewer children have led to the emergence of the empty nest while the parents are still in middle age.

Earlier marriage and earlier completion of childbearing and child-rearing on the one hand, and greater survival in the later years of life on the other, have resulted in a higher proportion of a woman's life spent first with a husband but without children and then alone without either husband or children.

In contemporary society, the empty nest period comprises one-third or more of the married adult life span. Paul Glick concludes that the duration of this period has increased over the past eighty years by eleven years, from 1.6 years to 12.3 years, reaching one-third of the forty-four years of average married life. Increasing sex differentials in mortality above age fifty have dramatically increased the ratio of women to men and have made widowhood a more important feature in a woman's life. By contrast, in the nineteenth century, later age at marriage, higher fertility, and shorter life expectancy rendered different family configurations from those characterizing contemporary society. Thus for large families the parental stage with children remaining in the household extended over a longer time period—sometimes over the parents' entire life.[9] (This pattern is changing now again: because of limited employment opportunities and expensive housing, some children are now returning to live in the parental household or are not leaving at all.)

Demographic factors only in part explain the presence or absence of an empty nest. The major change since the late nineteenth century has been not so much the emergence of the empty nest as its duration. Even at the turn of the century, children present in the households of their aging parents were in their teens or early twenties, therefore old enough to leave home. Nevertheless, at least one child stayed behind because custom and familial obligations required that one adult child remain to care for aging parents. This was crucial when other sources of assistance were absent.

Autonomy in old age, in part expressed in household headship, hinged on some form of support from one or more working children in the household or on the presence of boarders. The transition into the later years of life was thus marked by the effort of aging parents to maintain the integrity of their family through the continued residence of at least one child at home.

Recent historical analyses of family patterns in the late nineteenth century suggest that older couples and, especially, aging widows with children were more likely to reside with their children than with other kin or strangers. Childless couples or those whose children had left home took in boarders and lodgers as surrogate kin. Widows or women who had never married and who were unable to maintain independent households moved in with their relatives or boarded in other people's homes. Solitary residence, a pattern that is becoming increasingly pervasive among older people today, was rarely experienced in the nineteenth century.[10]

Typically throughout American history, older people have struggled to retain the headship of their own households rather than move in with their relatives or strangers. Nuclear household arrangments were often broken or stretched, however, during parents' dependency in old age or during housing shortages that made it more difficult for newlyweds to afford separate housing. Under such circumstances, some children would return home with their spouses to live with their aging parents. Other children, most often the youngest daughter remaining at home, postponed marriage in order to continue supporting older parents.

The commitment of older people to maintaining the headship of their own households resulted in the residence of adult children in their parents' household, not in parents moving in with their children. Even older widows, generally the most vulnerable to dependency, continued to head households for as long as they could. If no children were available or able to help, widows took in boarders and lodgers. Once they were unable to continue to maintain independent households, they eventually had to move into the households of relatives or nonrelatives.[11]

The nature of interdependence in a familial setting imposed demands as well as constraints on the timing of life transitions. Synchronization of individual with collective transitions involved balancing and juggling a number of family roles. A potential source of conflict lay in the fact that older children had already left home and younger ones were entering adulthood while their parents approached old age.

Such strain was intensified by the conflict between two sets of norms in American culture that often placed generations in a double bind: one was the prevailing expectation that the integrity of the family of orientation be preserved; the other was the presumption that young adults would achieve autonomy as soon as possible and set up independent households. How could young men and women fulfill those seemingly conflicting sets of requirements?

The basic commitment in American culture to residence in a nuclear household intensified the dilemma. Nuclear household structure seems to have been the norm throughout the nineteenth century and has been the predominant residential form for the majority of the population in the twentieth century as well. While the majority of households did not include extended kin, a considerable portion of households included strangers residing as boarders and lodgers.

Boarding and lodging to some extent alleviated this generational strain by providing surrogate family arrangements: young people who had left their parents' household boarded with older people whose own children had left home. This practice thus enabled aging couples or widows to continue to head their own households even after their children had left. Only in cases where older people were too weak to continue heading households or to live alone was the function reversed; aging widows in particular went to board in other people's households.

In the late nineteenth-century setting, the norms of familial assistance and autonomy seemed to prevail over age norms of timing. This is an area where the historical difference with our time is drastic. Life-course transitions in contemporary society have become more strictly age related and more rigidly governed by age norms. Bernice Neugarten's definition of being "late" or "on time" in one's fulfillment of certain age-related roles reflects the standards of a society bound to age norms; in earlier time periods, economic needs and familial obligations prevailed over age norms.[12]

Thus the current trend toward specific age-related transitions is connected to the decline in instrumental relations among kin over the past century and their replacement by an individualized and sentimental orientation toward family relations. This trend has led to an increasing separation between generations and to age segregation in American society.

COHORT COMPARISON IN ATTITUDES TOWARD KIN ASSISTANCE TO THE ELDERLY

Some of the historical changes in perceptions of timing of life transitions are exemplified in the comparison of two generations in Manchester, New Hampshire, spanning the period from the turn of the century to the present. The older generation are the mill workers and their older children whose work and family patterns were analyzed in *Family Time and Industrial Time*. The younger generation are their younger children.[13]

For analytical purposes, each generation was divided into cohorts: the parents' (historical) cohort consists of people born before 1910; the children's (contemporary) cohorts were born between 1910 and 1919, and between 1920 and 1929. These cohorts were selected and defined in relation to the historical events that affected the community as well as the larger society.

The parent generation were predominantly immigrants who came to Manchester to work in the textile mills, especially those of the large Amoskeag Company. Even though they experienced considerable discontinuities in their careers, they spent most of their work lives in periods of labor shortage during the peak of the Amoskeag Company's expansion and activity. The children's generation, on the other hand, came of age during or after the decline of the Amoskeag Company and the collapse of the mills.

The two age cohorts of the children were defined in relation to lateral events: the older one came of age during the Great Depression, in a period of deprivation; the younger of the children's cohorts came of age during World War II, in a period of recovery and economic prosperity. Because of high fertility, two siblings in the same family often belonged to two different cohorts.

A preliminary comparison of the parents' and the children's cohorts reveals differences in their perceptions of life-course transitions as well as in their attitudes toward kin assistance in old age. Both sets of differences illustrate several of the general propositions discussed above.

Members of the parents' cohort perceived their life as a continuous whole, not segmented into stages. They did not view normative life events as major transitions or discontinuities. Rather, they viewed migration, external economic crises, a major strike, or the shutdown of the mill as much more critical events than normative life course transitions. The only exception in this respect was the birth of the first child. Women in particular noted this event as a major transition and used it as a chronological device from which to mark other events. The historical cohort expressed little consciousness of distinct stages of the life course such as adolescence, and middle age, or of family stages like the empty nest.

The contemporary cohorts, on the other hand, especially the younger of the two, were conscious of stages and discontinuities in their life course, and some used terms drawn from popular culture to label them. They viewed adolescence as a major turning point and referred to critical periods as of a "middle-age crisis" and of the "empty nest." When asked which had been the major crises in their lives, they referred to "adolescence" and "middle age." Unlike the historical cohort, they also had a clearer anticipation of what their major life transitions would be.

The younger cohorts' awareness of discontinuities and segmentation of their life course was a result of two major transitions in their lives that were generally absent from the experience of the historical cohort: retirement, particularly for men, set specific boundaries for their later years of life; and the empty nest marked a major discontinuity for both men and women, but particularly for women.

The historical cohorts, on the other hand, did not identify the empty nest as a specific stage, because in reality their nests had rarely been empty. The absence of an empty nest is consistent with the pattern found at the turn of the century both in Manchester, New Hampshire, and nationally: the nest was rarely empty because one child usually still lived at home. In the case of Manchester and the other New England communities, the remaining child in the household was commonly a daughter who delayed marriage or gave it up altogether in order to stay at home and support aging parents.[14]

The younger cohorts' sense of discontinuity was also a result of the bureaucratic demarcations of life-course stages: they came of age during periods when stages of the life course were officially recognized in the culture, and when certain transitions and stages had become defined in relation to age boundaries and were publicly regulated. Legal limits to school age, child labor legislation, and formal retirement were all official landmarks of such life-course transitions, representing society's acknowledgment of age norms. The private as well as public consciousness of marked life-course transitions was thus more characteristic of the lives of the contemporary cohorts than of the historical ones.

For the historical cohort, on the other hand, migration and economic crisis were more dramatic turning points than normative life-course transitions. The immigrant and working-class background of the historical cohort placed more emphasis on their economic constraints and family need than on age norms. Age was much less important than familial timing dictated by economic needs.

Attitudes toward Kin Assistance

The cohorts also differed in their respective attitudes toward obligations for kin support in general and expectations for care of aging parents in particular. The historic cohort viewed kin as their almost exclusive source of assistance over the life course. They had been the major supporters of their aging parents. They had a strong sense of integration with kin and expected their own children to support them in old age. The older members of the parents' cohort, those in their eighties and nineties, were especially articulate on this issue. Having come of age in an era preceding the welfare state, when institutional supports in old age were virtually absent, they were socialized to view the family as their almost exclusive source of support and social security. Their belief in the self-sufficiency of the family led them to view public assistance as demeaning.

The attitudes toward kin assistance within the historical cohort were a product of their earlier life histories. In ranking their preferences for sources of assistance, they expressed a commitment to support from within the nuclear family as their highest priority, followed by assistance from extended and more distant kin. They considered public relief as a last resort. Even during the Great Depression, the members of the historical cohort claim to have avoided public relief. Those who resorted to welfare agencies for assistance did so surreptitiously and later denied having received assistance from outside the family.

The ethnic background of the older cohort also influenced their reliance on kin. Their ideology of kin assistance was part of their ethnic tradition and formed a survival strategy that they had carried over from their preimmigration cultures. They modified this ideology to fit the needs, requirements, and constraints imposed by the insecurities of the industrial environment. Their reliance on kin thus represented the continuation of an earlier practice of exchange relations, as well as an ideology that shaped their expectations of each other and of the younger generation.

The older generation's aversion to public assistance was also a cohort phenomenon: it resulted from their unfamiliarity with procedures and bureaucratic institutions for receiving support. Having spent the prime of their lives in a period that antedated the welfare state, they found the very concept of reliance on the state alien to their principles and upbringing.

The contemporary cohorts were socialized with expectations and ideologies of kin assistance similar to those of their parents, but they were faced with the tasks of implementing such standards under conditions of declining employment opportunities and dwindling financial resources in the family. In many cases, the coping strategies they worked out were intended to meet the ideology passed on by their parents, but changing pressures, changing ideals, and the availability of assistance from the public sector led them to revise these ideals. They were thus caught in a conflict and were ambivalent toward the older generation's expectations of kin support.

While the historical cohort expected their children to assist them in old age, the two contemporary cohorts did not expect to have to rely on their own children for *economic* support. They prepared for old age through pension plans, savings, and homeownership and expected to rely on social security. This attitude once again was a cohort phenomenon. Over their life course, the children's generation had become accustomed to the welfare state and had developed skills in dealing with bureaucratic institutions.

Members of the younger of the children's cohorts in particular expressed ambivalence toward carrying economic obligations for aging parents, or taking them into the household when they became unable to take care of themselves. They aided their aging parents, principally by providing them with services rather than with regular financial support, and they did not expect to carry such responsibilities in the future.

The ambivalence of these younger cohorts may also have been a result of an increasing individualization in the society, the erosion of ideologies of mutual interdependence, and an expectation of assistance from the public sector. Although they had been raised with strong values of familial responsibility, they made their transitions into a more individualistic mode of thinking and a greater acceptance of public welfare as a substitute for kin assistance.

These attitudes on the part of the contemporary cohorts also reflected their status as second-generation immigrants and their own transition into the middle class. Though some of the children's cohorts had started their work careers in textile mills during the Great Depression, they had been coached by their own parents to aspire toward occupational advancement and to develop a "middle-class" life-style. A considerable portion of these cohorts entered middle-class employment during the post–World War II recovery period and developed a life-style that entailed privacy and a separation of the family of orientation from the family of procreation.

HISTORICAL IMPLICATIONS FOR THE FAMILY AND THE LIFE COURSE

Historically, the family was the central arena in which many of the life transitions were converging. Transitions that we could consider today as individual were in the past collective and familial. They were either shared by a number of family members or, even if they involved strictly individual careers, they still affected the entire family as a unit, or at least several members within it. Marriage, for example, was not merely subject to individual or couple decisions; rather, its timing hinged on the needs of each partner's family of origin, particularly on the needs of aging parents.[15]

The family also played a major role as the locus for economic and welfare functions. This central role of the family persisted even after many of the family's earlier educational, welfare, and social control functions had been transferred to other institutions under the impact of industrialization.

Despite the growing tendency of the urban middle-class family to serve as a retreat from the outside world, and to concentrate on domesticity and child nurture as its exclusive role, the majority of families in the larger society continued to function as economic units. Families and individuals therefore had to rely heavily on kin assistance as their essential social base.

Timing was a critical factor in the family's efforts to maintain control over its resources, especially by balancing the contributions of different members to the family economy. Under the historical conditions when familial assistance was the almost exclusive source of security, the multiplicity of obligations toward other family members that individuals incurred over the life course was more complex than today. In the current setting of the welfare state, such responsibilities are primarily the domain of public agencies. (This is not to say that at present kin do not continue to fulfill such obligations, but the major welfare functions earlier carried out by kin have been transferred to the public sector.) This historical shift from a collective family economy and help patterns to public welfare and increasing individualization in family relations is exemplified in the differences between the historical and the contemporary cohorts.

The nineteenth-century family economy was out of necessity flexible, because individual resources were precarious and institutional buttressing was slim or nonexistent. Family adaptation was crucial, therefore, in coping with critical life situations or even with regular life-course transitions.

The family was the most critical agent both in initiating as well as in absorbing the consequences of transitions among individual members. Clearly, when viewed from this perspective, the essential aspect of the timing of a transition was not the age at which a person left home, married, or became a parent, but rather how this transition was related to those that other family members were undergoing and, especially, to the needs of aging parents.

Under the insecurities of the late nineteenth century, pressing economic needs and familial obligations took precedence over established norms of timing. The timing of early life transitions was bound up with later ones as part of continuing familial needs over the life course. More significant than age was the sequence or coincidence in which transitions were expected to occur.

The timing of life transitions was influenced by the economic opportunity structure in the community and was limited by institutional constraints such as compulsory school attendance, child labor legislation, or retirement. The absence of institutional supports such as welfare agencies, unemployment compensation, and social security added to the pressures imposed on family members.

The timing of transitions along the life course converged around interdependence and mutual obligations among different family members. Individual life transitions were not always self-timed. In modern society, we are accustomed to thinking of most family roles and work careers as subject to individual decisions. Historically, each apparently individual transition was treated as a family move and had to be synchronized with family needs. In addition to the ties retained with their family of origin, individuals took on obligations toward their families of procreation and toward their spouses' families. The complexity of obligations cast family members in various overlapping, and at times conflicting, roles over the course of their lives. One role might gradually come to dominate while another receded in importance, but the shifting was not always a smooth one.

The major historical change over the past century has not been the decline of coresidence of kin, but the decline in the interdependence of kin. The increasing separation between the family of origin and the family of procreation, combined with the discontinuities in the life course discussed above, occurred in the context of changes in the quality of kin relations. In the nineteenth and twentieth centuries, family relations were characterized by a higher degree of interdependence among kin. Relatives served as the most essential resource for economic assistance and security and carried the major burden of welfare functions, many of which now fall within the purview of the public sector. Exchange relationships among parents and children and other kin thus provided the major, and sometimes the only, base for security.[16]

The gradual erosion of instrumental kin relationships has tended to increase insecurity and isolation as people age, especially in areas of need that are not met by public programs. In examining this particular aspect of historical change, it is important to distinguish between the availability of kin and the nature of kin support systems. Recent historical studies have documented the multiplicity of functions of kin in the nineteenth century, especially their critical role in migration, job placement, and housing.[17]

These studies and studies of contemporary kinship patterns have shown that, contrary to prevailing theories, urbanization and industrialization did not break down traditional kinship ties. There are thus many parallels between the role that kin fulfilled in the nineteenth and early twentieth centuries, and patterns of kin assistance found by sociologists in modern American society. Their studies, particularly those by Ethel Shanas,[18] have emphasized the frequency of interaction among older parents and adult children and the flow of assistance to older people from their relatives. The difference lies, however, in the degree of integration with kin and the dependence on mutual assistance. While many intensive patterns of kin interaction have survived among first-generation immigrant, black, and working-class families, there has been an overall erosion of instrumental ties among relatives, especially in the almost exclusive dependence on kin for consistent support over the life course.

Contemporary studies insisting on the persistence of kin assistance in old age have not documented the intensity, quality, and consistency of kin support that older people are receiving from their relatives.[19] Until we have more systematic evidence in this area, it would be erroneous to assume that kin are carrying or should be expected to carry the major responsibility for assistance to old people. The current involvement of the elderly with kin, as Shanas and others have found, represents a cohort phenomenon rather than a continuing historical pattern. The elderly cohort of the present has carried over into old age the historical attitudes and traditions that were prevalent when their members were growing up early in this century, especially a strong reliance on relatives. This cohort also has kin available because of the larger family size of earlier cohorts. Future cohorts, as they reach old age, might not have the same strong sense of integration with kin and might not have sufficient numbers of available kin on whom to rely.

It would be a mistake, therefore, to leave kin to take care of their own at a time when the chances of doing so are considerably diminishing. Nor should the historical evidence about the continuity in kin relations be much used in support of proposals to return welfare responsibilities from the public sector to the family without additional public supports. An examination of the historical patterns reveals the high price that kin have had to pay in order to assist each other in the absence of other forms of societal support. The historical precedent thus offers warning against romanticizing kin relations, particularly against the attempt to transfer responsibility for the elderly back to the family without adequate governmental assistance.

NOTES

1. Matilde Riley, M. E. Johnson, and A. Foner, eds., *Aging and Society: A Sociology of Age Stratification* (New York, 1972).

2. Tamara K. Hareven, "Family Time and Historical Time," *Daedalus* 106 (1977): 57–70.

3. Glen H. Elder, Jr., "Family History and the Life Course," in Tamara K. Hareven, ed., *Transitions: The Family and the Life Course in Historical Perspective* (New York, 1978), pp. 17–64.

4. Glen H. Elder, Jr., *Children of the Great Depression: Social Change in Life Experience* (Chicago, 1974).

5. Peter Uhlenberg, "Cohort Variations in Family Life Cycle Experiences of U.S. Females," *Journal of Marriage and the Family* 36 (1974): 284–292; idem, "Changing Configurations of the Life Course," in Hareven, ed., *Transitions*, pp. 65–95; Hareven, "Family Time and Historical Time."

6. John Modell, Frank Furstenberg, and Theodore Hershberg, "Social

Change and Transition to Adulthood in Historical Perspective," *Journal of Family History* 1 (1976): 7–32.

7. Paul Glick, "Updating the Life Cycle of Family," *Journal of Marriage and the Family* 39 (1977): 9.

8. Howard Chudacoff and Tamara K. Hareven, "Family Transitions and Household Structures in the Later Years of Life," in Hareven, ed., *Transitions*, pp. 217–244; Tamara K. Hareven, *Family Time and Industrial Time: The Relationship between the Family and Work in a New England Industrial Community* (Cambridge, England, 1982); Daniel Scott Smith, "Life Course, Norms, and the Family System of Older Americans in 1900," *Journal of Family History* 4 (1979): 285–299.

9. Glick, "Updating the Life Cycle," p. 9; Chudacoff and Hareven, "Family Transitions"; Hareven, *Family Time and Industrial Time*; idem, "Family Time and Historical Time."

10. Frances Kobrin, "The Fall in Household Size and the Rise of the Primary Individual in the United States," *Demography* 13 (1976): 127–138.

11. John Modell and Tamara K. Hareven, "Urbanization and the Malleable Household: An Examination of Boarding and Lodging in American Families," *Journal of Marriage and the Family* 35 (1973): 467–479.

12. Bernice Neugarten, "Adult Personality: Toward a Psychology of the Life Cycle," in Neugarten, ed., *Middle Age and Aging* (Chicago, 1973), p. 146.

13. Hareven, *Family Time and Industrial Time*. Data on these cohorts are based on extensive interviews and the reconstruction of life histories of members of the historical cohorts, their spouses, and the siblings of the spouses and the spouses of the siblings in an effort to reconstruct kinship networks as far as they could be retrieved. The original informants of the historical cohorts were also interviewed again, for comparisons. The research for this project was funded by a grant from the National Institute on Aging.

14. Chudacoff and Hareven, "Family Transitions"; Hareven, *Family Time and Industrial Time*; Smith, "Life Course."

15. Modell, Furstenberg, and Hershberg, "Social Change and Transition"; Hareven, *Family Time and Industrial Time*.

16. Michael Anderson, *Family Structure in Nineteenth-Century Lancashire* (Cambridge, England, 1971); Hareven, ed., *Transitions*.

17. Anderson, *Family Structure*; Hareven, ed., *Transitions*; Hareven, *Family Time and Industrial Time*.

18. Ethel Shanas, "The Family Arrangements of Older People," in Ethel Shanas and Gordon F. Streib, eds., *Social Structure and the Family: Generational Relations* (Englewood Cliffs, N.J., 1965), pp. 1–27; Marvin B. Sussman, "The Isolated Nuclear Family: Fact or Fiction," *Social Problems* 8 (1959): 333–347; Eugene Litwak, "Extended Kin Relations in an Industrial Democratic Society," in Shanas and Streib, eds., *Social Structure*, pp. 290–325.

19. Ethel Shanas, "The Family as a Support System in Old Age," *Gerontologist* 19 (1979): 169–174.

PART IV

POLICIES TOWARD THE ELDERLY

The Transformation of Old Age Security

At present there exists a plethora of national programs for older people that provide economic and social support and protection against financial insolvency due to the costs of prolonged illness. They include social security, the numerous programs funded through the Older Americans Act, Supplemental Security Income, Medicare, and Medicaid. It was not until the twentieth century, however, that the aged emerged as a separate category in welfare programs. In fact, the history of economic support for older people can only be understood in the broader context of the history of relief, for until recently aid to those in need remained undifferentiated. Even though it is difficult to disentangle the fate of the aged from that of other categories of poor in the past, the lessons of history are relevant today because policy legacies are imbedded in present programs. Throughout the past four hundred years, old age security has been transformed from a locally financed and administered system of care to a massive, bureaucratic national program of income maintenance. Yet some of the same conflicts over eligibility for aid that threatened the sense of community in the colonial era are still present in contemporary programs for the aged.

RELIEF UNDER THE COLONIAL POOR LAW

English settlers in the American colonies brought with them the Elizabethan concept that giving public relief to those who could not support themselves or secure support from relatives, friends, or private philanthropy was a proper function of local government. With only one exception, every community in the Plymouth and Massachusetts Bay colonies provided for relief in the initial stages of settlement and subsequently administered relief as a regular town function.[1] As early as 1647, at the first session of its colonial legislature, Rhode Island announced the poor law principles that stressed, most importantly, public responsibility for the poor. Public responsibility for the poor was buttressed by the other principles of English poor law—local responsibility, family responsibility, and the residency requirement of legal settlement.[2]

The proper objects of relief were the aged, infirm, or insane who were separated from their means of support and also from a household, and various arrangements were made to care for the needy, including providing light employment, giving provisions and a pension, boarding with a relative or neighbor at town expense, or care in an almshouse, the first of which was erected in Rensselaerswick, New York, in 1657.[3] One common solution to old age dependency was to assign the person's property over to the community in exchange for care for life, usually through some boarding arrangement. For example, in 1660 the case of Mr. Burrowes, a resident of Providence, was considered at the town meeting because of his need of relief through "age and weakness."[4] Burrowes was moved into the home of a townsman who had been found willing to take care of him, and his property and possessions were turned over to the town. Similarly, William Baker petitioned the free inhabitants of Portsmouth to take his sheep in return for care. The town meeting granted his request and bargained with "Hinory Pearcey" to provide "diat and lodgin" for a year for £8. Sometimes the sense of communal responsibility was taken quite literally, and a rotation system for boarding was established among members of the town. In Hadley, Massachusetts, in 1687, the town meeting voted that the widow Baldwin be removed from house to house "to such as are able to receive her" and "remain a fortnight in each family."[5]

The decline of Joseph Patchin can be documented through the changing responses of the Fairfield, Connecticut, town meetings to his needs. In 1673, the records indicate that "Goodman Patchin is to continue his worke about the meeting house." Eight years later, due to his "weakes and ages," Joseph Patchin applied to the townsmen, "desiring his owne estate may mayntayne him as far as it will reach."

Just one year later, it is apparent that his health had deteriorated still further, and it is now "old Patchin" that the town refers to when it provides Thomas Bennet with £13 for a year's food and lodging.[6] Other older people received similar consideration in Fairfield. Thus, assistance to the aged was flexible and might shift from finding work for an ailing man to providing food and lodging when deteriorating health made employment impossible.

Although it is difficult to make any accurate assessment regarding the proportion of older people receiving relief, in Plymouth, where the population grew from five hundred to about seven hundred between 1630 and 1645, fifty-seven cases of relief were recorded, and many of the relief recipients were old.[7] Similarly, in Watertown, Massachusetts, twenty-one individuals received relief between 1660 and 1675, and most was given to older people, usually widows and widowers.[8] If no generalization about the extent of support can be drawn, it is apparent that some older people in every colonial town had no family members either willing or able to provide support and that relief to the aged was one of the more common functions of poor relief. It also appears that the concept of family responsibility was applied liberally as best fit the needs of individual family members and was associated, at this stage, with economic factors rather than any punitive intent.

In these early years in the colonial period, administrators of relief to the needy were neighbors in small communities, and the concept of family governance reigned, as seen by the frequency with which boarding was used as a means for relieving the aged. Yet as early as 1617, British poor law officials began the practice of dumping their undesirables—vagrants, paupers, and convicts—upon the colonies.[9] As a means of protecting themselves against this British practice and as a way of maintaining religious and moral solidarity within the community, the colonies established laws regulating the terms under which a resident might attain inhabitancy. This was accomplished through a procedure termed "warning out," which was based on the belief that each town was a corporation that had the right to choose whom it admitted to permanent residency. The purpose of warning was to free the town of any obligation to provide relief, and once warned, an individual might become an inhabitant to all intents and purposes except for the right to receive support.[10]

One of the basic reasons for denying settlement to a stranger was likelihood of early dependency, and older people were among those at risk. This was recognized in an order passed in 1680 in Portsmouth, New Hampshire, which declared "that if any children, or older person shal be sent or come from one town to another, to school, or to nurs . . . if such shal stand in need of relief, they shal be relieved at the charge of the Town, from whence they came and do belong; and not by the town, to which they are sent." [11] Thus, even though they might need aid, older people who were not town residents were given no special consideration and in fact were even perceived as a threat. This was demonstrated in the case of John Harmon, "a decriped man," who had no established clear inhabitancy. In 1680, the Massachusetts towns of Taunton and Plymouth disputed which was liable for the support of Harmon. [12] The dispute continued for two years, until the court finally ordered that "the towne of Taunton shall receive and entertaine him for the space of one whole yeer, and Plymouth then to take him for one whole yeer; and soe to be kept from yeer to yeer." [13] This was a practical but hardly humane solution, illustrating the difficulty of determining just who the town's poor were.

In the late seventeenth century, a series of colonial wars uprooted hundreds, who came pouring into the cities and towns needing relief. These paupers were not familiar citizens who had earned the right to be maintained by the community, but neither were they disreputable strangers who could easily be warned away. In 1701, the province of Massachusetts agreed to reimburse the cities and towns directly out of its treasury due to the influx of refugees driven from their homes during the King Philip's wars. [14] In what represented a significant turning point, for the first time paupers were given support that was not funded out of local taxation. Similarly, in 1708, the mayor of Philadelphia, on behalf of the city corporation, complained to the Provincial Council that "the Corporation not only maintains all their own poor without any charge to the county, but almost all the poor of the province, most of them when distressed in the Countrey, repairing to the town for relief." [15] The solution was to build a workhouse at province expense to house all the poor who were not claimable by a town. Other colonies passed similar laws throughout the eighteenth century, with some requiring relief in workhouses and others reimbursing towns directly.

The effect of changes in funding patterns was to emphasize even further the distinction between the two classes of paupers, those who were legitimate residents of towns and thus proper recipients of local poor relief, and transient nonresidents who could either be warned away or if incapacitated sent to almshouses, which increasingly came into use for this purpose. For example, housed in the New York almshouse between 1724 and 1729 were either seriously ill or disabled local people, particularly the very old who required too much care to be boarded with a neighbor, or strangers who had suddenly been injured or fallen ill.[16] As in the seventeenth century, when cases of contested residency arose, many involved older people who because of ill health or widowhood required extensive poor relief. John and Ruth Pitman, for example, became trapped between Marblehead and Lynn, Massachusetts, when the Lynn constable physically removed them to Marblehead. "Ruth [was] then very sick and weak, not able to stand and having fitts upon her in the Street at the Door of one of the Selectmen of . . . Marblehead."[17]

Government units beyond the level of the town intervened in the provisions for old age security in other ways in the eighteenth century. For example, the General Court of Massachusetts granted tax exemptions to widows of soldiers and ministers and sometimes paid them direct relief out of public funds.[18] Courts also worked to change the way in which inheritances were transmitted, creating more self-sufficiency for widows, on the one hand, while stimulating investment capital on the other. Typically, a widow held one-third of her husband's estate during her lifetime but did not have the right to sell the property. This meant that while many widows were not technically poor, the property they possessed could not generate an adequate annual income without a great deal of labor—often an impossibility in a labor-scarce economy. As the Massachusetts economy expanded and diversified, businesses required increasing amounts of investment capital. In the eighteenth century, the General Court began to pass acts enabling women to sell their real property in order to support themselves.[19] The changing economy thus provided investment opportunities for widows who could live off the interest of their property sales. Widows became more able to support themselves, and investment capital was released to business rather than being tied up with family inheritance laws.

The increased impersonality of public relief led some groups, on the basis of national origin or religious ties, to form charitable organizations, soliciting funds in anticipation of need. One of the first of these philanthropic organizations was the Scot's Charitable Society of Boston, which was formed in 1657 and became the prototype for thousands of other groups. The society's records indicate that by the early

eighteenth century one of its major functions was the provision of relief to the aged on a long-term basis as a type of pension. For example, in 1718 a petition from James Maxwell was read. Maxwell, who
had been "a Contributor while he was in capacity," was praying for
relief in his old age. The society voted to give him 20 shillings immediately and an additional 10 shillings every quarter.[20] Eliza Wilson,
who died in 1756, had been relieved by the society for twenty-three
years.[21]

By mid-eighteenth century, the transient population had swelled further due to population growth and a decline in available land as well
as inflation and the increase in commerce. Transients and laborers mi-
grated between commercial towns, seaports, and farming villages in
search of employment. As the problem of identifying strangers led to
increased stringency in relief practices, the treatment of the aged poor,
whether resident or nonresident, became harsher. In larger towns, the
sick and aged were no longer the major recipients of poor relief, and
there was less of an inclination to differentiate their care from that given
to transients. If the almshouse or workhouse was the dominant form
of relief in a township, then it was likely that older people would be
provided relief in that fashion. A vivid example of the lack of differentiation occurred in Great Barrington, Massachusetts, in 1769. Barnet
and Sarah Campbell, an aging couple, applied to the town for poor
relief, expecting to receive outdoor relief. Instead, the Overseers of
the Poor ordered them to the workhouse. Barnet Campbell protested
before the Berkshire County Sessions Court, arguing that "instead of
that kindness and tenderness which Old Age and impaired health required and that provision and support which human nature Demands,
[he and his wife] have been treated with . . . Roughness, threatened
with the workhouse, whips and chains . . . and left without any support." To prove that he was not among the idle poor, he obtained dep-
ositions from twenty-three friends who testified to his good moral
character and frugal nature. Although the justices agreed that the
Campbells did not deserve confinement in the workhouse, the overseers refused to grant them outdoor relief.[22]

In contrast, in many small villages, like Danvers, Massachusetts, older
people were still regularly boarded out. In 1767, the average age among
the fifteen boarded paupers whose age could be ascertained was seventy-five.[23] Even though the continuation of the practice of boarding
may appear to be benevolent compared to the almshouse, however, the

nature of boarding had changed. Rather than the property exchanges common in the sixteenth century, the town's poor were simply auctioned off to the lowest bidder.

As was true earlier, older people were defined as a particularly heavy burden, and in some instances settlement laws singled them out for special treatment. In 1792, for example, the province of Pennsylvania passed an act requiring a bond from any person importing an older person into the community. If that individual subsequently became a charge, the bond money was to be used for transportation to the person's original county of residence.[24]

The extent of familial aid is, of course, impossible to estimate, but some evidence of problems in enforcing family responsibility does exist. For example, the Massachusetts towns of Wenham and Beverly had to negotiate a contract in order to force a nonresident son to care for his widowed mother. Also, in 1752, overseers of the poor of Marblehead petitioned the court of general sessions of the peace to force the relatives of two elderly women to care for them.[25] The increased rigidity in the interpretation of poor law policy seemed to affect the way in which the concept of family responsibility was interpreted and implemented.

Toward the end of the eighteenth century, fundamental changes occurred in how poverty was defined and treated. The practice of boarding out declined, at least in the East, and workhouses now housed the impotent local poor and transients together. According to a description of the Boston Poorhouse in 1790: "Persons of every description and disease are lodged under the same roof and in some instances in the same or contiguous apartments, by which means the sick are disturbed by the noise of the healthy, and the infirm rendered liable to the vices and diseases of the diseased and profligate."[26] Massachusetts terminated the warning-out system in 1767, ending the primary enforcement system for the settlement laws. One reason for ending this system had to do with the increased need for a mobile labor force, which was impeded when strangers were not allowed to establish residency. Massachusetts further amended the settlement laws in 1789 to allow individuals to establish residency on the basis of property ownership or by paying taxes for five years.[27] The onus of responsibility for identification of settlement was now shifted from the town to the individual. At the same time, towns were required to provide care and immediate poor relief to anyone, regardless of legal residence, for a period of up to three months. Paupers were thus officially recognized as part of everyday life, and the definition of pauperism was expanded to include not only those traditionally recognized as having a claim on the resources of the community—widows, orphans, the sick, and the aged—but those previously considered ineligible—vagabonds, the unemployed, strangers.

DIFFERENTIATION AND INSTITUTIONALIZATION

In the early nineteenth century, several social movements arose that had the simultaneous effect of differentiating among various categories of individuals in need of aid or reform and incarcerating them in separate institutions. Hoping to eradicate crime, mental illness, and poverty and provide sanctuary for abandoned and orphaned children, reformers pressed for the construction of well-ordered institutions. Between 1820 and 1840, prisons, mental hospitals, orphan asylums, and renovated or newly constructed almshouses proliferated, with 144 new almshouses erected in Massachusetts alone. Even though many were replacements for previously existing structures, they were also considerably enlarged.[28]

Reformers focused on the role of the community in creating pauperism and denounced outdoor relief as an inducement to dependency. Although outdoor relief was never eliminated and in some areas not even reduced, the increase in the proportion of paupers relieved in institutions in many urban areas was substantial. The proportion of paupers receiving indoor relief in Boston rose from 21.4 percent in 1832 to 44.5 percent by 1851.[29] In New York, 4,500 persons received indoor relief in 1830 as opposed to nearly 10,000 by 1850.[30]

Various theories centering around the ideology of reform have been postulated to explain the rise of institutionalization in the early nineteenth century, but whatever other explanations may appear salient, there is little doubt that the influx of European immigrants who were trickling in to the eastern shores played a significant role in the acceptance of institutional care. Urban areas were particularly burdened by the influx of rural migrants and foreigners who accounted for major portions of cities' relief bills. For example, most recipients of public welfare in the 1820s in Philadelphia were blacks, immigrants, and women. Blacks made up 15 percent of the almshouse population, although they represented only 8 percent of the total city population. One-third of those receiving outdoor relief were immigrants, who also comprised 40 percent of the almshouse residents.[31] In Danvers, Massachusetts, where the expanding shoe industry had spurred the demand for labor, the proportion of the foreign-born paupers increased from 59 percent in 1841 to 86 percent by 1846.[32]

Representatives from urban areas urged state legislatures to pass acts requiring counties to erect institutions where the unsettled poor could be maintained. Counties, however, were often reluctant to erect almshouses, forcing cities to continue to care for the influx of residents. States continued to shoulder a large portion of the burden of relief, as towns were reimbursed from state funds for the care of state paupers not in almshouses. Since they could not make counties erect almshouses everywhere, some states simply tightened eligibility requirements to exclude paupers under age sixty and reduced the amount of reimbursements.

While those in control of public relief attempted to reduce the number of able-bodied on relief rolls, private charities like the New York Association for Improving the Condition of the Poor were more concerned with identifying the redeemable poor on the basis of background, character, and ability and separating them from those unlikely to benefit from moral reform. Consciously omitted among the redeemable were the aged, who had little left to contribute and who "are likely to continue unable to earn their own support, and consequently to be permanently dependent."[33]

If charities abandoned the aged as unworthy recipients for aid, they were still maintained through the traditional method of poor relief, and, in fact, in spite of the emphasis of public opinion on the number of unworthy poor receiving aid, statistics indicate that older people still received a disproportionate share of all public relief. In 1826, 61 percent of those on outdoor relief in Philadelphia were over fifty, a figure that had risen to 80 percent by 1929. Forty-eight percent of the almshouse residents were in the same age group.[34] In 1830, Philadelphia supported 549 outdoor paupers at an average rate of 46 ½ cents per week. Of those, 390 were over sixty years of age.[35]

On the more sparsely settled frontier, territorial governments and newly established states set up poor law principles that mimicked those of their eastern counterparts. In spite of an emphasis on the almshouse, there was also, as in the East and South, tremendous variation in provisions made for the care of the aged. When it was a part of the

Northwest Territory, Indiana, under the poor relief law of 1795, determined that those not able to work, including the "old, blind, impotent and lame," were to be kept in homes under the supervision of overseers. The Indiana Constitution of 1816 made provision for "an asylum for those persons who by reason of age, infirmity, or other misfortunes may have a claim upon the aid and beneficence of society."[36] Institutional care became the main form of relief for the aged, as every county erected a poor asylum. When Kansas entered the Union in 1861, it included in the state code a statute concerning the care of the poor, who were defined as "the aged, infirm, lame, blind, or sick persons who are unable to support themselves."[37] A county tribunal was established to provide relief to needy persons who had resided in the county at least twelve months, and poorhouses were to be erected. Each county was responsible for levying its own tax for the erection of poorhouses. Missouri and Ohio also included the aged under those deserving relief, and initially older paupers were boarded out. Gradually, in these states, too, almshouses became the main source of relief.[38] Missouri also experimented with a county pension, a form of relief practiced in counties both with and without almshouses. The pension system was particularly subject to abuse in cases where the pauper was infirm, because in these instances the pensioner received the pension through a guardian who, because there was often little supervision, sometimes kept part of the pension for his own use.[39]

Although the almshouse experiment was judged a failure as early as 1833 by a Massachusetts committee that toured the state and found grossly inadequate conditions, almshouses were not abandoned.[40] Rather, they continued to serve a function, albeit a different one than that intended by early reformers. Instead of being rehabilitative, they were now accepted as custodial, peopled even more than formerly by decrepit aged, particularly aged immigrants. Since immigrants had no legal residency, they were taken in with no charge to towns, and the lack of concern for this marginal group in terms of cure helped perpetuate the continuation of the institution.

While immigrants and other categories of marginal older people were relegated to the poor relief system of meager benefits and almshouses, there grew alongside this system an alternative for the respectable aged, the Civil War pension system, enacted into law in July 1862. It was designed to aid those who were disabled as a direct consequence of their military activities and to provide for the widows and children of deceased soldiers.[41]

As gradual amendments to the regulations regarding eligibility for pensions created substantial variations in individual benefits, both veterans and government officials became concerned about the inequities in the system. In 1879, an arrears act was passed, which provided full back payments for all new and existing pension claims. New claims flooded the Bureau of Pensions, jumping from 18,800 in 1878 to 110,600 by 1880. Concerns over pension policy also stimulated veterans' organizations, and the Grand Army of the Republic grew from 45,000 members in 1879 to 215,000 by 1885.

The emergence of pensions as a political issue with a well-organized lobbying group did not go unnoticed by the Republicans, who already had the loyalty of Civil War veterans. In the 1888 elections, the Republican party platform called for an enlarged system of payments "to provide against the possibility that any man who honorably wore the Federal uniform shall become the inmate of an almshouse or dependent on private charity." When the Republican party won a sweeping victory, gaining control of the White House and the Congress, it sought to repay its electoral debt to the old soldiers by further liberalizing veterans' pension benefits. The 1890 Pension Act reduced the stictures on eligibility, and within just one year over 655,000 applications for new or increased pensions were received. By 1893, Civil War pensions accounted for 41.6 percent of the entire federal budget.

With a clerical force of two thousand in Washington, over four hundred in the eighteen pension agencies responsible for actual payments, and a staff of 3,800 examining physicians spread across the country, the Bureau of Pensions was a formidable political tool, and like numerous other benefit programs, veterans' pensions became a part of the political spoils system that dominated nineteenth-century party politics. The Republicans used the pension bureaucracy to create an enduring alliance with the ex-soldiers and build a national political machine.

OLD AGE BENEFITS IN AN ERA OF REFORM

The period between 1895 and World War I has been termed the Progressive Era, because of the various reform movements that emerged during these years. Although alienated by the exposé of corruption in politics, the Progressives were not opposed to the expansion of government, which they viewed as a source of leverage for reform. Although the Progressive movement was dominated by middle-class professionals, organized labor also pressed for government intervention in such areas as housing, health, factory safety, regulation of working hours, and worker's compensation. Some businessmen also promoted limited government regulation when it served to protect their enterprises.

Among the targets of reformers were the poorly administered and often corrupt local systems of welfare, which distributed the burden of taxation inequitably and resulted in extreme regional variations in services. The result was increased state intervention into what had been defined as local affairs, as the state began attempts to regulate functions previously left to local government. State funds for paupers were now accompanied by attempts to standardize and regulate treatment in state institutions of charity and public welfare. In 1865, for example, Massachusetts established a state board to regulate health, lunacy, and charity.[42] A similar board was established by Indiana in 1889.[43]

One of the unintended consequences of state regulatory boards was to further accelerate the process of differentiation and state expansion. These boards had to deal with local institutions, both public and private. In sparsely populated rural areas, there were too few inmates for specialized programs, and the obvious solution was to congregate special classes in an agency under state auspices. The early lunatic asylums and schools for the blind and deaf were established in just this manner. Urban counties, in contrast, had large populations with specialized needs, enough to justify a local institution, but they were often corrupted by political spoils systems. The solution to abuse was, again, state control.

With state institutions, a problem with funding arose. It seemed reasonable to ask local taxpayers to pay for a local resident sent to a state institution, but since local almshouses were often cheaper (because less care was provided), local officials often declined the state option.[44] In 1890, New York passed the State Care Act, which mandated state financial responsibility for all mentally ill individuals. A similar act was passed by Massachusetts. These acts ended a system that had divided responsibility for the care of the mentally ill between the states and local communities, transferring funding entirely to the state. Until the passage of this act, local officials had been sending resident older people to almshouses because costs were lower. Defined as incurable, they were rarely sent to insane asylums. The State Care Act shifted responsibility for the funding of the mentally ill to the state, and local officials rapidly began classifying the senile aged as mentally ill and sending them to mental hospitals.[45] The result was a rapid rise in the proportion of aged persons in state mental hospitals and a reversal of the earlier trend of refusing to send older people to these institutions.

Economic factors also propelled the aged into institutions in increased proportions in California, where the passage of an act by the state legislature in 1883 appropriated the sum of $100 yearly for the support of every indigent person over sixty years of age.[46] Since the average cost per inmate in California almshouses was less than $100 per person per year, it became financially advantageous for institutions to admit old as opposed to young residents. The result was a substantial increase in the average age of inmates, from fifty in 1882 to fifty-nine by 1894.[47] As was true elsewhere, the majority of these residents were Irish immigrants.

In the early twentieth century, there occurred a gradual shift of administrative responsibility for public welfare, initially from local overseers of the poor to local or county departments of welfare and, eventually, to the state level. Kansas City, Missouri, established a city department of welfare in 1910 with the authority to provide for needy groups. St. Joseph, Missouri, established a county-city department of public welfare, and Chicago set up the Cook County Bureau of Public Welfare, both in 1913. In 1917, Illinois reorganized state government and grouped all state functions into nine departments, each with its own director.[48] Among the nine was a Department of Welfare with a director of public welfare. The Illinois code, which was emulated by other states, introduced a new era in public administration, in that welfare became identified as a statewide function, and the state took responsibility for administration as well as regulation.

Although the dominant thrust of Progressive Era reform was toward regulation, a few socialist reformers drew attention to the problems of old age dependency and argued that a national pension scheme would preserve the dignity and self-respect of the old while placing "no greater burden, on the community as a whole . . . than to support the aged dependents on the present system of public and private charity."[49] The first serious investigation of the pension issue was undertaken by the

Massachusetts Commission on Old Age Pensions, appointed in 1907. Significant in identifying the aged as a special group, the commission examined the status of the dependent aged in Massachusetts and rejected state pensions on the grounds that they would have a number of undesirable effects. A pension would have a demoralizing influence on character by breaking down the habit of thrift and would impair family solidarity by removing the filial obligation for the support of aged parents.[50] Social insurance advocates' arguments that it was not thriftlessness but inadequate wages that made it impossible for workers to save for old age were countered on the grounds that pensions were likely to depress wages further for a number of reasons. First, the establishment of a pension system would attract workers into the state, overcrowding the market and lowering the wage rate. Second, the direct competition of pensioners would reduce the wage rate. Third, the prospect of a pension would tempt workers to offer their services for lower wages. Finally, the increased burden of taxation on industry would reduce wages as employers attempted to shift the burden to workers.[51]

The more serious objection of industry was that state pensions were undesirable because they would place industries in states that implemented them at a competitive disadvantage with neighboring states "unburdened by a pension system."[52] Couched in the liberal ideology of thrift and preserving the traditional family, the commission preserved the interests of manufacturers by not imposing a tax that would reduce their ability to compete and by not guaranteeing welfare benefits that might prove to be a disincentive to labor.

A few states made provisions for pensions for the disabled, rather than for the aged as a category, but they were illiberally administered and still associated with the stigma of poor relief. For example, Kansas in 1913 gave county commissioners the authority to pay a monthly pension of no more than $50 to any person wholly disabled from performing manual labor who had been a resident of the state for fifteen years, and a resident of the county for ten years. When a Mr. J. West applied to the commissioners of Sedgwick County for such a pension, claiming that he complied with the residence requirements, that he was blind in both eyes, that because of disease and old age he was unable to perform any labor, and that he had no relatives to maintain him, the commissioners decided it was "unwise" to give him a pension.[53] The legislature upheld the right of the commissioners to deny the pension, stating that the granting of a pension was a matter of grace, not a right, and was discretionary with the commissioners.[54] In Kansas the aid defined as a "pension" was merely another form of poor relief.

The first attempt to establish general old age assistance independent of the poor law was made by Arizona in 1914. In that year, a law was enacted abolishing almshouses and granting a pension of $15 a month to all persons over the age of sixty who were without visible means of support. The Supreme Court of Arizona later declared this law unconstitutional. These early pension schemes, while ineffectual, were symbolically significant in legitimating the view that older people needed economic aid.

Overall, the social insurance advocates had difficulty in pushing forth any pension legislation at either the state or national level because of concerted opposition from a number of sources. The official position of national organized labor as represented by the American Federation of Labor (AFL) was antagonistic to pensions. Union president Samuel Gompers organized a particularly vociferous attack on any form of social insurance on the grounds that "compulsory social insurance cannot be administered without exercising some control over wage earners,"[55] and that it would "aim a death blow at the trades union movement."[56] Although state federations of labor supported pension proposals, the opposition of the national leadership was a serious impediment.

Another problem was the lack of citizen support for pension initiatives, stemming from the unsavory reputation of the Civil War pension system. People doubted that social spending measures could be implemented honestly and feared that they might well reinforce the hold over the electorate of patronage politicians.[57] As Charles Henderson, an advocate of national old age pensions, noted, "the extravagance and abuses of the military pension system have probably awakened prejudice against workingmen's pensions."[58]

Finally, a third source of opposition came from business and manufacturers' organizations, which sent representatives to state pension hearings to argue against passage of pension legislation.[59] In Pennsylvania, for example, the Pennsylvania Manufacturer's Association defeated a pension amendment in 1927, "a costly and vicious scheme" that would "make necessary a Manufacturer's Tax, or an Income Tax, or both."[60]

The most successful lobbying organization for old age pension bills was the Fraternal Order of Eagles. Since the mid-nineteenth century, fraternal organizations had been offering protective features for their members, including insurance against sickness and disability, and funeral benefits. The benefit societies expanded substantially during the early decades of the twentieth century, and between 1910 and 1920 they wrote about one-third of the total amount of life insurance in the United States.[61] Since they were not subject to state regulation like life insurance companies, many were not funded on a sound actuarial basis, and as their memberships aged, they found themselves unable to meet their benefit obligations. As a result, numerous fraternal orders went out of existence, and several states passed laws forcing them to reorganize their financing schemes.[62]

The Eagles was formed in 1898 by a small group of theater owners and had gained a rather disreputable image. Like other fraternal oganizations, they had encountered a membership crisis in the second decade of the twentieth century, losing eighteen thousand members between 1917 and 1919.[63] As a means of stimulating membership interest, the Eagles launched a drive for old age pensions at their national convention in 1921.[64] The pension drive gave them not only an *esprit de corps* and sense of purpose but also tremendous publicity, and their organization expanded as the pension drive moved forward.

Many of the Eagles were also members of labor organizations, and they combined forces with state federations of labor in numerous states to fight for old age pension legislation. By lobbying legislators, mobilizing public opinion, and supporting pro-pension candidates for office, the Eagle-labor coalition succeeded in getting several states to pass old age pension bills.

The first laws passed were on a county-option basis, and most counties refused to assess the taxes necessary to fund pensions. As late as 1929, only six states actually had pension laws in operation, and only 53 of the 264 counties eligible to adopt a pension had actually done so.[65] Other commonly adopted requirements included fifteen years' residency in the state, possession of no more than $3,000 in property, a maximum payment of $1 per day, and the exclusion of clients with children or other close relatives with the means to assist.[66] Clearly, poor law philosophy was incorporated directly into these pension programs, including residency and family responsibility clauses, and they continued to be more of a dole than a pension. Some states allowed counties an option but included state aid to assist them. These, too, proved largely ineffective, and in the late 1920s there was a gradual move toward *mandatory* pension laws with statewide control and contributions from state government.

PRIVATE SECTOR INITIATIVES

One of the factors that motivated labor unions to participate in the drive for state pensions was their own failure to provide pensions for union members. At the urging of Samuel Gompers and the national leadership of the AFL, many unions began implementing pension programs in the early decades of the twentieth century. The Granite Cutter's International was the pension pioneer, establishing an old age pension plan in 1905.[67] The International Typographical Union (ITU) followed suit in 1907 and began paying out pensions in 1909.[68]. By 1920, seven more unions had initiated pension plans.[69]

The period after World War I was a prosperous one for unions, and membership in the AFL increased from 2,072,702 in 1916 to 3,260,168 by 1919.[70] As new industries that employed primarily unskilled workers emerged, the earlier growth declined. Business opinion became increasingly inhospitable to unionism, and throughout the next decade union membership dropped precipitously. By 1929, barely 10 percent of the nation's labor force was unionized.[71]

The unions' ability to pay out pensions was predicated on increasing numbers of new dues-paying members. As labor organizations shrank, so did their coffers. Faced with an aging membership and increased demands for benefits, many unions discontinued their pension funds or tightened their eligibility criteria.[72]

By 1929, organized labor had clearly recognized that paying pensions on a cash disbursement basis out of funds generated each year created a fragile system subject to collapse when such factors as technological change, economic crisis, or political hostility affected the dues structure of unions. Reversing its earlier advocacy of union pensions, the AFL now warned its members: "Old age pension plans should be undertaken with the greatest caution. Plans developed without adequate knowledge of the particular circumstances to be met may involve the union in serious financial difficulties."[73]

In 1929, the AFL reversed its historic opposition to state pensions and endorsed a proposal to design a model bill for state pensions and to promote its enactment.[74] Organized labor had learned that pensions placed an insupportable burden on unions and that the only resolution to providing old age security for workers was to rely on the taxing power of the state.

The other substantial private pension initiative that arose during this period was in industry. Although business associations in highly competitive industries fought against any welfare program that might raise taxes and interfere with existing wage scales, a few monopoly corporations began to implement their own welfare capitalist programs. In 1929, a study by industrial relations counselors found that 329 industrial pension programs were in existence. Eighty percent of covered employees were in railroads, public utilities, metal trades, oil, banking and insurance, and electrical apparatus and supply companies. In contrast, among the highly competitive and largely unregulated manufacturing companies, only one-eighth of all employees were covered by a pension plan, and these were in the larger manufacturing establishments.[75]

These pensions were usually funded as an operating expense, making them highly unstable during business downturns. Sixty-nine new industrial pension plans were implemented between 1929 and 1932, but a greater number of existing plans were discontinued. As the Depression grew worse, a few farsighted welfare capitalists began to recognize that some type of state intervention was necessary.[76]

By the early 1930s, it had become apparent that private initiatives would not be able to provide a secure source of economic support for older people. Labor union pension programs were underfunded, and many business plans were in shambles. The Depression brought increased pressures on state treasuries as thousands demanded relief. A nation that had resisted federal intervention in welfare for decades had come to agree that a national pension plan was a necessity. The only question to be resolved was what type of a pension program would be legislated.

THE EXPANSION OF PUBLIC AND PRIVATE BENEFITS

As the nation moved toward a national program of old age pensions, various citizen-initiated proposals arose. The most significant was the Townsend movement, whose constituency was primarily older people. Led by retired physician Frances Townsend, Townsendites demanded that anyone over the age of sixty be paid a flat pension of $200 a month from the federal treasury on the single condition that the recipient spend the entire amount within that month.[77] The purchasing power generated by the pensions would stimulate the economy and help produce economic recovery. Hundreds of thousands of elderly people supported Townsend, and members of Congress were bombarded with petitions from elderly constituents.[78]

The other proposal that received serious consideration was the Lundeen bill, which called for compensation equal to average local wages for all unemployed workers, for supplementary benefits for part-time workers unable to secure full-time employment, and for payments to all workers unable to work because of sickness or old age, the source of funds being the general treasury of the United States. Any further funds necessary were to be provided by taxes levied on inheritances, gifts, and individual and corporate incomes of $5,000 a year and over.[79] The Lundeen bill had the support of numerous local unions and unemployment councils but not the support of the national AFL, and none of its provisions nor those from the Townsend measure were incorporated into the final measure.

In August 1935, President Franklin Roosevelt signed into law the Social Security Act. It contained two separate measures, neither of which resembled the citizen-initiated proposals. The old age assistance title provided grants of federal funds to the states for old-age pensions to needy persons aged sixty-five or older, on a fifty-fifty matching basis up to a maximum federal contribution of $15 per month. States were also granted 5 percent of the pension amount for administrative costs.[80] Eligibility requirements made mandatory by the federal act included age sixty-five as the eligible age and a minimal residence requirement of one year or five of the past nine years in the state; the pension was available to all citizens. Those without residency still had to turn to the poor law.

By 1937, forty states had plans approved by the Social Security Board, and although there was wide variation in these plans, many incorporated requirements in line with poor law philosophy. For example, twenty-five states required an investigation to determine the ability of other members of the family to support the applicant. These twenty-five plans variously specified that the applicant could not have "children" or "relatives legally responsible," or in some cases "persons legally responsible," who were able to provide support. There were also variations in property and income limitations in terms of the maximum or minimum amount allowed.[81] In Missouri, 137,427 applications for assistance were received between 1935 and 1939. In a sample taken of those rejected, 63 percent were rejected because of resources and nearly 20 percent on the grounds that they had relatives able to support them. Only 3.6 percent were rejected because of a failure to establish residency. Thus family responsibility clauses were a major method used by states to keep pension costs down.[82]

In contrast, the insurance portion of the Social Security Act was financed by means of contributions assessed equally against the employer and employee. Taxes began to be collected in 1937, and the first payout occurred in 1940. Since only a small proportion of older people were eligible for benefits in 1940, most older people received their income, if any, from old age assistance. In fact, it was not until 1953 that there were more people receiving federal old age insurance than state old age assistance.[83]

The old age insurance title (OASDI) has gradually been expanded to include dependents of wage earners and the disabled. As of 1983, 82 percent of the population in the United States was fully insured under Old-Age, Survivors, and Disability Insurance (OASDI), with 92 percent of all men and 73 percent of all women being eligible for retirement benefits.[84] Of those receiving benefits, the average monthly benefit for white males was $432.60, for white females $279.20, for black males $351.10, and for black females $245.20.[85] Thus OASDI covers nearly all men and three-quarters of all women with benefits inequitably distributed on the basis of race and gender.

In contrast, the joint federal-state old age assistance program was replaced in 1972 with Supplemental Security Income (SSI). Financed entirely out of general revenues, SSI provides a minimal income floor for the indigent aged, blind, and disabled. In 1983, approximately 79 percent of all SSI recipients had incomes below poverty level.[86]

In addition to the public support provided for older people through OASDI and SSI, an extensive system of contributory pensions in private industry has also developed. Private pension plans were stimulated by federal tax policy, which first (in 1916) allowed corporations to deduct pension payments as operating expenses and later (in 1943) allowed employer contributions to pension funds to be discounted in calculating income.[87] In 1981, 44.3 percent of all civilian workers were covered by a private pension plan, including 50.1 percent of all men and 37.3 percent of all women. Coverage varied by income level, with

77.4 percent of those making $20,000 and over eligible for a pension but only 30.2 percent of those in the $5,000 to $9,000 income bracket covered by a pension plan.[88] The combined effect of a wage-related system of social insurance and a private pension system that favors high-income workers is increased income inequality in old age for those who have always been at the bottom of the income scale.

THE HISTORY OF OLD AGE SECURITY AND POLICY OPTIONS

It is clear from this brief historical sketch that our present program structure emerged from policy choices that evolved gradually over the last several centuries. In the early colonial period, those who came under the jurisdiction of the poor law were needy dependents but not necessarily poor. Rather than having to depend solely on the goodwill of their neighbors, older people exchanged their goods and property for care in old age. Providing for the elderly was the responsiblity of the family and the local community, because this responsibility could be clearly circumscribed. When family networks or informal provisions failed, the poor law offered a reasonable degree of protection for the needy among the community's elderly. Family responsibility clauses in the context of a close-knit community where each individual was known to village leaders made sense and were interpreted liberally, meaning financial support in one situation, household support in another.

The very aspect of the poor law that made it amenable to personalized care, the concept of local responsibility, also made it difficult to administer. The principle of local responsibility coupled with regulations about legal settlement was simply inapplicable to a growing nation, a nation increasingly composed of strangers who could not simply be "warned away." Commercial and industrial growth expanded the demand for labor, and immigrants and rural migrants poured into northern cities and towns, further accelerating the erosion of local responsibility and making the concept of legal settlement even more difficult to enforce. As poor law regulations became increasingly rigid, older people in need were auctioned off to the lowest bidder or sent to almshouses. Family responsibility laws also became more difficult to enforce, and when they were implemented, their intent was harsher and more punitive.

It is not until the twentieth century that the aged were recognized as a separate category in need of specialized programs for economic support outside of the poor law. Yet the strong values of voluntarism and thrift served as an impediment to developing an old age pension system that was free from the stigma of relief. When a national pension plan was finally enacted, it reflected our society's ambivalence about redistributing income without incorporating some test of need. The Social Security Act was a complex mixture of nearly every social welfare device known and included poor law criteria for eligibility in its old age assistance title.

The legacy of the poor law is still with us, specifically in terms of several programs targeted for the aged poor and more generally in terms of the debate regarding the relationship between equity and adequacy in OASDI. Should social security function primarily as an insurance program, returning benefits to individuals on the basis of past contributions? Or should income be redistributed to equalize social inequities by paying benefits on the basis of need? Our present program partially serves both functions. Benefits are only marginally related to past contributions, but although low-income workers receive relatively higher returns on their contributions, women and minorities still tend to receive significantly lower benefits than white males.

It is only by understanding the legacies of social policy we have inherited that we can begin to make sense of present policy debates. Programs for economic security for the aged were formulated in a political and economic context that set constraints on the alternatives available today. In order to formulate policy choices for the future, we must reevaluate the validity of assumptions imbedded in programs that are a legacy from a past when social and economic conditions were quite different.

NOTES

This chapter is based upon work supported by a grant from the University of Kansas General Research Fund, and a grant from the Kansas Committee for the Humanities, an affiliate of the National Endowment for the Humanities. The author is indebted to Arthur Blum, David Hackett Fischer, Ann Schofield, and David Willis for extensive comments on an earlier draft.

1. The exception was the town of Taunton in Plymouth Colony, which was cited for not providing relief during the 1650s. Charles R. Lee, "Public Poor Relief and the Massachusetts Community, 1620–1715," *New England*

Quarterly 55, no. 4 (1982): 564. Other regions were not as quick to establish poor laws. Both North and South Carolina were slow to pass poor law legislation, and although poor laws existed in Virginia, they often were not implemented. Elizabeth Wisner, *Social Welfare in the South* (Baton Rouge, 1970).

2. Actually, local administration of relief was not implemented immediately. Initially, in Plymouth the town meeting shared responsibility for relief with colony officials, and it wasn't until 1649 that the town inhabitants delegated the task to their selectmen. The pattern was similar in Bay Colony. See Lee, "Public Poor Relief," pp. 569-570.

3. June Axinn and Herman Levin, *Social Welfare: A History of the American Response to Need* (New York, 1982), p. 21.

4. Records of the Colony of Rhode Island and Providence Plantations (Providence, 1856), vol. I. Reprinted in Margaret D. Creech, *Three Centuries of Poor Law Administration* (Chicago, 1936), p. 14.

5. Robert W. Kelso, *The History of Public Poor Relief in Massachusetts, 1620–1920* (Boston, 1922), p. 102.

6. Fairfield, Connecticut, Town Records, Minutes of Town Meetings. Reprinted in Ralph E. Pumphrey and Muriel W. Pumphrey, *The Heritage of American Social Work* (New York, 1961), p. 22.

7. Lee, "Public Poor Relief," p. 569.

8. Ibid., p. 577.

9. There is a lively debate regarding the extensiveness of this practice. Mildred Campbell, "Social Origins of Some Early Americans," in James Morton Smith, ed., *Seventeenth Century America* (Chapel Hill, N.C., 1959), pp. 63–89, argues that most British immigrants to the colonies were from the middle ranks of British society. Galenson challenges her conclusions and cites evidence that boys released directly from parish authorities and men released from jails where they had been confined for debt or vagrancy comprised a good portion of the immigrants. See David W. Galenson, "Middling People or Common Sort? The Social Origins of Some Early Americans Reexamined," *William and Mary Quarterly* 35, no. 3 (1978): 5, 8. Georgia was founded by men released from debtor's prison. Wisner, *Social Welfare*, p. 15. Regardless of who is correct in this debate, the perceptions of the colonists that dumping undesirables was a common British practice caused them to act as if it were true.

10. Josiah Benton, *Warning Out in New England* (Freeport, N.Y., 1911), pp. 114–116.

11. Ibid., pp. 88–89.

12. Kelso, *History of Public Poor Relief*, p. 100.

13. Ibid., p. 101.

14. Ibid., p. 122.

15. Hannah Roach, "Philadelphia's Colonial Poor Laws," *Pennsylvania Genealogical Magazine* 22, no. 3 (1962): 159–169.

16. David S. Rothman, *The Discovery of the Asylum* (Boston, 1971), p. 38.

17. Douglas Lamar Jones, "Poverty and Vagabondage: The Process of Survival in Eighteenth Century Massachusetts," *New England Historical and Genealogical Register* 133 (1979): 252.

18. Alexander Keyssar, "Widowhood in Eighteenth Century Massachusetts: A Problem in the History of the Family," *Perspectives in American History* 8 (1974): 112–113.

19. Ibid., p. 114.

20. Robert B. Adam, ed., *The Constitution and By-Laws of the Scots' Charitable Society of Boston* (Boston, 1896), reprinted in Pumphrey and Pumphrey, *Heritage*, p. 32.

21. Ibid., p. 33.

22. Douglas Lamar Jones, "The Transformation of the Law of Poverty in Eighteenth Century Massachusetts," paper presented to the Organization of American Historians, 1980.

23. Louis J. Piccarello, "Social Structure and Public Welfare Policy in Danvers, Massachusetts: 1750–1850," *Essex Institute Historical Collections* (1982): 251.

24. Carole Haber, *Beyond Sixty-Five: The Dilemma of Old Age in America's Past* (Cambridge, England, 1983), p. 24.

25. Douglas Lamar Jones, "The Strolling Poor: Transiency in Eighteenth Century Massachusetts," *Journal of Social History* 8 (Spring 1975): 45.

26. Allan Kulikoff, "The Progress of Inequality in Revolutionary Boston," *William and Mary Quarterly* 28, no. 3 (1971): 384.

27. Jones, "Transformation," p. 36–39.

28. Several scholars argue that the extent of almshouse use in this period is exaggerated. Piccarello demonstrates that the use of an almshouse by a village varied according to the nature of the town's poor, and that some towns with large numbers of unemployed built almshouses in the eighteenth century to care for them. Thus, the nature of the local economy was more important than any single reform movement. See Louis Piccarello, "The Administration of Public Welfare: A Comparative Analysis of Salem, Danvers, Deerfield and Greenfield," *Historical Journal of Massachusetts* 10, no. 2 (1982): 30–42.

29. Ibid., table VI.

30. Rothman, *Discovery*, p. 183.

31. Priscilla Ferguson Clement, "The Response to Need, Welfare and Poverty in Philadelphia, 1800 to 1850," Ph.D. dissertation, University of Pennsylvania, 1977, p. 184.

32. Piccarello, "Social Structure," p. 257.

33. Haber, *Beyond Sixty-Five*, p. 38.

34. Clement, *Response*, p. 184.

35. Matthew Carey, *Appeal to the Wealthy of the Land* (Philadelphia, 1833), pp. 3–34.

36. Alice Shaffer and Mary Wysor Keefer, *The Indiana Poor Law* (Chicago, 1936), p. 4.

37. Grace A. Browning, *The Development of Poor Relief Legislation in Kansas* (Chicago, 1935), p. 87.

38. Fern Boan, *A History of Poor Relief Legislation and Administration in Missouri* (Chicago, 1941), p. 46.

39. Ibid., p. 47.

40. Rothman, *Discovery*, p. 196.

41. The following discussion comes from Heywood T. Sanders, "Paying for the 'Bloody Shirt': The Politics of Civil War Pensions," in Barry S. Rundquist, ed., *Political Benefits* (Lexington, Mass., 1980), pp. 137–159.

42. Edward Berkowitz and Kim McQuaid, *Creating the Welfare State* (New York, 1980), p. 26.

43. Shaffer and Keefer, *Indiana Poor Law*, p. 5.

44. James Leiby, *A History of Social Welfare and Social Work in the United States* (New York, 1978), pp. 97–98.

45. Gerald Grob, Chapter 2 of this volume.

46. Mary Roberts Smith, "Almshouse Women," *American Statistical Association* 31 (September 1985): p. 223.

47. Ibid., p. 240. This act was repealed in 1894.

48. Axinn and Levin, *Social Welfare*, p. 136.

49. Lee Welling Squier, *Old Age Dependency in the United States* (New York, 1912), p. 331.

50. Spencer Baldwin, "The Findings of the Massachusetts Commission on Old Age Pensions," *American Statistical Association* 89 (March 1910): 16.

51. Ibid.

52. Massachusetts House No. 1400, Report of the Commission, January 1910, Boston; reprinted in Pumphrey and Pumphrey, *Heritage*, p. 325.

53. Browning, *Development*, p. 74.

54. Ibid., p. 75.

55. Samuel Gompers, "Not Even Compulsory Benevolence Will Do," *American Federationist* 24 (January 1917): 48.

56. Samuel Gompers, "Voluntary Social Insurance vs. Compulsory," *American Federationist* 23 (May 1916): 340.

57. Ann Shola Orloff and Theda Skocpol, "Why Not Equal Protection? Explaining the Politics of Public Social Spending in Britain 1900–1911, and the United States, 1880–1920," *American Sociological Review* 49 (1984): 743.

58. Charles Henderson, *Industrial Insurance in the United States* (Chicago, 1909), p. 227.

59. Jill Quadagno, "Welfare Capitalism and the Social Security Act of 1935," *American Sociological Review* 49 (1984): 635.

60. Pennsylvania Manufacturer's Association, *Monthly Bulletin*, 1 May 1927, p. 1.

61. Charles K. Knight, "Fraternal Life Insurance," *Annals of the American Academy of Political and Social Science* 130 (March 1927): 97.

62. Walter S. Nichols, "Fraternal Insurance in the United States: Its Origin, Development, Character and Existing Status," *Annals of the American Academy of Political and Social Science* 70 (March 1917): 111.

63. *Eagle Magazine* 11 (August 1923): 5.

64. *Eagle Magazine* 10 (November 1922): 17.

65. Edward F. Grady, "Old Age Pensions," *American Federationist* 37 (1930): 546.

66. Clarke A. Chambers, *Seedtime of Reform* (Minneapolis, 1963), p. 164.

67. U.S. Department of Labor, "Care of the Aged by Labor Organizations," *Bulletin of the Bureau of Labor Statistics, No. 489* (1929): 26.

68. Ibid.

69. Murray W. Latimer, *Trade Union Pension Systems* (New York, 1932), p. 8.

70. Selig Perlman and Philip Taft, *History of Labor in the United States 1896–1932* (New York, 1935), p. 410.

71. Irving Bernstein, *The Turbulent Years* (Boston, 1970), p. 84.

72. U.S. Department of Labor, "Care of the Aged," p. 96.

73. *Proceedings of the American Federation of Labor* (1929), p. 99.

74. *Proceedings of the American Federation of Labor* (1928), pp. 258–259.

75. Murray W. Latimer, *Industrial Pension Systems in the United States and Canada* (New York, 1932), p. 42.

76. Quadagno, "Welfare Capitalism," p. 637.

77. Frances Townsend, *New Horizons* (Chicago, 1943).

78. Abraham Holtzman, *The Townsend Movement* (New York, 1963), p. 88.

79. U.S. Congress, House Subcommittee of the Committee on Labor, *Hearing on H.R. 2872, Unemployment, Old Age and Social Insurance*, 74th Cong. (Washington, D.C., 1935), pp. 1–2.

80. Malcolm Morrison, "Fifty Years of Social Security," U.S. Senate, Special Committee on Aging, *Information Paper #99-6* (Washington, D.C., 1985), pp. 1–11.

81. Margaret G. Schneider, *More Security for Old Age* (New York, 1937), p. 77.

82. Boan, *A History of Poor Relief*, p. 141.

83. Paul Brinker, *Economic Insecurity and Social Security* (New York, 1968), p. 60.

84. *Social Security Bulletin*, Annual Statistical Supplement (Washington, D.C., 1982), table 34.

85. Ibid., table 37.

86. U.S. Congress, House Committee on Ways and Means, *Background Material on Poverty*, 98th Cong., 1st Sess. (Washington, D.C., 1983), p. 94.

87. William Graebner, *A History of Retirement* (New Haven, 1980), p. 134;

Beth Stevens, "Blurring the Boundaries: How Federal Social Policy Has Shaped Private Sector Welfare Benefits," paper presented to the Conference on Federal Social and Economic Policies from the New Deal to the 1960s, University of Chicago, 1985, p. 11.

88. U.S. Bureau of the Census, *Statistical Abstract of the United States* (Washington, D.C., 1984), p. 384.

The Elderly's Social Security Entitlements as a Measure of Modern American Life

A striking shift has occurred during the past decade in the ways that American scholars think and write about the history of old age. Ten years ago, there had been little effort to reconstruct continuities and changes in the place of older people in Western societies. With varying degrees of success, medical doctors and social scientists had garnered historical nuggets or extrapolated from some grand theory of societal development in order to underscore differences over time in attitudes toward age and in the aged status. No one claimed to have made a comprehensive search into the historical record. Rather, history was being used to illustrate the distinctiveness of contemporary circumstances.[1] A few researchers, moreover, had studied the elderly's collective action in the political arena, particularly during the Great Depression. But these projects were designed as case studies to refine issues in political and social welfare history, not to retrieve the elderly from anonymity.[2] A concerted and systematic effort to investigate the meanings and experiences of old age in past times, it would be fair to say, did not begin until 1975, when David Van Tassel invited roughly a dozen prominent, rising, and aspiring historians to participate in his National Endowment for the Humanities–funded ''Human Values and Aging'' project.

The articles and books this band of historians produced shared two traits: they tended to treat the history of old age as yet another frontier to be blazed as social historians reworked and reinterpreted the American experience, and they concentrated on pre-twentieth-century trends.[3] Nearly every historian Van Tassel commissioned had been trained as a colonial, early national, or nineteenth-century historian; many were leading practitioners of the so-called new social history. It is not surprising, then, that they should attempt to map out the subfield of historical gerontology by exploring periods with which they were quite familiar and by using tools with which they were comfortable. Although they were to disagree over details, nearly all attempted to see how the history of the elderly fit into broader social and cultural patterns. Most of these historians had some sense of when and how such processes as urbanization and democratization had transformed conditions in early America. They recognized that the lives of middle-class men and women, immigrants, and blacks had been affected by broad-scale changes at different times and in dissimilar ways. Thus they asked straightforward questions: How did the changes that were altering basic patterns of behavior among other segments of society affect the elderly? Why—and to what extent—were the patterns of adaptation among the old distinctive? Explicitly or implicitly, historians debated the pertinence of "modernization" in describing and explaining major trends in the history of the old.[4]

Historians thus far have done a much better job in detecting shifts in the aged's images and conditions prior to the passage of the Social Security Act than they have in explicating the social, cultural, political, and economic history of older Americans during the last half-century. Demographers and family historians have emphasized that some of the critical changes in the elderly's household structure and kinship links have taken place in recent decades.[5] David Stannard, William Graebner, and Carole Haber, among others, have documented how, for better and for worse, bureaucratic assumptions and innovations have continually influenced the elderly's behavior and self-images in twentieth-century America.[6] Given the obvious diversity and magnitude of present-day old age institutions that did not even exist in 1900, historians naturally are preoccupied with bureaucratic structures, political developments, and ideologies as they grapple with the modern history of old age.

And yet, insofar as they have dealt with such issues as the impact of national programs on retirement behavior or the symbolic importance of federal aging policies, historians rarely have challenged conventional ways of synthesizing developments in recent American history as they have affected the elderly. Like political scientists and sociologists, they have tended to treat the last four decades of the national experience as a monolithic whole. In studying major trends during this period, they have not been terribly sophisticated in identifying points of divergence among the history of recent America, the social history of the elderly, and the history of public policies for an aging society. They have been less interested in seeking out those anomalies and countervailing tendencies in American political, social, intellectual, and economic life since World War II that have influenced the development of aging policies and transformed prevailing perceptions and conditions of the aged in contradictory ways than they have been in mapping out broad patterns and seeking modal tendencies among the older population.

Historians, for example, were hardly the first to notice that the social security system constitutes this nation's most significant effort to address the needs of the elderly in a bureaucratic world. As social security has expanded over time, the literature on the program's history, current policies, management, and administration has mushroomed. Social scientists, presidential commissions, congressional staff, Social Security Administration researchers, and special interest groups have prepared impressive analyses dealing with actuarial, demographic, political, and economic features of the system.[7] Although considerable differences of opinion on important details have emerged, certain facts are now taken for granted.

Most commentators focus on the concatenation of demographic, socioeconomic, and political factors in discussing the social security phenomenon. Typically, we are told that the configuration and dynamics of the modern social-welfare state—of which programs for the elderly such as social security are clearly among the most salient features—reflect and result from the aging of the population base, past economic growth, and the political success of powerful interest groups that serve, represent, and/or cater to the needs of key voting blocs in the polity. "Economic level is the root cause of welfare-state development," argues Harold Wilensky among others, "but its effects are felt chiefly through demographic changes of the past century and the momentum of programs themselves, once established."[8] No one would question, moreover, that social security has became a central—and valued—feature of the American way of life. Both government re-searchers and independent scholars agree that the federal government's program has become the basic means of economic support for most men and women over sixty-five.[9]

Given existing levels of knowledge about the dynamics of social se-curity, historians to date have been unwilling to subject accepted truths to historical scrutiny. What can historians possibly contribute to the ongoing debate about the system's impact? For openers, they might suggest that excessive, indeed almost obsessive, attention has been paid to actuarial estimates, dependency ratios, recent fluctuations in the Consumer Price Index, and the political calculus of the gray lobby. Other factors—such as the role of women in contemporary society, the improved image and status of older people in America, and the shift-ing meaning of "work"—have been underplayed. As a result, few scholars have tried to relate systemic changes in social security to the context of developments shaping the range of experiences characteris-tic of modern old age.

In addition, historians might note that the development of social se-curity has been treated in a curiously deterministic manner. There has been a regrettable tendency to concentrate all historical interest in the formative years of the program and to act as if all subsequent devel-opments flow naturally from initial presuppositions and operating pro-cedures. As a consequence, too little attention has been paid so far to the complexity and ambiguity of the historical process that has both sustained the growth of social security and made the system so vul-nerable to the economic woes, political constraints, and distinctive so-ciocultural tenor of modern American society. Critics rarely indicate that the historical forces transforming the structural and normative bases of social security have very often affected the system in unexpected, even unpredictable, ways.

Hence, it would not be too much of an exaggeration for historians to claim that we really do not understand how social security fits into the political economy of modern America, or how it has affected the contemporary evolution of the elderly in society overall. Despite countless studies, academic experts and government officials are still unable to agree on the precise role of social security on levels of sav-ings and consumption, employment behavior, and other critical as-pects of the current political economy. Reviewing the various data and models set forth during the past decade, Henry Aaron, a Brookings Institution economist who has offered seminal recommendations on social security for the past two decades, concludes:

Achieving a theoretical consensus on how so complex a system should influence behavior has proven elusive. Theorists have developed alternative analytical frameworks for looking at the effects of social security. But all involve extreme assumptions introduced to ensure analytical tractability, and each seems to describe the behavior of some, but not all or even most people. The reasonable position for the policymaker or ordinary citizen to take is that no single model is generally applicable. The shortcomings of available data have created additional roadblocks to measuring the effects of the social security system on economic behavior.[10]

The difficulties in the task of writing the twentieth-century history of old age, therefore, are precisely the opposite of those presented to the first investigators of the field. Colonial and nineteenth-century historians did not know what was special about older people's history before 1930, but they grasped "the big picture." In contrast, the major institutions, events, and statistics about the aged in contemporary America are well known, but no scholar has yet succeeded in writing a sophisticated history of the United States since the Great Depression. We face three immediate historiographic challenges. First, we have not yet placed the modern history of old age into the context of the social history of modern America. Second, we have not paid sufficient attention to the complexity of the dynamics of programs like social security since World War II. And for these reasons, third, we cannot yet be certain about the interconnections between policy initiatives and the larger political economy as they affect the lives of the elderly and other age groups.

In the face of such uncertainty, a thoughtful—albeit tentative—review of the historical evolution of social security becomes vitally important. We need to recognize that social security does constitute a watershed in old age policy but at the same time realize that there is serious social and political evolution to cover after the act as well as before. An historian would be foolish to assume that he or she could quickly resolve all the complex issues, particularly since the history of older Americans in a bureaucratic world remains one of the major items on the research agenda. Rather than presume that they understand how all the factors shaping old people's experiences fit together, historians of aging would be well advised to break down broader macroeconomic and political issues into more manageable problems. In short, they should begin to test the validity of commonplace verities and determine whether the real world is truly as neat as we assume.

That we have been blind to the messiness of recent developments, and that we presume the truth of "facts" that should be scrutinized, is most apparent in the way professional analysts and journalists treat the issue of social security "entitlements." Writers frequently describe social security as a sacred cow. Suggesting changes in the status quo raises anxiety levels, draws fire from well-financed vested interests, and most importantly, costs votes. The political sagacity of this observation hardly depends on some arcane social science theory. The recent politics of social security, pundits report, confirms that the American voting public consider their entitlements sacrosanct rights. People count on the program being there in the future. Political consultants have been unanimous in their conclusion that Ronald Reagan's clumsy attempt in May 1981 to control the rate at which future social security benefits will rise cost the president valuable congressional and popular support and hurt the Republican party in the 1982 elections. The situation is tricky for Democrats and liberals as well.[11] But *is* Social Security a sacred cow? *Have* entitlements become inviolable?

An historical analysis of entitlements reveals that policymakers and the public at large labor under certain false and misleading assumptions about the development of benefits under social security. The evolution of rising old age assistance and insurance entitlements is traced in the next two sections. By reviewing the evidence in public opinion polls, as well as the evolution of rising old age assistance and entitlements, the complex relationship between changes in social security and the American public's changing expectations can be placed into longitudinal perspective. In the final sections, it will be demonstrated that erroneous assumptions about social security benefit structures, and the persistent failure to recognize the fundamental incongruity between entitlements and expectations, have complicated efforts to decide if and how to rectify the system's deficiencies and to institute necessary bureaucratic reforms.[12]

THE FORMATIVE YEARS OF SOCIAL SECURITY

Launching Social Security: 1934–1937

On June 8, 1934, Franklin D. Roosevelt told Congress that he intended to assemble a group of experts and public officials to devise a program for protecting Americans against some of the conditions that threatened their financial well-being:

> If, as our Constitution tells us, our Federal Government was established among other things, "to promote the general welfare," it is our plain duty to provide for that security upon which welfare depends. . . . Hence I am looking for a sound means which I can recommend to provide at once security against several of the great disturbing factors in life—especially those which relate to unemployment and old age.[13]

This was not the first time in American history that a public official had invoked the federal government's responsibility to ensure the economic and social security of the body politic. In his first annual Message to Congress (1825), John Quincy Adams had proclaimed that "the great object of the institution of civil government [was] the progressive improvement of the condition of the governed."[14] The 1912 Progressive platform, moreover, had affirmed the need for a nationwide system of old age pensions; similar pleas had been made thereafter in each session of Congress. But Roosevelt was the first incumbent president to take decisive steps to translate such political rhetoric into reality.

Three weeks later, Roosevelt appointed a cabinet-level Committee on Economic Security. While he gave the committee free rein, he made his policy goals well known. Roosevelt wanted to establish a program that dealt at the very least with the problems of unemployment and old age dependency; beyond these objectives, he thought that any social insurance scheme should cover all likely vicissitudes "from the cradle to the grave." The president clearly wanted far-ranging, omnibus legislation. And if all of his objectives could not be realized immediately, the seeds for subsequent growth had at least been planted. Hence, the expectation that expanding future entitlements would be related to current benefits was recognized from the start. Furthermore, Roosevelt believed that his public system should be built on the same principles that shaped private insurance programs. The president was especially insistent that both employees and employers make regular contributions to any federally sponsored institution. Such taxes, in his view, had a value that transcended economic considerations: "We put those payroll contributions there so as to give the contributors a legal, moral, and political right to collect their pensions and unemployment benefits. With those taxes in there, no damn politician can ever scrap my social security program."[15] Roosevelt saw even modest contributions as a way to guarantee entitlements now and in the future. Because the public had a stake in social security, they naturally would want to protect existing benefits and undoubtedly would press for more. And as more and more taxpayers received benefits, they would constitute a lobby eager to expand the system as conditions warranted.

The legislative proposal drafted by the Committee on Economic Security reflected the president's wishes, but it did not give him everything that he had wanted. At Roosevelt's request, for instance, a Medical Advisory Committee was formed to study the possibility of including health insurance in the original social security measure. Although a feasibility study was completed, the president heeded the warnings of his advisors and did not press for a health care bill; in fact, steps were taken to ensure that the committee's report was not publicized in the newspapers.[16] Roosevelt submitted his legislative proposals to Congress on January 17, 1935, with the clear implication that this was an all-or-nothing package. For strategic reasons, the old age assistance proposal—the item certain to gain strongest support in both the Senate and the House—was listed as Title I. At the same time, the president made it known that he did not expect the first title to be the only part of the measure that would receive favorable action. Predictably, subcommittees in both the House of Representatives and the Senate made changes in the original draft. The public hearings provided an occasion for debating the pros and cons of several items and for proposing amendments. Nevertheless, by mid-July a joint conference committee had ironed out differences in the various executive and legislative versions, and a "social security" bill (as it was now called) quickly made its way through both houses of Congress.[17]

The original Social Security Act signed into law on August 14, 1935, was divided into ten titles. Title I authorized a federal-state program to finance old age assistance. Along similar lines, categorical grant programs providing aid for dependent children (title IV) and to the blind were enacted. Two other programs were established with nonuniform federal grants to enable states to continue their efforts in the areas of maternal and child welfare and public health. The rest of the twenty-nine-page document detailed eligibility requirements and funding mechanisms for old age insurance (titles II and VIII) and for a federal-state unemployment compensation measure (titles III and IX). Though it is important to note that elderly men and women were not the only people targeted for public intervention, attention here is confined to the old age assistance and insurance program.

The wording and provisions of the original Social Security Act had an immediate impact on the status of older Americans. The measure defined the elderly for administrative purposes as that segment of the population over the age of sixty-five. Increasingly, this administrative criterion became the chronological baseline delineating the onset of old age.[18] Furthermore, the aged became entitled to consideration in federal policy circles that long had been denied them. Social security guaranteed old people certain age-specific benefits. Title I made public relief in old age not a gratuity but a right that could be legally enforced. Title II created a mechanism to enable aging Americans to reduce the likelihood that they would be impoverished in their late years. As the chairman of the Senate Finance Committee pointed out during deliberations, this measure reflected distinctly American values:

It comports better than any substitute we have discovered with the American concept that free men want to earn their security and not ask for doles—that what is due as a matter of earned right is far better than a gratuity. . . . Social Security is not a handout; it is not charity; it is not relief. It is an earned right based upon the contributions and earnings of the individual. As an earned right, the individual is eligibile to receive his benefit in dignity and self-respect.[19]

Because older Americans were now the actual and potential beneficiaries of a categorical program that was national in scope, the aged could expect to get more and be expected to demand more. It seemed highly likely that efforts to liberalize existing benefits and to broaden coverage would force policymakers and old age interest groups in the future to defend past entitlements and to fight for more.

Yet it is imperative to remember that not every older person in America directly or immediately benefited from the passage of social security in 1935. Title I did not uniformly cover all the aged poor. As late as 1938, Arizona, Georgia, Kansas, North and South Carolina, Tennessee, and Virginia still had not enacted old age assistance measures, and as a consequence, its citizens received no federal aid. Likewise, key elements of the work force—including farm laborers, government employees, and military personnel—were not covered under Title II. Policymakers justified such exclusions on administrative grounds. However reasonable this justification may have seemed, the restrictions in coverage adversely affected some groups more than others. For instance, since blacks and Hispanics in the 1930s were heavily concentrated in agriculture, their hard work did not earn them benefits or future entitlements that they would have received had they been employed in the commercial or industrial sectors of the economy.

Not surprisingly, the mandated benefits and presumed limitations in the old age assistance and insurance programs provoked criticisms across the political spectrum. Reformers such as I. M. Rubinow, Abraham Epstein, and Eveline Burns faulted the system for failing to extend protection to the entire population and questioned its financing mechanisms.[20] While such critics hoped that these deficiencies could be corrected in due course, others were not so sure. On the basis of their reservations, several business groups and Republican politicians recommended more radical steps. The National Association of Manufacturers, for instance, attacked the payroll tax on employers; many small town shopkeepers remained hostile to any type of old age pensions. Kansas governor Alfred Landon tried unsuccessfully to capitalize on conservative discontent by making social security a major issue in the 1936 presidential campaign: "To call it 'social security' is a fraud on the working man," claimed Landon in a speech in Milwaukee. "To get a workable old-age pension plan, we must repeal the present compulsory insurance plan."[21] Leaders of older people's grassroots movements, on the other hand, pressed for broader programs. About eighty different old age welfare schemes were presented to the public in California alone between 1936 and 1938. The Townsendites had mobilized sufficient support in Congress and across the nation to make some policymakers worry about whether the Townsend Plan might not yet replace the fledgling social security system.[22]

Some attempted to reform social security by challenging its constitutionality. Litigation against several provisions of the Social Security Act was initiated shortly after Roosevelt signed the measure into law. In May 1937, however, the Supreme Court validated the social security program in two landmark decisions. In *Stewart Machine Company v. Davis*, five liberal justices accepted the unemployment excise tax on employers and approved the federal-state funding apparatus. In *Helvering v. Davis*, the Court upheld (again by a 5-4 decision) the statute's old age insurance tax and retirement benefit provisions. Delivering the majority opinion, Mr. Justice Benjamin Cardozo noted that since the old age problem was "plainly national in area and dimensions," Congress had the right to "spend money in aid of the general welfare."[23] The Supreme Court did not rule on the wisdom of Title II, to be sure, but it clearly had certified the measure's constitutional legitimacy.

The day after the Supreme Court rendered its decision in *Helvering v. Davis*, Arthur J. Altmeyer, who chaired the Social Security Board, declared that the stage was set for expanding the system: "Passing the law is only, as it were, the 'curtain-raiser' in the evolution of such a program."[24] The original equilibrium between entitlements and expectations was about to be disrupted. Significantly, the most successful architects of systemic change were found inside the fledgling bureaucracy.

The Social Security Board Takes Off: 1936–1939

While fulfilling its "duty of studying and making recommendations as to the most effective methods of providing economic security through social insurance," the Social Security Board broadened prevailing definitions of old age dependency. In a 1937 study, the board reported that 34.7 percent of all elderly men and women were able to maintain their financial independence through earnings, savings, annuities, and pensions; another 19.8 percent were currently recipients of public or private assistance. The status of the rest of the aged population (45.5 percent) was not known. This meant, in the board's view, that this group was *potentially* dependent on federal assistance or charity.[25] On the basis of its definition of dependency and its data, the board determined that the economic plight of old people constituted a major social problem, and probably would continue to do so in the indeterminate future. For this reason, it stressed that public assistance was not enough. The board made the case that the insurance program established under Title II offered a "reasonable solution" for providing economic support for older people.

Indeed, the board became so committed to expanding the scope and benefits of Title II that it sought to alter the actuarial basis, target population, and philosophical underpinnings of the federal old age insurance program before the first benefit was ever paid. In 1938, the board recommended that monthly benefits (originally scheduled for disbursement beginning on January 1, 1942) be made payable two years earlier, and that more workers—particularly those employed by banks and loan associations, and seamen—be covered by the program. In order to promote family security, the board proposed that the emphasis be shifted from the worker as an individual to a notion of the worker as the chief breadwinner of a family. Specifically, the board wanted to provide money not only for retired wage earners but also for their wives at age sixty-five or for their children. And, in the event of the wage earner's death, provisions were to be made for their survivors (typically widows and dependent children). The board's recommendations served as the basis for amendments incorporated into the social security program in 1939.

These 1939 amendments fundamentally altered old age entitlements without nullifying all of the original provisions. Social security's old age welfare function no longer was limited to the provisions of Title I. By providing family members as well as contributors at least a minimum guaranteed income, greater emphasis was placed on the "social adequacy" features of social insurance than had been the case in the 1935 version. The issue of equity was not forgotten, however. The level of benefits to which family members were entitled still bore a direct relation to the amount of covered wages an employee had contributed over time. More important, existing provisions were liberalized without making access to federal old age insurance a universal right. After all, only dependents who could stake a claim to benefits based on their relationship to a wage earner could expect to receive monthly pensions.

Thus during the "takeoff" period of the social security program, its central bureaucracy took actions that set into motion a dynamic relationship between entitlements and expectations. Not only were entitlements expanded, but so was the basis for expecting future entitlements. Social security was not simply an insurance program; nor was it basically a welfare package. It was intended to be both simultaneously. And therein lay both the basis for the system's subsequent evolution and, at the same time, the source of widespread misunderstanding of the program's objectives and accomplishments.

A reviewing of the data gathered in public opinion surveys conducted during the late 1930s reveals that most Americans did not fully understand the difference between the government's old age assistance and old age insurance programs. "Despite the numerous articles which have been written," bemoaned Edwin E. Witte, "the two parts of the old age security are confused and many of the essential features have been grossly misrepresented."[26] And yet, even if the public did not understand exactly how social security worked, they clearly believed that the federal program was vital. A December 1935 Gallup poll found that 89 percent of those interviewed endorsed the idea of providing old age assistance for "needy" senior citizens; six years later, an incredible 91 percent were "in favor of Government old-age pensions." Furthermore, the survey data indicate that the public recognized the need for a contributory retirement program. In 1937, 73 percent of those asked approved of the present social security tax on their wages; 85 percent rejected the notion of having employers pay for the whole cost of the program. In August 1941, 76 percent of the public said that they were willing to contribute 3 percent of their annual income in order to collect after the age of sixty a governmental pension worth $50 a month.[27] Social security, in the public's mind, had already become an important way of dealing with the problems of old age.

EXPANDING SOCIAL SECURITY IN AN AGE OF AFFLUENCE

The Politics of Incrementalism: 1940–1960

Even if there had been no changes in the social security system during the two decades after the first old age insurance check was paid out, existing provisions would have ensured the steady growth of the program. With the sheer passage of time, more and more workers were covered and thus ultimately entitled to benefits in retirement. In 1939, 43.6 percent of the civilian labor force was actually contributing to the system; twenty years later, the figure had risen to 64.1 percent.[28] The number of beneficiaries correspondingly increased. Roughly 222,000 Americans received old age insurance benefits in December 1940; the figure had exceeded 14.8 million by December 1960. Expenditures (in current dollars for the 1960 fiscal year) rose from $40.4 million to $11 billion between 1940 and 1960. And as the experts had predicted, the proportion of Americans receiving old age assistance benefits under Title I steadily declined as the proportion of workers and their dependents eligible for benefits under Title II rose: in February 1951, the number of old age insurance beneficiaries surpassed the number of people receiving old age assistance pensions for the first time; six months later, the dollar value of Title II disbursements exceeded Title I payments.[29]

Various amendments to the social security system, moreover, expanded coverage. Legislation enacted in 1950 required regularly employed farm and domestic workers, workers in Puerto Rico and the Virgin Islands, and federal civilian employees not covered by the federal civil service retirement system to contribute to the program; state and local employees not covered by a program and employees (other than ministers) of nonprofit organizations could elect to be covered. As a consequence of amendments enacted in 1954 and 1956, compulsory coverage was extended to self-employed farmers, self-employed professionals (except physicians, who would not be covered until 1965), and military and naval personnel. These amendments also permitted ministers and members of religious orders not bound by a vow of poverty and state and local public employees (including firemen and police officers in designated jurisdictions) to join the system. At the same time, average monthly benefits rose. Part of the increase reflected the higher wage histories upon which benefits were based. Social security amendments also boosted benefits. In September 1950, for instance, Harry S Truman signed a 77 percent increase in the benefit levels established in 1939. Two years later, another 12.5 percent increase was authorized, which in turn was followed by a 13 percent raise in September 1954 and 7 percent in December 1959.

Besides expanding the coverage and raising the dollar value of social security benefits, Congress liberalized existing provisions and moved to broaden the scope of the system itself. In order to encourage early retirement, for instance, workers were permitted to apply for actuarially reduced benefits if they retired between their sixty-second and sixty-fifth birthdays. (Women were eligible under this program in 1956; men became eligible five years later.) In 1954, moreover, Congress extended disability protection to anyone unable to engage in substantial gainful employment because of any medically determinable permanent physical or mental impairment. And in a series of amendments, changes were made in the eligibility requirements for the Aid to Families with Dependent Children (AFDC) program—all designed to extend protection to children and their care-takers.

The Dynamics and Limits of Incrementalism

Perhaps the most remarkable aspect characterizing the growth of social security between 1940 and 1960 was the lack of conflict over the series of decisions to expand coverage and increase entitlements. During this period, successive sessions of Congress tended to approve by overwhelming margins those amendments that were endorsed by the House Committee on Ways and Means and the Senate Committee on Finance. No president ever vetoed a social security bill. Regardless of their party affiliation, appointees to the Department of Health, Education, and Welfare (HEW) generally agreed about the next legislative and administrative steps to be taken. Conservative opposition in Congress typically was ineffective. Special interest groups, such as the American Medical Association and the U.S. Chamber of Commerce, proved to be successful in preventing dramatic changes in the then prevailing scope of federal programs. But they rarely mounted a consistent or effective assault on the status quo; nor did their opposition foreclose the possibility that liberalization would someday take place.

Scholarly analysts by and large attribute this fortuitous development to the successful implementation of the politics of incrementalism.[30] Political conflict was minimal, according to this view, because the chief architects of social security (figures such as Arthur J. Altmeyer, Robert M. Ball, J. Douglas Brown, Wilbur J. Cohen, and Robert J. Myers) remained active in the policymaking process. Deeply committed to assuring the financial integrity and social viability of the program, these insiders shared common values and goals, possessed a formidable degree of technical expertise about the actuarial and fiscal aspects of the program, and were politically astute enough to know what could and could not be proposed at any given point in time.

The success of social security reform, however, was not just the result of shrewd calculations and lobbying by members of a policy elite. American prosperity made it possible to extend the federal program. As the economy boomed and incomes rose after World War II, the system was able to take in larger and larger amounts of revenue without making a noticeable dent in an individual's take-home pay. Indeed, as the system expanded and the labor force grew, the number of new contributors far exceeded the number of new beneficiaries. Since initial start-up costs were low and tax rates remained modest—thanks to the favorable demographic balance between those contributing to the

system and those claiming current benfits—the system actually managed to operate with a surplus during the period. Above all, social security's future seemed bright because so many different groups had a
stake in the program's well-being. Obviously, differences of opinion
existed across the political spectrum that could not be minimized; nor
is it legitimate to discount the philosophical ambiguities inherent in the
system's normative and structural foundations. But insofar as tough
choices could be avoided in relatively affluent times, the politics of
consensus prevailed over potential sources of dissent. Older people realized that the system would provide the financial basis for their future
security. Younger Americans recognized that the system reduced the
degree to which their parents in their later years would need to depend
on them. Democrats and Republicans alike saw obvious advantages in
supporting a program that appeared sound and enhanced the quality of
voters' lives. Business and labor groups disagreed about many legislative particulars, but each group realized that their respective constituencies viewed social security as a right. No wonder the system itself
increasingly appeared to be a sacred cow.

Despite all of the factors that undeniably sustained bureaucratic
growth, it is imperative to realize that this felicitous set of circumstances was not inevitable. Social programs for older Americans were
not simply a political response to the elderly's presumed needs or a
reflection of their current entitlements. Various factors constrained the
growth of entitlements. Thus it is essential to specify the limits as well
as the dynamics of incremental policymaking—particularly in order to
understand social security's recent troubled history. The precise development of the social security system was greatly influenced by prevailing national priorities and the ways that policymakers defined the
relationship of older people to other segments of American society. The
idea of entitlements also proved to be tightly constrained by the power
of Congress. To underscore the significance of this point, two historical episodes must be briefly recounted.

World War II demonstrated the extent to which addressing the needs
of the elderly depended on the state of the political economy. A review of the legislative record between 1941 and 1945 also reveals the
ease with which policy experts' goals could be ignored in the face of
more pressing matters. After the enactment of the 1939 amendments,
influential members of Congress and members of the Social Security
Board pressed for greater coverage and benefit increases. The Wagner-

Murray-Dingell bill introduced in 1943, for example, called for a national system of old age assistance, the extension of old age insurance coverage for farmers and domestic workers, and an ambitious health insurance scheme. Proponents of this measure justified the liberalization of social security in terms of the nation's wartime economic requirements and its need to prepare for widely forecast postwar dislocations. They were able to cite a Gallup poll conducted in early August 1943, which reported that 64 percent of those interviewed favored extending coverage to "farmers, domestic servants, Government employees, and professional persons."[31] Although a splendid case could be made for expanding the program, Congress chose not to enact any changes. Indeed, even though increases in contribution rates and benefit levels had been mandated, existing schedules remained in effect throughout the conflict. Winning the war took precedence over any desire to augment the social welfare agenda.

Wartime exigencies were not the only factors that stemmed the rate of growth of the social security system. The program's future was shaped by unexpected twists of fate. Indeed, in deliberating the plight of an obscure former social security beneficiary, the judicial branch of the federal government had to reexamine the inherent tension between statutory entitlements and popular expectations. In the process, the legal basis of every American's entitlements was shown to be less sacrosanct than most people at the time thought. In *Flemming v. Nestor* (1960), for instance, the Supreme Court extended its line of reasoning in *Helvering v. Davis* (1937) by reaffirming Congress's right to exercise its power—and specifically to determine the precise nature of governmental entitlements under social security—as long as the legislative body operated within constitutional bounds.[32] According to the Supreme Court, current and future beneficiaries were entitled to receive whatever Congress decided it could afford to pay them in light of prevailing social, economic, and political realities. Had the 1960s been a period of social tranquility, economic stagnation, and political passivity, it is possible that more conservative and fiscally minded Congresses might have restrained the growth of social security. But in an era of rising expectations and seemingly boundless prosperity, Congress took steps that dramatically underlined their desire to do more for the aged.

Great Society Initiatives

Throughout the 1960s, Congress continued to engage in the politics of incrementalism. A 7 percent benefit increase was authorized in January 1965; Lyndon B. Johnson signed a 13 percent raise in February 1968; two years later, a 15 percent hike was enacted. Amendments in 1960, 1965, and 1967 extended compulsory and elective coverage under the old age insurance program to new groups of employees. Provisions concerning eligibility for AFDC and disability benefits were also liberalized.

Without question, the most important change in social security was the establishment of a health care program for older Americans and those in need. Though Roosevelt and Truman had presed for some sort of national health insurance plan, it was not until the Dwight D. Eisenhower administration that officials looked for ways to graft health care options onto social security's bureaucratic apparatus and financing mechanisms. John F. Kennedy in one of his first messages to Congress urged that a hospital insurance program be added to the social security system. In the spring of 1965, a bill was drafted combining the three different health care proposals that enjoyed the most support on Capitol Hill. The keystone of the bill was a hospital insurance plan that provided benefits to social security beneficiaries, protection against hospitalization costs to those covered by the federal railroad retirement program, and coverage of nursing home care to all persons over the age of sixty-five. This plan was enacted as Part A of Public Law 98-97, Medicare. Part B of Medicare was designed to supplement the scope of Part A: for $36 a year (initially), this program covered payments for physicians' and surgeons' services, diagnostic tests, prosthetic devices, and the rental of hospital equipment. Subscription to Part B was voluntary. At the same time that Medicare was enacted, Congress created a federal-state program (Medicaid) that financed medical service for public welfare recipients of all ages, and those who were demonstrably unable to defray their health care costs.

From a systemic perspective, therefore, Medicare was designed with those eligible for old age insurance benefits in mind, and Medicaid was intended to mesh with Title I (old age assistance) guidelines. This strategy made sense on several counts. Social security had a reputation for efficiency and effectiveness within and beyond official policy circles. Gallup polls taken in 1962 and 1965 indicated, moreover, that the public approved of increasing social security taxes in order to meet the hospital costs of beneficiaries through a government-sponsored program.[33]

Besides successfully lobbying for a federal program that helped older people deal with their medical expenses, the architects of Johnson's Great Society made promises to elderly Americans that went far beyond previously enunciated commitments. For instance, the Older Americans Act, which was passed in 1965, created an Administration on Aging in HEW; allocated funds for community planning, services, and training programs, and provided a network of federal-state matching grants for community social services and demonstration projects. Some of these initiatives were funded subsequently through titles XIX and XX of the Social Security Act. In 1968, Wilbur J. Cohen, who recently had been named secretary of HEW, unveiled "A Ten-Point Program to Abolish Poverty," which called for an end to racial discrimination in jobs and education as well as an overhaul of the federal government's public welfare, health care, and social insurance programs. His proposal specified six changes in social security, including an increase in benefit levels, a method for keeping the system "inflation-proof," a way to ensure that the program was *the* basic system of income security, increased protection against relatively short-term total disability, improved benefits for those over the age of fifty-five who were presently disabled, and a liberalization of the earnings ceiling for current beneficiaries. Such an ambitious agenda was feasible, Cohen believed, because "the Nation has the economic capacity, the technological capability, and the intellectual resources to accomplish this goal before the end of the next decade."[34]

Nixon's Good Deed

Needless to say, a combination of domestic crises and international problems in the late 1960s and early 1970s undermined the bold visions enunciated by liberal reformers who hoped to reconstruct American society and culture through concerted governmental intervention and the expenditure of federal revenues. Johnson could not win his War on Poverty as he squandered lives and millions of dollars in Vietnam. The race riots and youth protests gave conservatives an excuse to decry governmental excesses, caused liberals to pause, and raised many doubts in the public mind about the efficacy of federal initiatives. As a result, many domestic proposals formulated in the heady mid-1960s stalled. Even those programs for older Americans and other needy groups that were put into place languished because they were insufficiently funded and poorly evaluated. In this context, the election of Richard M. Nixon in 1968 seemed to presage the end of a drive to deal with structural causes and effects of poverty. And despite the fact that Nixon's victory was at least partly a measure of his ability to capitalize on the fears of "middle Americans," his desire to contain the growth of federal programs probably meant that middle-class Americans' social security entitlements would not continue to rise as they had in the past.

Yet one of the many ironies of Nixon's first term is that his administration encouraged the passage of legislative "reforms" that greatly increased the scope and cost of federal involvement in the welfare arena and in the area of income maintenance. When Nixon signed House of Representatives Bill 1, a compromise measure, he brought to a close a three-year struggle to improve the system. The Social Security Amendments of 1972 constituted a compromise measure that reflected the desires and objectives of liberal elements in the executive and legislative branches of government more than it did the conservative wing of the Republican party. Included in the package was a 20 percent across-the-board increase in social security benefits, effective September 1972; the Medicare program was altered to provide extended coverage and improve its operating effectiveness. A federal Supplemental Security Income (SSI) program was created, which guaranteed minimum income levels for the needy on a nationwide basis. Effective January 1, 1974, SSI replaced the current Title I program and other federal-state provisions for the blind and permanently and totally disabled; administered by the Social Security Administration, this program was to be financed through general revenues.[35]

In terms of expanding current social security entitlements, one feature in the 1972 amendments merits special scrutiny. Beginning in calendar year 1975, an annual determination was to be made as to whether or not a cost-of-living increase in cash benefits should be established. Whenever the Consumer Price Index (CPI) rose 3 percent or more, benefits would correspondingly be increased. Proponents of this measure cited a host of impressive precedents for this idea. They noted that a prototype of the purchasing-power guarantee in wage agreements had been part of the 1948 General Motors-United Auto Workers settlement and was a feature of some other private pension arrangements, notably college professors' retirement plans. In the early 1960s, automatic cost-of-living provisions were added to major public retirement plans: 1962 amendments to the Civil Service Retirement Act included a provision for increasing annuities automatically as the CPI rose; the Uniformed Services Pay Act of 1963 provided similar benefits for military veterans and their dependents. In addition, fourteen other (mostly industrialized) countries had introduced cost-of-living escalators that adjusted benefits in relationship to changes either in rising prices or wages.[36] Social security experts, notably Wilbur Cohen and Robert Ball, had been advancing this concept during the 1960s; the idea was scrutinized in hearings about amendments to social security in 1970 and 1971. And now that the actuaries reported that the social security trust funds appeared to have a larger surplus than previously estimated, it made sense to implement a provision at this juncture: it was a well-tested idea; it made sense economically; and politically, it could be presented as Nixon's "good deed," thereby enhancing his prospects for an overwhelming victory in the upcoming presidential election.[37]

It is impossible to exaggerate the importance of these 1972 amendments. They seemed to usher in a new era in the politics of incrementalism. By guaranteeing a minimum level of income support funded by the federal government through its new SSI program, leaders at the national level were poised to achieve a dream first envisioned in 1935—a "minimum standard of decency and health" could really be realized across the country simply by raising the level of minimum benefits. And by instituting an automatic cost-of-living index to current social security benefits, the economic well-being of millions of older Americans would no longer be subjected to the lag between their benefits' worth and soaring prices as the public waited for the legislative branch to enact and the executive branch to sign increases in benefits on an *ad hoc* basis. Entitlements now seemed to be insulated from the cumbersome political process. Social security had been converted from a system in which economic growth and reserve accumulations preceded legislative expansion of benefits to one in which entitlements would reflect changes in consumer prices as measured by the government. More than ever before, social security had become a "pay-as-you-go" system: Congress had provided that benefits would be financed exactly by each year's social security taxes from current wage earners.[38] (The Old-Age, Survivors, Disability Insurance [OASDI] trust fund, which then had about $42.8 billion worth of reserves, would serve as a cushion against short-term fluctuations in the contributions caused by recessions or higher than projected unemployment and inflation rates.) In this context, there was little doubt that entitlements would increase. Indeed, there was every reason to believe that one's retirement benefits would far exceed any contributions made to the system.

THE PAST DECADE AS A WATERSHED IN THE HISTORY OF SOCIAL SECURITY

The events of the 1975–1985 decade, needless to say, eroded the balance in the relationship between rising entitlements and changing expectations. In retrospect, four factors—the deleterious effects on short-term and long-range social security financing caused by operationalizing the 1972 amendments amid international stagflation; the sharp decline in public confidence in the future health of Social Security; the failure of "experts" to reach a consensus concerning either the proper role or the actual impact of the program on the political economy; and the inability of the federal government to regain control over the rate at which benefit levels increased—precipitated a new crisis mentality about the nation's largest and most important domestic program.

Future Shock and the 1972 Social Security Amendments

Shortly after the enactment of the 1972 amendments, serious defects were discovered in the new method of computing social security benefits. Economists within the Social Security Administration and outside governmental bureaucracies demonstrated that the formula was sensitive to the workers' period of covered employment, that it provided windfall benefits to young disabled workers and survivors of young deceased contributors, and that it overcompensated for the effect of inflation on benefits. If prices rose 4 or 6 percent a year, for instance, low-income workers would retire with benefits that exceeded their most recent wage; anticipated earnings-replacement ratios for both low- and middle-income workers would rise far higher than was the case prior to 1972. "Rather than just compensating persons who retire in the future for the effects of inflation, the present system provides huge rewards for inflation to these persons, at the expense, of course, of future workers who, if the indexing error is not corrected, will incur the cost of paying for these inflated benefits."[39] Hence, far from being neutral, the new formula "double-indexed" for inflation.

In December 1977, Congress corrected the technical error. Automatic cost-of-living adjustments remained intact, but the system was "decoupled." Wage indexing of earnings histories and the benefit formula was introduced. In order to compensate for the depletion of trust funds and to restore the future financial integrity of the program, a new set of tax rates was imposed, which culminated in a 7.65 percent tax on both employees and employers in 1990. By making these changes, policymakers were able to reduce nearly half of the long-term deficit that social security actuaries now believed had been caused by the 1972 formula and the recent inflationary period.

Unhappily, even after the double-indexing problem was solved and a new tax rate was imposed, the economic problems of the times wreaked havoc for social security. The automatic indexing of benefits had been pegged to changes in prices rather than to changes in wages because, historically, wage increases had outstripped rising prices. This traditional pattern was reversed in the 1970s. Inflation in the United States had risen to an annual rate of 5.9 percent in 1971, and then gyrated between 5.5 and 11 percent at mid-decade. By the end of the 1970s, the inflation rate was still hovering around double-digit figures and seemed virtually out of control. The wages of most workers, in stark contrast, did not keep pace with inflation. Real wages actually declined about 0.6 percent during the decade. In a sense, then, older people seemed to benefit from the adverse economic climate, for their entitlements grew as inflation soared. Unlike men and women in the labor force, whose earning power had been reduced, indexing gave the elderly an additional measure of security.

From a broader perspective, however, it was becoming painfully evident that inflation was a bane that not only hurt those in the labor force but also threatened the immediate and long-range health of all financial institutions, including social security. Actual economic conditions upset the "optimistic" and "intermediate" economic assumptions that policymakers had used to maintain a proper balance between contributions and disbursements in the social security's pay-as-you-go manner of financing. As a consequence of sustained price increases, benefits proved to be higher than estimated. At the same time, more and more people joined the eligibility roles, because the earnings-replacement ratio now afforded by the system made it financially possible for them to take early retirement. Increases in social security taxes, however, were not keeping up with rising benefit levels. And even though a greater percentage of all Americans was in the labor force than ever before, unemployment rates steadily rose, thereby reducing the relative number of those contributing to the system. As a result, trust funds were being depleted at a far faster rate than had been anticipated.

Public Confidence in Social Security Plummets

A crisis mentality about the future of social security took hold. The new posture on social security was most evident in the media. Newspaper articles and television specials graphically conveyed the impression that social security was on the verge of bankruptcy. Charts showing the actual and projected increase in the number of people over the age of sixty-five and the striking decline in the ratio of workers to beneficiaries between 1940 and 2030 were intended to demonstrate why the system had become so vulnerable. Figures depicting the recent tax increases and scheduled hikes touched raw nerves, particularly since it appeared that social security beneficiaries were better off than workers in inflationary times. While the data presented were usually accurate, the interpretation tended to sensationalize facts. Erroneous assumptions about the purpose and operations of social security were perpetuated. Stereotypic images of older people were reinforced: those who wanted to show how blissful the elderly were compared to the rest of the population interviewed healthy looking residents of "Sun City"; those who viewed all old people as drains on productivity and economic growth took a hard-nosed position on dependency and looked askance at able-bodied couples enjoying their leisure time. Rather than educating the public by showing how complicated the issues really were, and by indicating that a variety of solutions was possible (each of which would have different effects on different groups of Americans), the media eschewed subtlety, ignored ambiguity, seized on clichés, and illustrated their points with worst-case scenarios. It would be fallacious to argue that the media undermined Americans' support for social security. There can be no doubt, however, that it reinforced the sharp decline in popular confidence that occurred during the 1970s.

Consider the trends that emerge from seven public opinion surveys conducted between 1978 and 1982, which asked people about their confidence in the future financing of social security. Each poll indicated that younger people had less confidence than their elders that the system would still be solvent when they reached retirement age. In a January 1982 ABC News/*Washington Post* telephone survey of 1,508 people, for example, 69 percent of those respondents under the age of forty-five stated that they did not expect social security to exist by the time of their retirement. Only 38 percent of those between the ages of forty-five and sixty, and a mere 10 percent of those over the age of sixty-one, expressed similar fears.[40] Precipitous drops in confidence were detected by Louis Harris and Associates as well as other pollsters who replicated earlier surveys. What made this pattern all the more disturbing is that it paralleled a longer trend of popular disenchantment with governmental effectiveness. Public opinion polls had documented a dramatic decline, beginning in 1964, in Americans' trust in government. Surprisingly, the steepest drop was registered among those over the age of sixty-five.[41] Thus, in a marked switch from the overwhelming support that social security had enjoyed in its formative years, Americans suddenly evinced considerable fears about the security of social security.

Renewed Controversies among the "Experts"

Public concern over the financial woes of social security was echoed in controversies among experts and in policy circles. Several distinguished scholars in the 1970s formulated sophisticated econometrics models to demonstrate that the pay-as-you-go method of financing social security adversely affected private savings and capital accumulation.[42] In the midst of the debate among technicians, experts increasingly recommended radical reforms of the social security program. Conservative writers renewed their assault on a program they had long abhorred and now found more vulnerable than ever before. Hence, critics such as Peter J. Ferrera resurrected arguments first set forth in the 1930s and denounced *The Inherent Contradiction* in social security.[43] Ferrera's call for "privatizing" social security as a way to preserve personal liberty and improve economic performance was voiced (albeit with slightly different policy recommendations in mind) by economists including Michael Boskin, who held an appointment in the Hoover Institution, and Robert S. Kaplan, who served as dean of Carnegie-

Mellon University's Graduate School of Industrial Administration.[44] Former social security officials recommended other ingenious "solutions" that would have altered the fundamental structure of the system. A. Haeworth Robertson, who had served as chief actuary of the Social Security Administration between 1975 and 1978, proposed a "Freedom Plan" to take effect on July 4, 1984.[45]

Government's Inability to Regain Control over Social Security

A "crisis of political legitimacy" crippled Washington and the capitals of nearly all Western democracies.[46] Leaders in this country and in other advanced-industrial nations had to grapple with energy shortages, rampant inflation, and a decline in productivity rates. Keynesian macroeconomic remedies no longer proved efficacious. The Vietnam War and Watergate exposed to Americans the dangers of an "imperial presidency"; the nation's dependence on foreign oil supplies, international currency problems, and mounting trade deficits reduced Pax Americana to a shambles. Efforts by successive presidents to effect a recovery and restore a sense of unity at home appeared increasingly counterproductive; their promises and slogans seemed to complicate matters by exacerbating mistrust and indifference among the electorate. The executive and legislative branches failed to reach a consensus on how best to proceed. No segment of the population was willing or ready to jeopardize their entitlements or make sacrifices for the common good.

Indicative of the dilemma facing governmental leaders was the difficulty officials had in altering the shape and dynamics of the annual budget. In fiscal year 1967, entitlements accounted for 37 percent of all federal outlays. Thirteen years later, entitlements represented nearly 60 percent of total disbursements and almost 80 percent of all "uncontrollable spending." As political scientist Dennis S. Ippolito described the problem:

Serious issues of public policy—the shift of resources from the private to the public sector, the impact of government budgets on the economy, a large proportion of the population dependent on government for some or all of its income, and the removal of most of the budget from annual review or control—are tied to current spending levels. And *spending* is the key; virtually everyone agrees that it is too high, but there is sharp disagreement on how to reduce or control it.[47]

Since the New Deal, the federal government had initiated nearly three dozen entitlement programs, but approximately 90 percent of this spending was earmarked for a few measures. Not surprisingly, the costliest programs were also ones that reached the greatest number of people. But commentators saw great significance in the fact that the largest of these entitlement programs either directly or indirectly benefited elderly people.

Analyses of government spending between 1969 and 1980 revealed that appropriations for income maintenance and health care programs, as well as benefits guaranteed through the Older Americans Act, had risen from 20 percent to more than 40 percent of the total budget. In light of "the graying of the federal budget," liberals and conservatives alike urged greater scrutiny of cost-benefit ratios. Public sympathy for the aged was further undermined; several experts feared fierce conflicts along intergenerational lines. Analyses of imminent and long-term deficits in social security underscored the need to take action before it was too late. "Established interest groups and governmental factions alike, unaccustomed to strong partisanship on social security issues since the earliest years of the system, may have to come to grips with divisions that are unusual in American politics and an atmosphere unusual in its intractability."[48]

Thus, in order to shore up the financial woes besetting social security and to begin to reduce the rate of growth in federal spending, three different blue-ribbon panels in 1981 alone called for a change in the way that Title II benefits were indexed. The President's Commission on Pension Policy recommended that the Bureau of Labor Statistics develop a cost-of-living index for the retired; that retirement benefits be adjusted for inflation only on an annual basis; and (until a new index was constructed) that future increases in entitlements be pegged to average federal wage increases or increases in the CPI, whichever was lower.[49] The final report of the National Commission on Social Security, issued in March 1981, also endorsed the promulgation of a new index based on the CPI for all urban consumers, not just urban clerical and manual workers.[50] The Committee for Economic Development, an independent research and educational organization of two hundred business executives and educators, urged "some adjustment of benefit levels, such as indexing at less than 100 percent for a period of several years, to partially reflect the past differential between average wage rate changes and increases in Social Security benefits."[51]

Reagan chose to ignore the findings of these various panels. Instead, in May 1981, while Congress was still debating his monumental changes in existing budget and tax laws, the president announced his own strategy for restoring the financial health of social security. Among other things, Reagan proposed reducing the benefit formula for those who took early retirement at age sixty-two after December 1981 from the then current 80 percent level to 55 percent of "normal" retirement benefits. He also recommended tightening disability rules. The timing and specifics of the president's package caught nearly everybody by surprise. Was Reagan really trying to restore public confidence in the system, or did he view social security as just another welfare program that needed to be trimmed in order to deal with new defense priorities and budgetary constraints?[52] Regardless of where social security fit into the president's agenda, reaction to his ideas was swift. Senior-citizen groups uniformly denounced the package. The Senate rejected the president's proposals by a 96-0 vote. In the face of such a decisive rebuff, Reagan decided to appoint another commission to study the problem and to propose reform measures that Congress would endorse and that the president could sign; he asked it to report its findings after the 1982 congressional elections.

On January 20, 1983, the National Commission on Social Security Reform issued its report to the president. The eight Republicans and seven Democrats on the panel unanimously agreed that Congress "should not alter the fundamental structure of the Social Security program or undermine its fundamental principles."[53] It also agreed that the OASDI trust funds would need an additional $150–$200 billion between 1983 and 1989 and that the actuarial imbalance for the seventy-five-year valuation period averaged 1.8 percent of taxable payroll. Twelve members of the commisison also agreed to a dozen specific measures to deal with the immediate funding problems and restore faith in the system. With remarkable speed, and only a few minor changes in the area of entitlements, the Congress crafted the 1983 amendments to the Social Security Act, which were based largely on the arguments, data, and recommendations set forth by the National Commission on Social Security Reform. In so doing, the president and Congress were able to defuse the immediate short-term financing problems besetting the nation's Old Age Insurance and Survivors program.[54]

It is worth noting that the 1983 amendments to the Social Security

Act dealt gingerly with the issue of how to control rising entitlements. Congress mandated a six-month delay in making cost-of-living adjustments in 1983 and required that, henceforth, adjustments be made on a "third quarter to third quarter" basis. It also devised a way to control the rate at which benefits would automatically rise. The amendments created a "stabilizer" against the possibility of continued poor economic performance like that we had endured for the previous decade. After 1988, automatic increases in social security benefits will be tied to the balance of the OASDI trust fund as a percentage of the estimated disbursements from the fund for any given year.

By indexing benefits, supporters of the best interests of older people hoped to elevate their economic well-being above the political fray. But this has not happened. The political environment is more volatile and factitious than ever. By indexing benefits, conservatives hoped to save money, because the rate of increase in benefits legislated on an *ad hoc* basis since 1950 had actually exceeded the rise in consumer prices in that period. This has not happened. By reaffirming the legitimacy of automatic indexing in the 1983 amendments to the Social Security Act, it will be harder to control spending, not just for social security, but for all other entitlement programs. Have policymakers, therefore, boxed themselves into a corner? Is it too late to redefine entitlements in light of current political, social, and economic realities?

From a historian's perspective, prevailing assumptions about social security entitlements are not warranted. They are simply too pat, because commentators ignore the temporal process by which the particular set of entitlements existing at any point in time has come into being. This chapter, by documenting the messiness of social security's evolution, indicates that constructive debate would be difficult but not impossible—as long as we eschew facile, misleading generalizations about the historical record. We can draw three lessons from the past:

First, monthly retirement benefits to which older Americans can now lay claim are fundamentally different from the ones to which they were initially entitled in 1935. Revisions in the ways in which benefits were calculated over time occurred because of shifts in program objectives and alterations in the financial resources of the social security system itself. Successive amendments have led to extended coverage, a gradual liberalization of eligibility requirements, and a steadily more generous basis for determining benefits. The cumulative impact of these technical changes has been to provide older people with an increasing measure of economic security. While such amendments were enacted in an incremental manner, however, they were not inevitable.

Proposals for reforming benefits under the federal government's old age insurance and assistance programs did not materialize out of thin air. New schemes usually were first advanced by prominent "experts" and endorsed by some public agency or private organization, gestated in the policy arena, tested in another area, and then (only after congressional deliberations) incorporated into the social security system. And though it is true that modifications in the system very often were the brainchild of a policy elite that guided social security's development, this cadre of insiders has never been oblivious to larger social, economic, and political currents transforming American society at large. Before any new entitlement was enacted, policymakers had to agree that existing measures had becomme inadequate, determine which of the available options made the most sense, and attempt to forecast the impact of changes in the status quo. Since policymaking in social security is a dynamic but gradual process, entitlements have evolved slowly over time.

Second, insofar as existing entitlements usually become the basis for greater and greater demands, it is likely that future entitlements will not simply be present rights writ large. Hence, today's entitlements at once embody previous decisions and nurture future expectations. Under certain circumstances, there is no tension between entitlements and expectations: the "reasonableness" of extending current benefits overrides cost considerations or any other constraints. But just as entitlements are never created in a vacuum, so too yesterday's expectations do not ineluctably become tomorrow's entitlements. Rising expectations are not always realized. For additional entitlements to be gained, socioeconomic conditions must be auspicious, and the political maneuvering must be successful.

Third, "entitlements" are a slipperier entity than most analysts suggest in at least one other sense. Those who study social security or administer the program tend to be fairly well informed about what benefits actually exist. This does not mean, however, that the general public is equally knowledgeable. What people think they are entitled to is not always what is prescribed in the relevant statutes. For this reason, the potential for tension between entitlements and expectations that exists among the public at large is of a different nature than is to be found in policy circles. This does not mean, of course, that the range of disagreement among the "experts" is narrow. Not only do such people express divergent views about future entitlements, but they also espouse different expectations. Those who think that current entitlements justify continued expansion of the program tend to have great expectations. Those who think the program has gone out of control try to devise ways to reduce its scope, or at least control its rate of growth.

Grasping the significance of these three historical lessons does not lead necessarily to the conclusion that the present system of entitlements is wrong, or that obvious reforms are needed. But history affords us more latitude for serious reflection on a wide range of alternatives than we might otherwise think that we have. Accordingly, it might well prove profitable for Americans to reconsider the structural and normative bases of current social security entitlements.

Automatically expanding benefits might have made sense in an era when resources seemed infinite and long-term economic prospects were ebullient, but this does not mean that it still makes sense to do so. It would be wrong to cut back current benefits. But future increases in entitlements do not have to conform to some formula that is itself a product of a particular historical moment. We should debate whether it makes sense to return to a system of liberalizing benefits on an *ad hoc* basis. The economic needs of older Americans must be taken seriously, but so too must competing national priorities.

It is not at all clear that Congress or the public at large has the courage to act in such a manner. After all, it is hard to buck the tide of the politics of incrementalism. Bureaucracies, especially ones like social security that are so vital to the well-being of so many age groups, have legitimate, vested interests to protect. But if we take projected long-term deficits seriously, and if the public is by chance right in doubting that future generations will get an equitable return on their social security contributions, then a failure to think about the nature of entitlements will have dire consequences. Squarely facing this reality will be painful. But such are the dictates of modern life in aging America.

NOTES

1. For a bibliography of works of this genre, see Joseph T. Freeman, *Aging: Its History and Literature* (New York, 1979). Several of these pioneering studies remain useful to historians. See, for instance, Gerald J. Gruman, *A History of Ideas about the Prolongation of Life: The Evolution of Prolongevity*

Hypotheses to 1800 (Philadelphia, 1966); Leo W. Simmons, *The Role of the Aged in Primitive Societies* (New Haven, 1945); and Donald Cowgill and L. Holmes, *Aging and Modernization* (New York, 1972). I wish to thank David Hackett Fischer, William Graebner, Gerald N. Grob, and Peter N. Stearns for their suggestions for revising an earlier draft of this essay that I presented at the April 1983 Case Western Reserve University conference, The Elderly in a Bureaucratic World.

2. See Jackson K. Putnam, *Old-Age Politics in California* (Stanford, 1971); Abraham Holtzman, "An Analysis of Old Age Politics in the United States," *Journal of Gerontology* 9 (1954): 56–66; Roy Lubove, *The Struggle for Social Security* (Cambridge, Mass., 1968).

3. The essays written by historians appeared in Stuart F. Spicker, Kathleen M. Woodward, and David D. Van Tassel, eds., *Aging and the Elderly: Humanistic Perspectives in Gerontology* (Atlantic Highlands, N.J., 1978); and David D. Van Tassel, ed., *Aging, Death, and the Completion of Being* (Philadelphia, 1979). At the time of the conference, David Hackett Fischer had completed the first draft of *Growing Old in America*; I was completing a dissertation that would become *Old Age in the New Land*.

4. See Fischer's analysis of this approach in the "Bibliographical Essay" in the paperback edition of *Growing Old in America* (New York, 1978), pp. 232–269. See also W. Andrew Achenbaum and Peter N. Stearns, "Old Age and Modernization," *Gerontologist* 18 (1978): 307–313; and W. Andrew Achenbaum, "Further Perspectives on Modernization and Aging," *Social Science History* 6 (1982): 347–368; and Brian Gratton, chap. 1 of this volume.

5. See Daniel Scott Smith, chap. 5 of this volume, and Tamara K. Hareven, chap. 6 of this volume; see also Peter Laslett, "Societal Development and Aging" in Robert H. Binstock and Ethel Shanas, eds., *Handbook of Aging and the Social Sciences* (New York, 1977), pp. 87–116.

6. David E. Stannard, "Dilemmas of Aging in Bureaucratic America" in Spicker, Woodward, and Van Tassel, eds., *Aging and the Elderly*, pp. 9–20; William Graebner, *A History of Retirement* (New Haven, 1980); and Carole Haber, *Beyond Sixty-Five: The Dilemma of Old Age in America's Past* (New York, 1983).

7. Much of this bibliography has been conveniently annotated in U.S. Department of Health and Human Services, *Basic Readings in Social Security* (Washington, D.C., 1981). This volume lists 2,593 different books, articles, and technical reports.

8. Harold L. Wilensky, *The Welfare State and Equality* (Berkeley, 1975), p. 47.

9. See, for instance, Lenore E. Bixby, et al., *Demographic and Economic Characteristics of the Aged*, Social Security Administration Research Report no. 45 (Washington, D.C., 1975); James H. Schulz, *The Economics of Aging*, rev. ed. (Belmont, Calif., 1980), ch. 2.

10. Henry J. Aaron, *The Economic Effects of Social Security* (Washington, D.C., 1982), p. 82.

11. See, for instance, Bob Kutner, "The Social Security Hysteria," *New Republic* 187 (27 December 1982): 20.

12. I hope to provide a further historical interpretation of social security in a Twentieth Century Fund report I am currently preparing. This will include treatment of other issues, such as social security's impact on retirement and discrimination regarding women and minorities, which go beyond this essay's focus on entitlements.

13. Franklin Delano Roosevelt, *Review of Legislative Accomplishments of the Administration and Congress*, 73d Cong., 2d sess., H. Doc. 397 (1934), p. 4.

14. Adams's remarks are cited in Arthur M. Schlesinger, *The Coming of the New Deal*, Sentry ed. (Boston, 1958), p. 315.

15. Roosevelt's guidelines are cited in Schlesinger, *Coming of the New Deal*, pp. 308–309.

16. Edwin E. Witte, *The Development of the Social Security Act* (Madison, 1962), pp. 174–189. I do not mean to imply that the president always endorsed his committee's recommendations. On January 16, 1935, the day before he was supposed to submit his legislative proposal for consideration in the House and Senate, Roosevelt discovered that a large deficit would probably arise in the old age insurance system after 1965. Alarmed by the size of the projected shortfall and assured that the calculations were accurate, Roosevelt insisted that the potentially disturbing tables be deleted from the official report. Despite reservations, the committee bowed to presidential pressure. See Witte, *Development*, pp. 74–75.

17. The legislative history of the original bill is recounted in Witte, *Development*, and, more recently, in Carolyn L. Weaver, *The Crisis in Social Security* (Durham, N.C., 1982), ch. 5.

18. It is important to remember that in 1935, alternative ages—sixty, sixty-two, seventy, seventy-five—served as benchmarks for retirement in the private sector, or for public relief. Age sixty-five's appeal, in part, was that it was a middling compromise.

19. 102 *Congressional Record*, p. 15110.

20. See, for example, Abraham Epstein and Eveline Burns in American Association for Social Security, *Social Security in the United States* (New York, 1936).

21. Edwin C. Rozwenc, *The Making of American Society*, vol. 2, (Boston, 1973), p. 362; Robert S. Lynd and Helen M. Lynd, *Middletown in Transition* (New York, 1937), pp. 128–129, 246; Governor Landon's remarks were reported in *New York Times*, 27 September 1936, pp. 1–2.

22. Richard L. Neuberger and Kelley Loe, *An Army of the Aged* (Caldwell,

Idaho, 1936); Jackson Putnam, *Old-Age Politics in California* (Stanford, 1970).

23. U.S. Congress, Senate, *Constitutionality of the Social Security Act*, 75th Cong., 1st sess., Doc. 74, pp. 32–35; see also Alfred H. Kelly and Winfred A. Harbison, *The American Constitution*, 4th ed. (New York, 1970), pp. 767–768.

24. Arthur J. Altmeyer, "Progress and Prospects under the Social Security Act," address before the National Conference of Social Workers, 25 May 1937, p. 4, cited in Weaver, *The Crisis in Social Security*, p. 111.

25. U.S. Social Security Board, *Economic Insecurity in Old Age* (Washington, D.C., 1937), pp. 12–13. The board was careful to note that its perception of "dependency" was not the only way to define the situation. Nonetheless, this 1937 report presented the first "conclusive" evidence that a majority of older people in the United States were dependent.

26. Quoted in Michael E. Schlitz, *Public Attitudes toward Social Security, 1935–1965*, Social Security Administration Research Report No. 33 (Washington, D.C., 1970), p. 34.

27. These data are taken from George Gallup, *The Gallup Poll: Public Opinion, 1935–1971*, 3 vols. (New York, 1972), vol. 1, pp. 9, 76, 292–293. See also Schlitz, *Public Attitudes*, for a cogent analysis.

28. Unless otherwise noted, the statistics and legislative amendments described in this and the following two paragraphs are taken from U.S. Department of Health and Human Services, *Social Security Bulletin: Annual Statistical Supplement, 1980* (Washington, D.C., 1981), pp. 19–21, 55–58.

29. Wilbur J. Cohen, "Income Maintenance for the Aged," *Annals of the American Academy of Political and Social Science* 279 (1952): 153–160.

30. The best analysis along these lines is Martha Derthick, *Policymaking for Social Security* (Washington, D.C., 1979).

31. See, for instance, the cogent argument made by the head of the Social Security Board: Arthur J. Altmeyer, "The Desirability of Expanding the Social Insurance Program Now," *Social Security Bulletin* 5 (November 1942): 3–8. The 1943 poll data come from Gallup, *The Gallup Poll*, vol. 1, p. 400. Similar support was registered in 1944 and 1948. See Gallup, *The Gallup Poll*, vol. 1, pp. 482, 783.

32. Flemming v. Nestor, 80 *Supreme Court Reporter* 1367ff. See also Jeremy Rabkin, "The Judiciary in the Administrative State," *Public Interest*, no. 71 (Spring 1983): 75–77.

33. Gallup, *The Gallup Poll*, vol. 2, pp. 1759, 1932.

34. Wilbur J. Cohen, "A Ten-Point Program to Abolish Poverty," *Social Security Bulletin* 31 (December 1968): 13. Cohen's social security proposals appear on pp. 7–8.

35. For more on the legislative history and details of the 1972 amendments, see Robert M. Ball, "Social Security Amendments of 1972," *Social Security*

Bulletin 36 (March 1973): 3–25; Vincent J. Burke and Vee Burke, *Nixon's Good Deed* (New York, 1974); and Daniel P. Moynihan, *The Politics of a Guaranteed Income* (New York, 1973).

36. Daniel N. Price and Robert O. Brunner, "Automatic Adjustment of OASDHI Cash Benefits," *Social Security Bulletin* 33 (May 1970): 1–12; Max Horlick and Doris E. Lewis, "Adjustment of Old-Age Pensions in Foreign Programs," ibid, pp. 12–15.

37. Lest any voter fail to notice that his or her benefits had increased, each social security check mailed out in October 1972 included a letter from the president informing the beneficiary of the 20 percent increase and future indexing provisions. See Edward R. Tufte, *The Political Control of the Economy* (Princeton, 1978).

38. Thus, to pay for the benefit increases approved in 1972, new contribution rates based on the new financing principles adopted under Public Law 92-336 were imposed. The percent of covered earnings subject to social security taxes rose from 5.5 to 5.85 percent between 1973 and 1978. See Ball, "Social Security Amendments of 1972," p. 23.

39. Robert S. Kaplan, *Indexing Social Security* (Washington, D.C., 1977), p. 16. See also Dean Leimer and Ronald Hoffman, *Designing an Equitable Intertemporal Social Security Benefit Structure* (Washington, D.C., 1976); and *Reports of the Quadrennial Advisory Committee on Social Security* and *Report of the Panel on Social Security Financing to the Committee on Finance, U.S. Senate*, 94th Cong., 1st sess., February 1975.

40. The data and interpretation set forth in this paragraph come from my reading of National Commission on Social Security Reform, Memorandum no. 13, "Surveys of Public Confidence as to Financial Status of the Social Security Program," dated 7 April 1982; the results of the ABC News/*Washington Post* poll are reported on p. 11. See also Louis Harris and Associates, *1979 Study of American Attitudes toward Pensions and Retirement* (New York, 1979); National Council on the Aging, Inc., *Aging in the Eighties: America in Transition* (Washington, D.C., 1981).

41. Harold R. Johnson, et al., *American Values and the Elderly* (Ann Arbor, Mich., 1979), p. S-64.

42. See, for instance, Weaver, *The Crisis in Social Security*, ch. 9; Martin Feldstein, "Social Security, Induced Retirement, and Aggregate Capital Accumulation," *Journal of Political Economy* 82 (1974): 905–926; and Martha Derthick, "How Easy Votes on Social Security Came to an End," *Public Interest*, no. 54 (1979): 94–105.

43. Peter J. Ferrera, *Social Security: The Inherent Contradiction* (San Francisco, 1980).

44. Michael Boskin, "Social Security: The Alternatives before Us," in Michael J. Boskin, ed., *The Crisis in Social Security* (San Francisco, 1977); Robert

S. Kaplan, *Financial Crisis in the Social Security System* (Washington, D.C., 1976).

45. A. Haeworth Robertson, *The Coming Revolution in Social Security* (McClean, Va., 1981). Robertson's "Freedom Plan" is presented in chapters 27–30. Similarly, Stanford Ross, who served as a commissioner of social security under Jimmy Carter, urged that the public acknowledge the "limits" of social security and encouraged greater reliance on private pensions. See "Social Security Commissioner Departs with Strong Views of System's Future," *Wall Street Journal*, 31 December 1979, p. 8.

46. The themes alluded to in this paragraph receive fuller treatment in Morris Janowitz, *The Last Half-Century* (Chicago, 1978); Lester C. Thurow, *The Zero-Sum Society* (New York, 1980); and David P. Calleo, *The Imperious Economy* (Cambridge, Mass., 1982).

47. Dennis S. Ippolito, *Congressional Spending* (Ithaca, N.Y., 1981), pp. 245–246.

48. Peter N. Stearns, "Political Perspectives on Social Security Financing," in Felicity Skidmore, ed., *Social Security Financing* (Cambridge, Mass., 1981), p. 183. Nor was social security the only retirement plan in jeopardy. A variety of state and local public pensions were clearly in a precarious financial state. Furthermore, the bail-out provisions of ERISA (the government program established in 1974 that guaranteed the fiduciary status of retirement plans of even those corporations that went bankrupt before workers became eligible for their vested pensions) meant that the federal government potentially was liable for millions of dollars of retirement benefits for which no adequate cash reserves could possibly be maintained.

49. President's Commission on Pension Policy, *Coming of Age: Toward a National Retirement Income Policy* (Washington, D.C., 1981), p. 51.

50. National Commission on Social Security, *Social Security in America's Future* (Washington, D.C., 1981), pp. 25–26.

51. Committee for Economic Development, *Reforming Retirement Policies* (New York, 1981), p. 36. CED based this recommendation on data presented in David Koitz, "Indexing Social Security," in Senate Budget Committee, *Indexation of Federal Programs* (Washington, D.C., 1981).

52. See W. Andrew Achenbaum, *Shades of Gray: Old Age, American Values, and Federal Policies since 1920* (Boston, 1983), pp. 152–153; William Greider, "The Education of David Stockman," *Atlantic* 248 (December 1981): 27–54.

53. *Report of the National Commission on Social Security Reform* (Washington, D.C., 1983), p. 2–2.

54. The "solutions" forged in 1983 did not eliminate all of the system's long-term problems or even guarantee that the program was financially sound for the rest of the decade. Among other things, it seems likely that the health

insurance trust funds will be exhausted in the 1990s, if there are no significant changes made in the financing of Medicare. If this happens, we once again will have to deal with a "crisis" situation, and public confidence once again will be undermined.

Citizenship at the Crossroads: The Future of Old Age Security

During the decades following World War II, the rapid growth in old age security entitlements in all capitalist democracies was widely hailed as a necessary—indeed, inevitable—consequence of industrialization and economic growth. Industrialization, it was thought, had simultaneously rendered the labor of older workers redundant and provided the wealth to make it unnecessary. A retirement wage sufficient to permit or induce withdrawal from the labor force in advance of physiological decline could, and should, be made available to all.

In the midseventies, however, a contrary view began to take form. Rather than being natural or inevitable, the combination of rising entitlements and an increasing number of retirees, it was argued, was part of a long-term process bound to self-destruct. In the long term, the old age security systems that were the pride of the postwar welfare state were doomed to collapse under the weight of changing demographic and fiscal realities. The "crisis" of old age security had been discovered.

In the usual formulation, the roots of the "crisis" are attributed to demography: the system of old age security entitlements currently in place in the capitalist democracies simply cannot withstand the rise in

This is a revised version of a chapter published in John Myles, *Old Age in the Welfare State: The Political Economy of Public Pensions* (Boston, 1984).

the number of old people projected for the decades ahead. Just as Harold Wilensky argued that changing demographic realities gave rise to the modern welfare state,[1] so too, it is now argued, demography will bring about its demise.

But what is the nature of this demographic imperative? The usual formulation of the demographic argument is, at best, highly misleading. This is not to say that demography is irrelevant to our understanding of the current situation. The size and composition of populations represent real constraints on any national political effort, whether for warfare or welfare. What is required, however, is to correctly identify the forms of social organization and institutional arrangements that make a particular demographic formation into a "problem." To understand the current situation, it is necessary to situate it within the broader context of the postwar welfare state and the political and economic foundations upon which it was constructed. The current conflict over the future of old age security is a symptom of a larger conflict over the proper role of the democratic state in a market economy. The postwar Keynesian consensus upon which the welfare state was constructed has broken down, with the result that the various social institutions it spawned, including retirement wages for the elderly, have now become the focus of renewed debate and political confrontation. The implication of this is that the long-term future of old age security—and, hence, of old age as we now know it—depends less on innovative fiscal management practices than on the eventual political realignments of a post-Keynesian political economy.

POPULATION AGING AND THE CRISIS IN OLD AGE SECURITY

In the conventional formulation, the crisis of old age security is explained by a rather straightforward exercise in demographic accounting. As Nathan Keyfitz has argued,[2] the current generation of adults is simply not producing enough children to support it in its old age. Due to declining fertility, the size of the elderly population will grow to a point where the economic burden on the young will become intolerable. Eventually, the demographic bubble will burst, old age security programs will go broke, and an intergenerational "class struggle" will ensue.[3] To avoid this eventuality, it argued, we must begin to show restraint now.[4] Promises should not be made to the current generation of workers that future generations will be unwilling or unable to keep.[5]

To evaluate this argument, it is necessary to identify its core assumptions. Old age pensions, in this view, are the product of an implicit social contract made between sequential age cohorts.[6] Each cohort, as it were, agrees to support the cohort it precedes, under the assumption that it will receive similar treatment from the cohorts that follow. But since age cohorts vary in size, the contract is inherently unstable. While it is relatively easy to provide generous benefits to a small retired population, to provide the same benefits to a very large cohort of retirees may become an intolerable burden.[7] The result is a conflict between cohorts leading to dissolution of the contract. This, it is argued, is what Americans and Canadians can expect when the baby boom generation retires.

The notion of a social contract between age cohorts is clearly intended as a metaphor, but one that will enable us to understand and predict changes in popular support for old age entitlement programs. The question to be answered is whether the empirical evidence gives any indication that the metaphor captures reality. Where the conditions specified by the model have been met, it would seem reasonable to expect some evidence of the intergenerational conflict and resistance to public spending on the elderly that it predicts.

Several Western nations are already quite "old" by demographic standards. The elderly constitute more than 16 percent of the populations of West Germany, Austria, and Sweden, a figure not far from the 18 percent at which the United States and Canadian populations are expected to peak in the next century. As John Heinz and Lawton Chiles observe:

Western European social security systems have already experienced the impact of population aging for some time now. The Federal Republic of Germany, for example, currently has a ratio of social security contributors to beneficiaries of less than 2:1, which is the level not projected to be reached in the United States until the year 2030, when the postwar baby boom generation reaches old age.[8]

Moreover, the tax burden necessary to finance old age security in these countries has already reached levels that exceed those projected for the United States in the next century. Prior to the 1983 amendments of the Social Security Act, the U.S. social security tax rate was expected to peak at 20.1 percent in the year 2035.[9] But by 1978, the effective tax rate to support old age security was already 18 percent in Germany,

20 percent in Sweden, 23 percent in Italy, and 25 percent in the Netherlands.[10] The experience of these nations, however, provides little evidence of the growing backlash and intergenerational hostility anticipated by the proponents of the conventional view.

Although a number of countries experienced a "welfare backlash" in the late seventies, Wilensky has shown that this pattern was unrelated either to the size of the elderly population or to levels of public spending and taxation.[11] Indeed, according to Wilensky's estimates, the very "oldest" of the capitalist democracies—Germany, Austria, and Sweden—were among the countries that experienced the least amount of popular resistance to rising welfare expenditures. And informed observers generally agree that, despite official concern over rising costs, public support of old age security systems remains high in these countries.[12]

Moreover, where there has been popular reaction against the growth of public spending, support for the elderly appears to occupy a special place. In 1981, only 11 percent of Americans under the age of sixty-five agreed that social security benefits should be reduced in the future. And the majority of those under sixty-five were prepared to accept further tax increases to keep social security viable.[13] Richard Coughlin's comparative review of public opinion poll data indicates that support for old age security programs is uniformly high and shows little variation from country to country, despite wide differences in the size of the elderly population and the quality of pension entitlements.[14]

There are some obvious reasons for such widespread support of old age security, even in the face of rising costs. First, familial bonds provide a strong basis for solidarity between generations. In the absence of suitable public provision for the elderly, adults of working age would be required to provide for their aging parents directly. For these individuals, a generous old age security system is experienced not as a burden but as relief from a burden. Second, those of working age are generally capable of recognizing that they will require similar support in the future. In the long run, they will suffer if the terms of the "contract" are not met.

Less obvious, but more important perhaps, is the fact that the key claim of the demographic model—that population aging increases the burden of dependency on the working population—is incorrect. As table 9.1 demonstrates, population aging has not generally been associated with a rise in either total or age-based dependency but, rather,

Table 9.1

Age dependency and total economic dependency, 1959–1979

	Youth Dependency1 (Age 0-14)		Old Age Dependency1 (Age 65+)		Total Age 1 Dependency		Total Economic 2 Dependency	
	1959	1979	1959	1979	1959	1979	1959	1979
Australia	30.1	25.7	8.5	9.4	38.6	35.1	n.a.	55.0
Austria	21.8	21.1	12.1	15.5	33.9	36.6	51.8	58.5
Belgium	23.3	20.5	11.9	14.3	35.2	34.8	60.2	58.0
Canada	30.3	23.5	7.8	9.3	38.1	32.8	63.6	52.3
Denmark	25.7	21.3	10.4	14.2	36.1	35.5	54.3	47.9
Finland	30.7	20.6	7.1	11.8	37.8	32.4	52.1	51.6
France	26.1	22.6	11.6	14.0	37.7	36.6	56.3	56.9
Germany	21.0	18.9	10.7	15.5	31.7	34.4	52.0	56.9
Netherlands	30.0	22.9	8.9	11.4	38.9	34.3	63.2	64.8
Norway	26.1	22.6	10.7	14.6	36.8	37.2	59.2	53.1
Sweden	22.8	20.0	11.6	16.1	34.4	36.1	51.4	48.5
Switzerland	24.0	20.1	10.1	13.7	34.1	33.8	54.0	54.9
United Kingdon	23.2	21.5	11.6	14.7	34.8	36.2	52.5	54.9
United States	30.8	22.8	9.1	11.2	39.9	34.0	60.1	52.4

1. Defined as a percentage of the total population.

2. Total non-working population as a percentage of the

   total population.

Source: OECD, Labour Force Statistics, 1959–70, Paris, 1972. OECD, Labour Force
Statistics, 1968–79, Paris, 1981.

with a decline. This is due to a decline in the size of the very young population and an increase in female labor force participation.

Canadian and American projections indicate a similar trend for the future. While the size of the elderly population will continue to grow, total age-dependency ratios will first decline and then rise slowly, back to current levels (table 9.2). At no point are they projected to reach the levels achieved during the early sixties, the peak of the baby boom period.

Table 9.2
Projected age dependency ratios, Canada and the United States

		Dependency Ratios[1]		
		Age 0-17	Age 65+	Total
Canada	1976	53.5	14.6	68.1
	1986	41.9	16.1	58.0
	2001	36.7	18.5	55.2
	2031	33.3	33.7	67.0
United States	1976	51.3	18.0	69.3
	1985	43.5	19.0	62.5
	2000	43.2	19.9	63.1
	2025	42.0	29.5	71.5

1. Dependency is defined as proportion of the working age population, i.e. population aged 18-64.

Sources: Canada—Health and Welfare Canada, *Retirement Age,* Ottawa: Ministry of National Health and Welfare, 1978:17. United States— Robert Clark and Joseph Spengler, *The Economics of Individual and Population Aging,* 1980:25.

The issue for the future then is not the *size* of the dependent population but, rather, its changing *composition*—fewer children and more retirees. The usual strategy in evaluating this change is to compare public expenditures on the old with public expenditures on the young. Since public expenditures on the old are, on average, three times public expenditures on the young, it is clear that total *public* expenditures on the nonworking population must increase as the population ages. But to assess the true economic impact on the working population, it is necessry to establish *total* expenditures on the young and old, not just that portion passing through the public purse. Information on this subject is at best incomplete. Based on the analyses of the French demographer Alfred Sauvy, Robert Clark and Joseph Spengler conclude that total expenditures on the old exceed those on the young.[15] In contrast, Hilde Wander finds that the total cost of raising a child to age twenty is one-fourth to one-third *higher* than that necessary to support an elderly person from age sixty to death,[16] indicating that total intergenerational transfers (public plus private) will decline as the population ages.

The empirical foundations for the conventional view, then, would appear to be rather shaky. Whatever its consequences, population aging does not seem to be a source of rising economic dependency, intergenerational conflict, or popular backlash against welfare state spending.[17] This does not mean that the so-called crisis of old age security is all sound and fury; only that we must look elsewhere to understand its nature and origins.

CLASS, CITIZENSHIP, AND THE WELFARE STATE

At the most general level, the current controversy over the future of old age security is rooted in the broader economic crisis that has beset the capitalist democracies since the early 1970s. A protracted economic slump, characterized by declining output, rising unemployment, and inflation, brought about a radical reassessment of the postwar welfare state. As T. H. Marshall pointed out in his now justly famous essay,[18] the postwar period was a time of remarkable optimism that the traditional problems and conflicts of the capitalist democracies could be resolved and reconciled. It appeared that a truce had been called in the ongoing war between the principles of citizenship and those of class. With an appropriate blend of Keynes and Beveridge, the rights of persons and the rights of property could be reconciled to the advantage of both. Welfare expenditures were construed as an investment in "human capital" that would improve the quality of the work force and reduce the waste of human resources produced by inadequate diet, health care, and education. Public pension systems would help to regulate unemployment and allow employers to replace older workers with more efficient, and less costly, younger workers. Most important, redistributive policies would provide the means to regulate the traditional boom and bust cycle characteristic of the capitalist economies.

Such optimism was not without foundation. Until the appearance of the massive inflation generated during the Vietnam War, and the stagflation that followed the energy crisis of the seventies, both capitalism and the welfare state experienced unprecedented levels of real growth. As the economies of the capitalist democracies grew, expenditures on social welfare grew even faster. Sweden's expenditures on income maintenance rose from 10.5 percent of GNP in 1957 to 30.7 percent in 1977. In the United States, comparable expenditures grew from 5 percent of GNP to almost 14 percent.[19] Moreover, social wages gained considerable ground on market wages as a primary source of workers' incomes. Samuel Bowles and Herbert Gintis estimate that over the three decades between 1947 and 1977 the rate of growth of real per capita "citizen's wage expenditures" was five times the rate of growth of real take-home pay in the United States,[20] with the result that social welfare expenditures increased from 11 to 27 percent of total consumption outlays.

By the midseventies, however, this optimism was beginning to wane. The capitalist democracies, it was argued, were suffering from a severe case of democratic overload.[21] The proliferation and growth of citizenship entitlements had created a revolution of rising expectations that was now a fetter on capital accumulation. Following the onset of the 1974–1975 recession, there was a growing tendency to regard welfare and efficiency as contradictory, rather than complementary, principles of economic decision making.[22] Hugh Heclo's conclusion is prototypical: "What came to be labelled as the welfare state was an arrangement for living with mutually inconsistent priorities, a system of tolerated contradiction."[23] As Marshall had anticipated, the principles of citizenship and social class were once again at war.

THE ANATOMY OF THE CRISIS

As Theodore Geiger and Frances Geiger observe, the critical issue raised by the growth of the welfare state is whether the market retains enough of its own output to satisfy its requirements.[24] For the market, that portion of the national product administered by the state is "out of control": it is no longer directly available to provide incentives to labor (in the form of wages) or to capital (in the form of profits); nor is it directly available in the form of savings to be used for reinvestment. Access to these resources is mediated by the state. As a result, the distribution of these resources is subject to the logic of the political process rather than that of the market. The expansion of the public economy increasingly politicizes economic affairs and, by so doing, reverses the great achievement of the bourgeois revolutions of the seventeenth and eighteenth centuries: removal of the state from the realm of economic decision making.[25]

Under current arrangements for the distribution of income, population aging exacerbates this process. Since increased public expenditures on the old are not offset by a corresponding reduction in public expenditures on the young, population aging increases the size of the public economy and reduces the share of national income directly subject to market forces. Thus, while population aging is unlikely to break the "national bank," it will alter the bank's structure of ownership and control. Linda McDonald and E. Bower Carty, for example, estimate that *public* intergenerational transfers to the old and young in Canada will rise from 12.8 percent of GNP in 1976 to 17.8 percent of GNP in 2031.[26] The main result of population aging, then, is not an increase in intergenerational transfers but, rather, an increase in political control of the economy.

But for whom does the expansion of public control over the distribution of income pose a problem? Any major social transformation is likely to generate conflict between those who stand to lose and those who stand to gain from such change. The trick is to correctly identify the likely winners and losers. It is instructive to ask, then, who stands to benefit and who stands to lose as the result of yet further expansion of the public economy in general, and the old age security budget in particular? If this question can be correctly answered, we are in a good position to identify the likely direction of any future conflicts that might ensue. More important, we shall be better able to appreciate the logic of the current controversies and struggles over the future of old age security. Traditionally, there have been three quite different answers to the question of who benefits from public control over income distribution. Neo-Marxists have argued that the benefits of the welfare state have gone primarily to the owners and managers of capital; "conservatives"—that is, the proponents of classical liberalism—have argued that the welfare state undermines the power of capital; and postwar liberals have generally claimed that the welfare state benefits everyone—both labor and capital. As Frances Piven and Richard Cloward have recently pointed out, however, there is a growing recognition among analysts of all political persuasions that the conservatives were right: the major consequence of the expansion of the public economy has been to alter the structure of power between capital and labor in favor of the latter.[27] Evidence of this shift is found in both the market for labor and the market for capital.

In the *labor* market, social entitlements enhance the bargaining power of labor both individually and collectively. The effects at the individual level have been recognized for some time in the life-cycle model of earnings and labor supply formulated by the Chicago school.[28] According to this model, individual workers make employment and wage decisions (whether to work and at what wage) in light of the anticipated impact of such decisions on total lifetime earnings. Universal income entitlements, such as those typically contained in old age security provisions, mean that some portion of each individual's total lifetime earnings is fixed by law. Thus, current decisions to work and at what wage can be made in light of the fact that some portion of future income is assured. This reduces dependency on the labor market and enhances the worker's bargaining position with respect to would-be employers. Where good jobs at good wages are not available, individuals may simply choose to withdraw, partially or completely, from the labor force. The "work disincentives" that result from the availability of unemployment, sickness, and old age entitlements reduce the labor supply and drive up wage levels.

To understand the effects of the citizen's wage at the collective level, it is necessary to consider the relationship between unemployment and the bargaining power of labor.[29] Under normal conditions, a rise in unemployment should lead to a reduction in wages by increasing the supply of unemployed workers and the subsequent competition for available jobs. But as Bowles and Gintis observe, social entitlements increasingly insulate the working class from the "reserve army" of the unemployed.[30] By absorbing the unemployed, the welfare state also absorbs much of the downward pressure on market wages that an increase in unemployment would otherwise create. Thus, wage levels tend to be higher, and profit levels lower, than would otherwise be the case.[31] Old age security provisions are very much part of this process. Among the first to be absorbed in periods of rising unemployment are older workers who join the ranks of the elderly by moving into early retirement.[32]

From the point of view of employers, this problem is compounded by the fact that the social wage bill and the market wage bill are interactive. Unemployment lowers the market wage bill but simultaneously triggers an increase in the social wage bill for unemployment, welfare, and retirement benefits. Irrespective of how they are immediately financed, public benefits are ultimately financed out of current production.[33] Thus, both market wages and social wages must, in the last instance, be construed as a cost of doing business. The problem for employers, then, is that the wage bill as a whole (market wages plus social wages) becomes increasingly rigid and insensitive to market forces.

The problems of employers do not stop with the obstacles they face in the labor market. The effects of the public economy also loom large in the capital market. When they attempt to borrow funds for investment in new plant and equipment or to meet temporary cash-flow problems, the owners and managers of capital find themselves faced with a very powerful competitor for the supply of available savings, namely, the state. Moreover, state borrowing to finance the public economy tends to increase when individual firms can least afford the resulting rise in interest rates. Downturns in the economy produce rising unemployment, a declining tax base, and an increased level of social spending, thereby increasing government deficits and the need to increase state borrowing. This in turn produces the rising interest rates that, in recent years, many firms have found prohibitive. In this competition for the available pool of capital, governments hold a decided advantage: the state can afford to pay the higher interest rates because of its powers of taxation, powers unavailable to private firms.

The public economy also affects the *amount* of capital available for investment purposes. Most national pension schemes are funded on a "pay-as-you-go" basis; that is, current expenditures (benefits) are paid for out of current revenues (contributions). Such a system is a form of pseudosavings: wage earners make contributions but no pool of capital is created. Since these contributions generate income entitlements that can be claimed on retirement, the necessity to save in other forms (e.g., a private pension plan) is reduced. According to Alicia Munnell, a dollar of social security contributions displaces approximately seventy-four cents of private pension savings in the United States.[34]

But to shift pension financing from a pay-as-you-go to a funded basis, as practiced in Sweden and Canada, simply compounds the problems of the business community. As has long been recognized, financing a public pension system on a funded basis results in a significant shift of economic power from the private sector to the state, since the capital pool created from contributions is in the hands of government. In Sweden, for example, the National Pension Insurance fund accounts for almost half of the total advances on the Swedish credit market,[35] effectively nationalizing the flow if not the stock of capital. In Canada, the funds of the Canada Pension Plan have become the major source of provincial debt-financing. The funds of the parallel Quebec Pension Plan have also been used to finance a state-directed program of private sector investment. In the latter part of the seventies, this situation resulted in what came to be called the Great Pension Debate. Faced with the obvious inadequacies of Canada's old age security system, Canadian labor proposed, in 1975, to rectify the situation by significantly expanding the Canada Pension Plan. Objections to this proposal had little to do with the need for improvement, nor was the superiority of the public system over private-sector counterparts seriously questioned. Rather, the principal objection was to the increase in government control over capital formation that such a change would bring about. As the editors of the Toronto *Globe and Mail* argued: "Government is already too deep into pension plans—and the savings they represent—for the good of Canada's economic future. We need more savings . . . but the savings should be in a variety of hands and not subject to the political vagaries of government."[36]

As Barbara Murphy has shown, the reasons for this concern are not difficult to identify.[37] During the decade following the Canada Pension Plan legislation of 1965, corporate saving as a source of investment capital was in decline, and corporations had to turn increasingly to external sources of financing. During the same period, private pension funds grew to become the single largest source of private equity capital in Canada and the major source of corporate borrowing. To expend the public system further would transfer a significant portion of these savings into the hands of the state and, in the words of the *Globe and Mail*, subject them to the "political vagaries of government." Democratization of the savings and investment process in this way serves to further undermine the power of private capital. And, as Canadian business has made abundantly clear,[38] the defence of this power must take precedence over the income requirements of the elderly.

But perhaps the most critical aspect of all this is the fact that the welfare state brought an increasing share of the national wage bill (including the retirement wages of the elderly) into the realm of politics. This was an event of enormous significance in the evolution of the distributional system of the capitalist democracies. Despite frequent protestations to the contrary, a state administered pension scheme is not just another big insurance company. Instead, an ever-growing and increasingly important portion of the national wage bill is removed from the market and made subject to a democratic political process; one in which workers, in their capacity as citizens, are able to lay claim to a share of the social product independent of any claims they possess in their capacity as wage earners. While a democratic polity may choose to respect the norms of the market—that is, to link benefits to contributions—it is by no means constrained to do so and, in general, has not done so. All national pension systems, as they have evolved during the past decades, have incorporated democratic principles of equality, need, and adequacy into their distributional practices: all redistribute income from high-wage earners to low-wage earners; the majority make allowance for need in the form of supplements for dependent spouses and survivors; and, historically, the majority of countries have legislated increases for the elderly to provide them with a larger share of a growing economic pie. In effect, the retirement wage was transformed into a citizen's wage, an income entitlement partially independent of the commodity value of the worker's labor power. The extent of this transformation varies from country to country as a result of differential levels of working-class power inside the state,[39] but the tendency has been universal.

The real crisis in old age security, then, is an outcome of the adverse effects of the citizen's wage on the power of capital. State intervention to meet social needs not met by the market, or created by it, tends to transform the market itself. When workers in their capacity as citizens can claim a social wage that is independent of the sale of their labor power, capitalist social relations are transformed. The "mixed economy" that emerges from this transformation is not a happy marriage between complementary principles of social organization but a unity of opposites, a system of "tolerated contradictions." Democratic control over wage and capital formation is the antithesis of capitalist control over wage and capital formation: where the one expands, the other must contract. The principal beneficiary of this shift is labor; the principal losers are the owners and managers of capital. The result is not an intergenerational "class struggle" but simply an expression of the traditional struggle between labor and capital.

The problem is not one of state control *per se* but, rather, one of *democratic* control of the state. State policies that assign resources on the basis of need and social equality undermine a system of assignment based on property entitlements and market value. The future of old age security, then, is a problem of democracy, not of demography.

CITIZENSHIP AT THE CROSSROADS: THREE DIRECTIONS FOR THE FUTURE

Elsewhere, I have argued that the postwar welfare state may be understood as the offspring of two contradictory logics of participation and distribution that became wedded in the modern liberal democratic state.[40] The liberal state, born of the bourgeois revolutions, was a state in which political participation and individual rights were based on economic capacity and the ownership of property (the class principle). In contrast, the democratic state, which was wedded to it, attached rights and duties to persons in their capacity as citizens. These included income entitlements—entitlements based not on market capacity but, instead, upon the democratic principles of equality, security, and need. In adopting democratic principles of participation and distribution, the state did not abandon its liberalism, however. Rather, these two opposing sets of principles were subsumed within a single structure, producing the internal tension that is the source of its own transformation. As Marshall observes, the postwar welfare state appeared to mark a truce in the ongoing war between citizenship and class.[41] But, as he also anticipated, this truce now seems to have come to an end: class and citizenship are once again on a collision course.

Under such circumstances there are at least three possible outcomes.

First, an acute navigator may intervene and avert the collision. If this comes to pass, people will grow old in the future much as they have in the recent past. There will be minor technical adjustments to retirement provisions and old age security benefits, but nothing substantial will be altered. Second, it is possible that the class principle and the rights of property will be restored to the position of preeminence they held in the past. This would not require abandonment of the retirement principle or the annihilation of social security. Rather, the citizenship principles of security, adequacy, and need would be abandoned to make the "wages" of the elderly subject to the principles of distribution that prevail in the market. The third possibility is that the rights of property will be further subordinated to democratic control, and the boundaries of the market pushed back so as to reduce and eventually eliminate the source of conflict.[42]

Can the collision be averted? In the current political economy, this is equivalent to asking whether the engines of economic growth can be fired again without a significant transformation of the existing social order. A survey of recent economic analysis does not offer much hope in this respect.[43] Keynesian theory is in retreat, and the alternatives being advanced generally call for substantial change in the relationship between state and economy upon which the welfare state was constructed.

The neoconservative solution is to roll back history and dismantle the gains in social citizenship achieved during the past several decades. According to this view, the economic problems of the capitalist democracies are attributable to an "excess of democracy."[44] The democratic quest for equality has generated "excessive expectations";[45] a "revolution of rising entitlements"[46] that no longer can be realistically met. As a result, democracy itself may be threatened. As Dan Usher argues, political democracy is

unworkable and impossible unless the range of issues to be settled by majority rule is severely circumscribed. In particular, government by majority rule cannot be relied upon to assign citizens' shares of the national income. *Political* assignment creates tension and conflict in society and, carried far enough, must lead to the breakdown of democracy and its replacement by another form of government.[47]

To function, a democratic polity requires what Usher refers to as a "system of equity"—"a set of rules for assigning income and other advantages independently of and prior to political decisions arrived at in the legislature." [48] In principle, that system of equity could be based on *equality*—assignment of equal shares—but this is "out of the question . . . in a modern industrial economy because it would destroy incentives and is logically inconsistent with the minimal degree of hierarchy an industrial society requires." [49] Rather, the only feasible system of equity is one that respects historically given property rights within the economic framework of a competitive capitalist economy. "Abolish economic freedom," concludes Usher, "and, regardless of one's wishes, political freedom will sooner or later be abolished as well." [50] Only by confining democracy and respecting the system of capitalist equity can democracy be sustained.

Usher's assertion that it is necessary to restrain freedom—democracy—in order to assure freedom would appear to be either a contradiction in terms or, at best, a compromise of principles. But such is not the case, because the term *freedom* is used in two different senses. When Usher speaks of *political* freedom, he has in mind the classical view of democracy according to which all persons have the right to be involved in making those decisions that have a significant impact on their lives and well-being. In this context, freedom is used in the tradition of Rousseau or Kant, to mean *rational self-determination*. [51] But the meaning of freedom changes when *economic* freedom is discussed. Here the term is used in the nineteenth-century liberal tradition, to mean the absence of restraint or interference. [52] To subject economic affairs to a collective, democratic process of decision making violates such freedom, and in particular, the freedom to dispose of one's own property. Thus, for Usher, freedom in the first sense is only applicable to strictly "political' affairs—the choice of rulers, the passing of laws that are noneconomic, and the like. The fact that private decisions over the disposition of property have significant effects on other individuals and society as a whole—for example, the level of investment, the location and availability of jobs, the distribution of income entitlements—does not qualify them as candidates for democratic decision making. The owners of property must be left free to dispose of it as they see fit and to impose their decisions on employees and others who are affected by such decisions.

How far the state must carry this attitude of respect for the capitalist order is a matter of debate. For Usher, some amount of redistribution is permissible so long as it does not alter the relative position of individuals on the scale of rich and poor.[53] But for others, public programs such as old age security violate the market principle both because participation is obligatory (unfree) and because of the lack of strict correspondence between contributions and benefits.[54] Such concepts as security, adequacy, and need are simply not market-conforming.

The conservative solution does not require abandoning the social wage principle altogether. Rather, what is required is to subject the social wage bill to the discipline of the market and restore the primacy of property rights in the wage-determination process. In the area of pension policy, several proposals have been made in this regard.

1. *Privatization.* The most direct means of restoring market control over the "wages" of the elderly is to shift responsibility for their administration from the public to the private sector, thereby insulating those wages from the claims of citizenship. In private pension plans, benefits are calculated according to strict market principles. Social transfers on the basis of need or adequacy are nonexistent. Privatization can be achieved gradually by restricting future growth of public sector pensions, thereby increasing the amount of private coverage necessary to achieve desired levels of income replacement in retirement.

2. *Limiting accessibility.* If citizenship entitlements cannot be abolished, it is possible to contain the problem by making accessibility to such entitlements more difficult. In the case of pension entitlements, this can be achieved by raising the age of eligibility for full benefits and restricting or eliminating early retirement provisions. All such efforts will mean an enlarged labor pool and, hence, greater responsiveness of market wages to fluctuations in labor demand.

3. *Make public entitlements market-conforming.* Yet another strategy is to administer public sector benefits according to market principles and to ensure that benefit levels and accessibility are responsive to changing market requirements. This could be achieved by eliminating the redistributive components of public pension systems, provisions for automatic indexing, allowances for dependent spouses, and other entitlements that violate market criteria.

Each of these strategies represents an alternative means of arriving at a common objective—the imposition of limits on the degree to which workers, in their capacity as citizens, are able to claim a share of the social product over and above any claims they possess as wage earners.

How practical is it to consider turning back the clock in this way? John Goldthorpe has pointed to at least three major obstacles to any such effort.[55] The first is a *cultural* problem arising from what he identifies as the decay of the status order. By this is meant the decay of traditional patterns of authority and deference based on symbolic and moral definitions of social worth attached to descent or hierarchical position. The decay of traditional attitudes toward authority makes the restoration of a more "balanced" democracy—one in which economic and political elites are insulated from mass demands—exceedingly difficult. The conservative solution, therefore, first requires some form of cultural restoration of traditional ways.

The second obstacle to which Goldthorpe points is the continuing demand for more, rather than fewer, citizen entitlements. The concept of citizenship has been extended to include the workplace itself, as workers demand rights to influence the decisions that affect their terms of work and employment opportunities. Any effort to dismantle existing entitlements will encounter considerable popular opposition, the broad support for old age security being a case in point.

Yet a third obstacle arises from what Goldthorpe refers to as the maturation of the working class. The institutionalized power resources now available to workers enable them to oppose and resist changes that threaten their interests. The more powerful the working class, the fiercer the opposition will be toward conservative reforms and the more likely it is that these reforms will be achieved only if accompanied by systematic repression of working-class political and economic organizations. As Goldthorpe concludes, neoconservative reforms will ultimately intensify class conflict and bring "organized labor into direct confrontation with government in defence of its achieved bases of power and security."[56] Thus, quite apart from their perceived desirability, the practicality of the neoconservative solution must be considered inversely proportional to the level of organizational power of the working class.

The third resolution to the current crisis is that proposed by Herbert Hoover's 1928 presidential opponent Al Smith when he remarked that "the only cure for the evils of democracy is more democracy."[57] If democratic control over distribution is incompatible with a market-based system of production, then one might conceivably restrict the latter rather than the former. If democracy is incompatible with the capitalist accumulation process more generally, this would suggest that democratic control be extended to the savings and investment process and to the workplace itself. This, in essence, is the social democratic solution to the current crisis.[58]

How would such a system affect the character of old age and old age security? It is difficult to identify the likely implications of such a solution since there is an absence of historical models upon which to base such analysis. In this respect, the situation of contemporary social democrats is analogous to that of the early philosophers of liberalism, who struggled to convince their contemporaries of the desirability of a social order for which there was no prior historical experience. Nevertheless, we might anticipate that under a system of socialist equity, to follow Usher, distribution would increasingly be based on principles of security, need, adequacy, and equality not just for the elderly, but for society as a whole. The result would be a crumbling of whatever divisions between old and young are created by treating different sectors of the population according to different principles of distribution. Since economic decisions could be based on principles of social need rather than profitability, work could be redesigned to accommodate an aging population, muting both the need and the desire for retirement among older workers. In sum we might anticipate a gradual decline in the importance of age-based criteria of social organization.

Is such a solution possible? To many North American ears, the social democratic solution rings of romantic utopianism. But in countries such as Sweden, where there has been more experience with democratic control of the economy, such proposals are the subject of widespread and serious debate and, with the reelection of the Social Democrats in 1982, must be considered as very real possibilities for the future. The absence of historical precedent is frequently used as empirical proof that the social democratic solution is not viable. Where the market and capitalist principles of economic organization have been abolished, it is correctly pointed out, dictatorship, not democracy, has followed.[59] The empirical demonstration, however, suffers from the fact that, thus far in history, socialist dictatorship has everywhere simply superceded some other form of dictatorship, as in Russia, China, or Cuba. With the short-lived exception of Chile, none of the so-called socialist societies in modern experience have moved toward socialism from a democratic base, through democratic means, or, one might argue, with a democratic intent. Hence, whether a full-fledged social democracy and the full realization of social citizenship that it entails is possible, is a question that can only be answered by future history. The problem of the analyst, of course, is that "history" takes an annoyingly long time to happen. Whether in the long run the current crisis produces a restoration of the rights of property, further expansion of the citizenship principle, or restabilization of the status quo, in the medium term, old age policies will reflect the halting the contradictory attempts at reform characteristic of all public policy formation. But the "muddling through" that frequently seems to characterize the policy process should not blind us to the fact that now, as in the past, old age policies are not produced randomly nor in an economic or political vacuum. Old age policies, whether in the field of pensions, health care, or social services, are ultimately distributional policies. And in an era when the politics of distribution and redistribution have intensified—marked by increasing conflict—it is hardly surprising that old age policies have attracted special attention. As with all distributional practices in the capitalist democracies, distributional policies for the elderly are a reflection of current arrangements for managing the contradictions of a democratic state in a market economy. If there is now a crisis of old age security, it is because the existing set of arrangements for managing this relationship has been brought into question and become a point of conflict. As Marshall anticipated, the principles of citizenship and social class are once again at war. The struggle over old age security is but one of the more important manifestations of this "new class war,"[60] between capitalism and democracy.

If it has done nothing else, the "crisis" of old age security has alerted us to the fact that the character and quality of old age in contemporary society are inextricably linked to the nature and character of the welfare state. In the period following World War II, old age became retirement, and both the right to retire and the rights of retirement are everywhere today the subject of national legislation. In an era in which the politics of distribution have intensified, marked by growing conflict, it is hardly surprising that old age policies receive special, sometimes confused, attention. Politics, not demography, determines the size as well as the condition of the population defined as "elderly."

The future of old age, then, will be determined by the future of the welfare state. If it survives in its present form, the experience of aging in the future will be much like that of the recent past; if it is dismantled, the elderly of the future will once again experience the insecurity generated by the dynamics of the marketplace; and, if the citizenship principle continues to evolve, the "elderly" are likely to slowly disappear as a distinctive status group in the larger society.

Whatever the outcome, history has not yet come to an end, and it would be presumptuous of us to assume that the character and experience of old age will mean the same thing in the next century as they do in this one. Despite its newness, we are apt to forget the novel meaning that became attached to the term *old age* in the twentieth century: a period in the life cycle prior to physiological decline, when productive activity ceases. This reconstruction of old age was made possible by the advent and expansion of the welfare state. The social, legal, and political constituency we now call "the elderly" was created by social, political, and economic forces; and it can be destroyed or dramatically altered by those same forces.

NOTES

1. Harold Wilensky, *The Welfare State and Equality* (Berkeley, 1985).

2. Nathan Keyfitz, "Why Social Security is in Trouble," *Public History* 58 (1980): 102–119.

3. Kingsley Davis and Pietronella van der Oever, "Age Relations and Public Policy in Advanced Industrial Societies," *Population and Development Review* 7 (1981): 1–18.

4. Robert Clark and David Barker, *Reversing the Trend toward Early Retirement* (Washington, D.C., 1981).

5. Arthur Laffer and David Ranson, "A Proposal for Reforming Social Security," in G. S. Tolley and Richard V. Burkhauster, eds., *Income Support for the Aged* (Cambridge, Mass., 1977), pp. 133–150.

6. Milton Friedman, "Payroll Taxes No, General Revenues Yes," in Colin Campbell, ed., *Financing Social Security* (San Francisco, 1978), pp. 25–30. This assumption is independent of the mode by which old age pensions are financed. Irrespective of whether the system is financed on a pay-as-you-go or fully funded basis, current consumption must ultimately be paid for out of current production, that is, by the labor of the working population.

7. Keyfitz, "Why Social Security."

8. John Heinz and Lawton Chiles, "Preface," in United States Senate Committee on Aging, *Social Security in Europe: The Impact of an Aging Population* (Washington, D.C., 1981), pp. iii–iv.

9. Dean Leimer, "Projected Rates of Return to Future Social Security Retirees under Alternative Benefit Structures," in Social Security Administration

Policy Analysis with Social Security Files, *Research Report No. 52* (Washington, D.C., 1979), pp. 235–257.

10. Barbara Torrey and Carole Thompson, *An International Comparison of Pension Systems* (Washington, D.C., 1980), p. 43.

11. Harold Wilensky, *The "New Corporatism": Centralization and the Welfare State* (Beverley Hills, 1976); idem, "Leftism, Catholicism and Democratic Corporatism: The Role of Political Parties in Recent Welfare State Development," in Peter Flora and Arnold Heidenheimer, eds., *The Development of Welfare States in Europe and America* (New Brunswick, N.J., 1981), pp. 345–382.

12. Stanford G. Ross, "Social Security: A World-Wide Issue," *Social Security Bulletin* 42 (1979): 3–10; Richard F. Tomasson, "Government Old Age Pensions under Affluence and Austerity: West Germany, Sweden, the Netherlands, and the United States," paper presented at the meetings of the Tenth World Congress of the International Sociological Association, Mexico City, August 1982.

13. Employment Bureau Research Institute, *Louis Harris Survey on the Aged* (Washington, D.C., 1981).

14. Richard Coughlin, "Social Policy and Ideology: Public Opinion in Eight Rich Nations," *Comparative Social Research* 2 (1979): 1–40.

15. Robert Clark and Joseph Spengler, *The Economics of Individual and Population Aging* (Cambridge, England, 1980).

16. Hilde Wander, "ZPG Now: The Lesson from Europe," in Thomas Espenshade and William Serow, eds., *The Economic Consequences of Slowing Population Growth* (New York, 1978), pp. 41–69.

17. Although population aging has not yet been ostensibly a source of intergenerational conflict, it has produced other forms of struggle and conflict and will no doubt continue to do so in the future. These conflicts have occurred within and between sectors of the younger, active population—professions, occupations, social institutions—dependent on a particular demographic dynamic and age structure for their power and access to resources. Efforts to adapt to changing population composition inevitably lead to conflict, since they require major reallocations of resources away from some sectors into others. Existing bases of power are eroded and new ones created. Such conflicts are already apparent in areas like education. Threatened by layoffs and lower salary increments, a result of declining enrollments, the teaching profession has responded with unionization, strikes, and a generally increased level of militancy. See John Myles and Monica Boyd, "Population Aging and the Elderly," in D. Forcese, and S. Richer, eds., *Social Issues: Sociological Views of Canada* (Scarborough, Canada, 1982), pp. 258–285.

18. T. H. Marshall, *Class, Citizenship and Social Development* (Chicago, 1964).

19. United States Senate Committee on Aging, *Social Security in Europe,*

p. 6. Between 1960 and 1978, U.S. federal expenditures on the elderly alone rose from 2.52 to 5.3 percent of GNP: Robert Clark and John Menefee, "Federal Expenditures for the Elderly: Past and Future," *Gerontologist* 21 (1981): 132–137.

20. Samuel Bowles and Herbert Gintis, "The Crisis of Liberal Democratic Capitalism," manuscript, University of Massachusetts at Amherst, 1980.

21. Samuel Huntington, "The United States," in M. Crozier, Samuel Huntington, and Joji Watanuki, eds., *The Crisis of Democracy* (New York, 1975), pp. 59–118.

22. Theodore Geiger and Frances M. Geiger, *Welfare and Efficiency: Their Interactions in Western Europe and Implications for International Economic Relations* (London, 1978), p. 108.

23. Hugh Heclo, "Toward a New Welfare State?" in Flora and Heidenheimer, eds., *Development of Welfare States*, pp. 383–406.

24. Geiger and Geiger, *Welfare and Efficiency*, p. 16.

25. Frances Fox Piven and Richard A. Cloward, *The New Class War* (New York, 1982), p. 42.

26. Linda McDonald and E. Bower Carty, "Effect of Projected Population Change on Expenditures of Government," in Canadian Government Task Force on Retirement Policy, *The Retirement Income System in Canada* (Hull, Canada, 1979), appendix 16.

27. Piven and Cloward, *New Class War*, p. 31.

28. E.g., Clark and Barker, *Reversing the Trend*.

29. Piven and Cloward, *New Class War*, p. 19.

30. Bowles and Gintis, "Crisis," pp. 39–49.

31. See Fred Block, "The Fiscal Crisis of the Capitalist State," in R. Turner and J. Short, eds., *Annual Review of Sociology* 7 (Palo Alto, Calif., 1981), pp. 15–17.

32. Clark and Barker, *Reversing the Trend*.

33. Thomas Wilson, ed., *Pensions, Inflation and Growth* (London, 1974), p. x.

34. Alicia Munnell, "Social Security, Private Pensions and Saving," paper prepared for the Conference on Public Policy Issues in the Financing of Retirement, Alexandria, Virginia, 16–17 January 1981.

35. Andrew Martin, *The Politics of Economic Policy in the United States: A Tentative View from a Comparative Perspective* (Beverly Hills, 1973), p. 18.

36. Toronto *Globe and Mail*, 12 October 1977.

37. Barbara Murphy, "Corporate Capital and the Welfare State: Canadian Business and Public Pension Policy in Canada since World War II," master's thesis, Ottawa, Carleton University, 1982.

38. Business Committee on Pension Policy, *Pension Policy—Issues and Positions: Consensus of the Business Committee on Pension Policy* (Ottawa, 1982).

39. John Stephens, *The Transition from Capitalism to Socialism* (London, 1979).

40. John Myles, *Old Age in the Welfare State: The Political Economy of Public Pensions* (Boston, 1983).

41. Marshall, *Class, Citizenship*.

42. Yet a fourth possibility is that in the force of the collision both principles will be destroyed and some undetermined and unpredictable social order constructed from the debris.

43. Peter F. Drucker, "Toward the Next Economics," *Public Interest* (Special Issue, 1980): 4–18.

44. Huntington, "United States," p. 113.

45. Samuel Brittan, "The Economic Contradictions of Democracy," *British Journal of Political Science* 5 (1975): 129–160.

46. Daniel Bell, *The Cultural Contradictions of Capitalism* (New York, 1960), p. 232.

47. Dan Usher, *The Economic Prerequisite to Democracy* (Oxford, 1981), p. xx.

48. Ibid., p. viii.

49. Ibid., p. 51.

50. Ibid., p. 89.

51. Andrew Levine, *Liberal Democracy: A Critique of Its Theory* (New York, 1981), p. 18.

52. Ibid., p. 18.

53. Usher, *Economic Prerequisite*, p. 123.

54. Milton Friedman and Rose Friedman, *Free to Choose* (New York, 1980), pp. 73–78.

55. John Goldthorpe, "The Current Inflation: Towards a Sociological Account," in Fred Hirsch and John Goldthorpe, eds., *The Political Economy of Inflation* (Cambridge, Mass., 1978), p. 197.

56. Ibid., p. 209.

57. Quoted in Huntington, "United States," p. 113.

58. Ulf Himmelstrand, Goran Ahrne, Leif Lundberg, and Lars Lundberg, *Beyond Welfare Capitalism: Issues, Factors and Forces in Social Change* (London, 1981).

59. Geiger and Geiger, *Welfare and Efficiency*, p. 117.

60. Piven and Cloward, *New Class War*.

A Comment: The Social Security Crisis in Perspective

Andrew Achenbaum and John Myles come at their subjects from different disciplines and different political perspectives. Achenbaum is a historian; Myles a sociologist. Achenbaum might be labeled a New Deal liberal; Myles a Marxist. Their focus in these chapters is on something that they agree has been happening in the 1970s and 1980s: a "crisis" has been taking place in the political economy of the United States since the early 1970s, and this "crisis" has something to do with social security and the aged. They agree, moreover, that the origins of this "crisis" may be found at least as far back as the Social Security Act of 1935. They agree that social welfare expenditures on the aged have increased dramatically since 1945. They agree that the "crisis," such as it is, is not fundamentally demographic in origin. Myles and Achenbaum also have roughly similar concepts of the nation's economic history since 1945: a postwar era of affluence, followed, beginning about 1970, by increasing economic dislocation.

On the issue of demography, Myles is much more elaborate. He demonstrates, convincingly for me, that overall demographic trends will be benign in their impact. Achenbaum avoids discussion of the demographic "problem," and its absence from his chapter can probably be taken as a sign of his rejection of the "crisis-of-demography" argument. Thus both authors agree with Myles's formulation: "population aging [does not increase] the burden of dependency on the working population." Myles and Achenbaum also apparently agree that the current crisis is not the product of an "intergenerational rebellion," though Achenbaum does briefly raise this specter. (As an aside, I think it important for Myles to explain why, if there is no such rebellion, there is so much talk of it. Who raised the issue of generational rebellion, and to what end? In addition, Myles may be correct in his assessment of *actual* burden, given public *and* private expenditures, and yet underestimate the extent to which the public will develop hostility to the dependent aged based solely on *public* expenditures.)

It is the next bit of agreement, however, that begins to take us into interesting territory. Curiously enough—in light of their political differences—Myles and Achenbaum agree on the *shape* of the crisis of the 1970s and early 1980s. They use different terms to describe the content of that crisis, but the end result is the same. Achenbaum no less than Myles believes that the crisis is a crisis of capitalism and, more specifically, a crisis in the relationship between capitalism and the state. This is explicit in Myles's work, and only slightly less so in Achenbaum's. Benefits, Achenbaum tells us, are "out of control" because, among other things, social security is endangering private savings and capital accumulation. Myles might shudder when I put it this way, but for him, Achenbaum is part of the problem—he is an academic apologist for capitalism.

Now, Achenbaum may appreciate that designation. Or may he point to the language he uses as evidence of a broader and more liberal motivation. From his brief discussion of World War II, for example, he draws the conclusion that the desires of social security advocates must be reconciled with competing *national* priorities. He laments that in the early 1970s, when the nation was faced with energy shortages, rampant inflation, and a decline in productivity rates, no one was "willing . . . to jeopardize their entitlements . . . for the common good." I am troubled by this analysis partly because the terms by which Achenbaum establishes "national" priorties and defines the "common good" are those of capitalism. Even if one grants the point that the "common good" requires rising "productivity rates," it is by no means clear that this goal can, or should, be achieved through a reduction in social security benefits.

Achenbaum's analysis of the crisis of the 1970s is replete with words that legitimize his interpretation: "distinguished" scholars formulated "sophisticated" econometrics models; "experts" recommended radical reforms of social security; liberals and conservatives alike said we should examine cost-benefit ratios; "blue-ribbon" panels reexamined Title II indexing in 1981; and another "blue-ribbon" panel proposed a tax on benefits. With all those distinguished scholars, sophisticated models, experts, blue-ribbon panels, and consensus, there seems little to do but surrender to the argument: the economy is in trouble and something has to be done with social security in order to save it.

I don't buy the connection. While there is no doubt that the American economy (or capitalism, or whatever label one chooses to apply) is having its troubles, it is not at all clear that the nation is too poor to continue the "present system of entitlements." Achenbaum can urge the need for reconsideration, but that does not make it so. I might add that his argument is the same one that is currently being used to attack pollution control and health and safety regulation. Would Achenbaum suggest that the "common good" requires cutbacks in these areas as well?

If Achenbaum believes something must be done, what kind of guidance does he offer us in arriving at a solution to the crisis? Historical guidance, of course. History tells us, Achenbaum argues, that the Social Security Act "clearly was designed to deal with key problems associated with the Great Depression," and that this was "the first time" that the federal government had addressed the problem of "old age dependency." These statements ignore the evidence, which I have presented elsewhere,[1] that old age insurance was conceived by the Committee on Economic Security in part as an instrument of retirement—as a labor market instrument—and that in this respect, far from being revolutionary, the act was the product of a historical evolution that included the campaigns for civil service retirement in the 1910s and railroad retirement in the early 1930s. Achenbaum argues—though in this chapter in a very veiled way—that the retirement interpretation of social security is somehow obviated by the liberal nature of the 1939 amendments. I do not find this argument persuasive.

But history tells us something even more important, according to Achenbaum. It tells us that we are free to do pretty much as we please—that we are not, curiously, bound by history at all. In setting up and expanding social security, no firm commitments were ever made as to what people could expect from social security when they retired. The historical process is complex and offers considerable "latitude," Achenbaum claims. The message is that things were up in the air and flexible from the beginning, and that they still are. History thus serves to liberate us from any feeling of guilt we may have that by reconsidering benefits to the aged we are doing something illegal or unethical.

I must confess my own inability to be persuaded by some of his arguments. I found the Supreme Court's 1960 pronouncement in *Flemming v. Nestor*, coming in a rather obscure case, less than compelling. The larger issue, in any event, is whether the Supreme Court has the "right" to shape our understanding of the Social Security Act in anything other than a strictly legal sense. On the relationship between "entitlements" and "expectations," I am confused. On the one hand, Achenbaum insists that social security entitlements "never were, and have not become, inviolable rights." On the other hand, the Senate Finance Committee has termed social insurance "an earned right based upon the contributions and earnings of the individual." Can a right be "earned" but not "inviolable"? The question of what is and is not a "right" is, I agree, an interesting and complex one; but an answer to it is not to be found here.

But let us, for the sake of argument, accept Achenbaum's not unreasonable position that history grants us a certain political flexibility in this current "crisis." With that in mind, we can refer to Myles's chapter and his valuable distinction between the market and the state. According to Myles, today's capitalists are disturbed because too much of the nation's product is administered by the state and is, therefore, "out of control." Although Achenbaum does not use the terms "market" and "state" and does not deal at all with the actual market, in an important sense his solution settles neatly into Myles's framework. What Achenbaum is suggesting is that the "state" need not, and should not, be considered outside the control of the capitalists (or whoever it is that makes decisions in Achenbaum's world). We should, he argues, open up the state to market influence so that the state's actions will reflect the needs of the market more accurately. Thus Achenbaum's chapter becomes an example of Myles's hypothetical "rollback" solution to the social security problem.

Finally, both authors raise the issues of democracy and the democratic state, as well as the relationship of each of these to the present social security "crisis." Neither does so very precisely. It is my sense that Achenbaum sees the "people"—the democracy—as more than a little at fault for making the irresponsible demands that have cumulatively put us in our current bind. He tells us that once the social security program existed, "the aged could . . . be expected to demand more." And there is an obvious elitist bias in all those references to experts and blue-ribbon panels.

Myles's conception of the state, and of the role of the democracy, is perhaps the weakest part of his chapter. That conception is ambivalent. On the one hand, Myles implies that, historically, the state has at least to some extent served the needs of a capitalist elite. For example, welfare expenditures were an "investment in 'human capital,' " and public pension systems were designed in part to "regulate unemployment." Over the years, however, the people seem to have been so successful in efforts to gain control of the state that wage earners seem now to have virtually insulated themselves from the marketplace, and employers are huddled together in abject fear that an expansion of the public pension system will shift capital into the hands of the "state." But who is this state? Are the retirement boards that control most of the state and municipal pension systems in the United States made up of labor leaders and working-class folks? Of course not. Moreover, the Swedish experience with public pension funds is not relevant to the United States, and there is considerable doubt how much anxiety capitalists need have of a program of "state directed . . . private sector investment" such as that carried out in Quebec. Capitalism and the state may not be coequal, but neither are they the separate entities described by Myles.

Strangely enough, both Achenbaum, the liberal capitalist, and Myles, the Marxist, find common ground in the belief that the American capitalist economy has been held hostage by the working class and, especially, the aged. Fortunately, they disagree on what to do about it.

NOTE

1. William Graebner, *A History of Retirement: The Meaning and Function of an American Institution, 1885–1978* (New Haven, 1980), pp. 184–190.

Two Roads Diverged: A Rejoinder

In his critique, William Graebner passed up an opportunity to delineate the parameters of an argument that is bound to divide historical gerontologists: how John Myles and I differ in our views of recent trends in the development of American society and culture, especially as they affect the elderly. Graebner could have stressed the significance of our theoretical disagreement: among other things, it influences the sorts of policy recommendations we offer. Thus rather than defend myself from a seemingly hostile reviewer,[1] I write this rejoinder to indicate why our respective interpretations signal important divergences that will become more prominent in the historiography of (old) age.

At the outset Graebner notes merely that Myles and I "come at [our] subjects from different disciplines and different political perspectives." To his mind, it is far more important we agree on so many details, including "the *shape* of the crisis of the 1970s and early 1980s." But is Graebner justified in asserting that my evidence and policy recommendations can properly be subsumed into the sociological framework of an advanced-industrial political economy that Myles uses here and develops more elegantly in his often brilliant *Old Age in the Welfare State*? Here is how Graebner sets up his straw man:

> According to Myles, today's capitalists are disturbed because too much of the nation's product is administered by the state and is, therefore, "out of con-

trol." Although Achenbaum does not use the terms "market" and "state" and does not deal at all with the actual market, in an important sense his solution settles neatly into Myles's framework. What Achenbaum is suggesting is that the "state" need not, and should not, be considered outside the control of the capitalists (or whoever it is that makes decisions in Achenbaum's world). . . . Thus Achenbaum's chapter becomes an example of Myles's hypothetical "rollback" solution to the social security problem.

Capitalists do indeed make decisions in "my" world, but they are not the only actors whose opinions and deeds count. And while the realities and exigencies of the marketplace surely affect politics on the Potomac, I stress in my chapter that any dispassionate history of social security must emphasize the messiness, ironies, and unpredictable twists and turns in its evolution. The differences between me and Myles (and Graebner) go beyond disciplinary canons and partisan predilections.

That pair seeks to illuminate important questions in the history of aging by uncovering and analyzing evidence in accordance with a conceptual model that they believe elucidates the "engine" driving recent history. "The history of retirement reflects the changing methodologies of American capitalism in the nineteenth and twentieth centuries," in Graebner's view.[2] Myles, in somewhat different language, attaches much significance to the designation *capitalist democracies*. "The source of dynamism and change in these societies is to be found in the fact that two forms of social organization [a capitalist economy and a democratic polity] represent contradictory rather than complementary principles of social participation and distribution."[3] Both the historian and the sociologist interpret the past in light of class relations in capitalist societies. It is the peculiar nature of the political economy that shapes the fate of the elderly. The history of old age, in their interpretations, is largely determined by methods of social control exercised by a self-serving elite grappling with the inherent contradictions of their basic organizational arrangements.

Now I happen to agree that "capitalism" and "democracy" are important—albeit not necessarily the catalytic—elements in the story. But rather than emphasizing the "contradictory" nature of these forces, I am intrigued by the asymmetry in their conflicting relationship.[4] And while I share Myles's view that social security is at a "crossroads," we are not using the term *crisis* in the same way. "The struggle over old age security is but one of the more important manifestations of this

'new class war,' '' Myles observes, invoking the title of an important
book by Frances Piven and Richard Cloward.[5] Rather than take such
a global stance, I limited my attention to far narrower issues: recount-
ing and explaining how we arrived at the bureaucratic manner in which
we calculate social security entitlements, and forecasting what our present conundrum presages.

In the confused and confusing swirl of developments in the past decade, I believe that it has become reckless to view social security as a
sacred cow. Policymakers are in a bind. The tried and true method of
obfuscating genuine philosophical debate over social insurance's purposes and effects with artful rhetoric no longer works. Focusing on
technical changes at the margins may still prove to be an efficacious
mode of policy-making, but it no longer allays the fears of an anxious,
middle-aged middle class. Entitlements, due to the concatenation of a
variety of historical forces, bear little resemblance to popular expectations.

Of course hard choices must be made. But what, I ask, is the proper
strategy for defining critical issues and generating reasonable ''solutions''? Relying on stereotypic images of age, as Reaganites are increasingly inclined to do, hardly solves the problems of those senior
citizens who do not have the wherewithal to retire to Palm Beach. Nor
does it address the needs of minorities or the diverse demands of women
in very different financial and marital situations. In facing these policy
changes under existing rules, lawmakers have little room to maneuver:
their debate takes place in annual fights over the federal budget. Even
if defenders of the status quo ''save'' benefits, social security's ene-
mies will simply look for systemic vulnerabilities elsewhere. The scenario I sketch is admittedly complex, but it does not constitute a ''crisis'' in the sense that Myles means.

More than semantics separates us. Myles apparently subscribes to
propositions typically associated with (neo-)Marxian analyses of Western political economies. The motif of ''inherent contradiction'' ani-
mates his discussion. His trend analysis implies that sooner or later the
''crisis'' of any capitalist democracy will lead to societal breakdown.
At times, he seems to stress the economic factors that scholars as different as Claus Offe and James O'Connor have characterized as the
''fiscal crisis'' of the polity.[6] At other times, Myles underscores the
disarticulation and dysfunction found in Western institutions—particularly those that deal with the problem of ''dependency'' and mitigate

tensions in the labor force. Thus, even though his thesis and emphasis are not identical to others on the Left, Myles nonetheless takes his stand with those who declare that it is the self-destructive tendencies of "modern" bureaucratic societies that ominously set the stage for the future of the welfare state.

I see several dangers in Myles's approach. His history of old age in the welfare state diverts attention from the elderly. The elderly are treated homogeneously as conniving pawns. The "ideology of dependency" mongers a radical myth no less disingenuous than the specter of all-out intergenerational conflict predicted in the media. And what are we to do until capitalism collapses? Short of a radical transformation of society, Myles eschews reforms we can sensibly initiate here and now.

There is an alternative metaphor for characterizing the locomotion of societal development. "The existence of conflicts or contradictory tendencies does not mean that the state must devour its own tail or collapse in total paralysis," Deborah Stone recently argued in *The Disabled State*. "States, too, can learn to walk with crutches and braces."[7] Just as the state hobbles along, so too I would argue that policymakers muddle through. Policies for the aged, in my view, reflect past mistakes as well as brilliant insights; they are the result of compromises forged long ago, yet which must be constantly adjusted to meet ever-present risks. Particularly in the United States, where ideological fights over "welfare" confound political action, it is the norm rather than the exception to tinker with existing policies and to make reforms on an incremental basis. For better *and* for worse, significant alterations are possible, but only when legislators and administrators avoid explicit reference to their ultimate goals. The public's opinion counts, to be sure, but the elite typically tries to lead an informed electorate by persuading them that changes in the status quo arise out of "traditional" practices and values.

Because I do not subscribe to the teleological assumptions central to Myles's argument, I am prepared to offer concrete policy recommendations that mesh with historical trends. I ended my chapter with a brief discussion of the 1983 amendments, which I believe should serve as the basis for re-forming social security to meet the needs of an aging society. The time has come for the American people and their policy elite to reach some agreement over the scope and direction of the social security program. On the basis of what I have learned about the history of this institution, I would urge that lawmakers henceforth do whatever is necessary—but no more—in order to establish and maintain a socially acceptable level of income for all Americans. This principle has several corollaries. To accommodate public expectations, policymakers should emphasize that social security is an essential expression of community that at once transcends and links together generational interests. It also means that the federal government should view social security as a "floor" for other public and private programs but frankly acknowledge the limits of any social welfare policy.

As historical gerontology becomes a legitimate field of inquiry, its central intellectual questions and modes of presentation have shifted. In this country, historians such as Thomas Cole, Brian Grattan, William Graebner, and Carole Haber have begun to interpret the historical record in light of theories of social change enunciated by political sociologists such as Carroll Estes, Laura Katz, Theda Skocpol, and John Myles.[8] In Europe, a distinguished and growing group of neo-Marxians and structural functionalists are developing a new political economy of aging.[9] These scholars have much to say, but they do not have—nor, surely, do they pretend to have—a monopoly on the truth. In response to their studies, "mainstream" historical gerontologists must become more sophisticated in analyzing the politics of "modern" aging in a bureaucratic world. It is no longer appropriate, it seems to me, for social scientists and historians who engage in the policy arena willfully to refuse to proffer a political opinion if appropriate.[10] Those of us who wish to challenge their premises must be explicit about why we disagree and formulate alternate modes of analysis and discourse.

The paths of historical gerontology have diverged. Earlier in my career, I preferred not to draw any links between my personal political views and my scholarly endeavors. But, as this rejoinder indicates, I am ready to go beyond enunciating the theoretical underpinnings of my research and to spell out the political implications of my position. I have come full circle, but I am keenly aware that the way I "do" applied history has changed in the process.[11] I am not wholly comfortable with recent developments, but I certainly want to join the fray. Whether it ultimately leads to better books, articles, and symposia—and how more sensible policy recommendations for young and old will emerge from such academic debates—remain to be seen.

NOTES

1. This is not the first time Graebner has delivered harsh assessments of my scholarship and gratuitous aspersions about my politics. See, for instance, his dismissal of *Shades of Gray* in *Journal of Interdisciplinary History* 14 (1984): 892–894.

2. William Graebner, *A History of Retirement* (New Haven, 1980), p. 13; see also ibid., p. 52.

3. John Myles, *Old Age in the Welfare State* (Boston, 1984), p. 4.

4. Hence (*pace*, Graebner), far from asserting that "the American capitalist economy has been held hostage by the working class and especially the aged," I simply cited data that showed how pressure from competing elites and various elements in the electorate pressed for the expansion of public services that several generations of Americans have come to expect as their "right." See also Herbert McClosky and John Zaller, *The American Ethos* (Cambridge, Mass., 1984), p. 302.

5. Frances Fox Piven and Richard A. Cloward, *The New Class War* (New York, 1982).

6. Claus Offe, "Advanced Capitalism and the Welfare State," *Politics and Society* 2 (1972): 479–488; James O'Connor, *The Fiscal Crisis of the State* (New York, 1973).

7. Deborah A. Stone, *The Disabled State* (Philadelphia, 1984), p. 189.

8. See, for instance, Carroll Estes, ed., *Federal Austerity and the Elderly* (Beverly Hills, 1984); Laura Katz, *The Political Economy of Aging* (New York, 1982); and Theda Skocpol and John Ikenberry, "The Political Formation of the Welfare State," in Richard F. Tomasson, ed., *Comparative Social Research* 6 (1983): 187–214.

9. See, among others, Anne-Marie Guillemard, ed., *Old Age and the Welfare State* (Beverly Hills, 1983); Chris Phillipson, *Capitalism and the Construction of Old Age* (London, 1982); Alan Wolfe, *The Limits of Legitimacy* (New York, 1977); and articles since 1981 in *Ageing and Society*, edited by Malcolm Johnson.

10. One need not be polemical, of course. See the stances taken in Bernice Neugarten, ed., *Age vs. Need?* (Beverly Hills, 1982); and Robert H. Binstock and Ethel Shanas, eds., *Handbook of Aging and the Social Sciences*, rev. ed. (New York, 1985).

11. W. Andrew Achenbaum, "The Making of an Applied Historian," *Public Historian* 5 (1983): 21–46.

PART V

RESEARCH STRATEGIES FOR THE FUTURE

The Aged in a Structured Social Context: Medicine as a Case Study

The study of aging seems inevitably to draw social scientists and historians toward theories of social change. At the same time, it has become clear in recent years that our theoretical views are in a state of disarray. Historians and sociologists still tend to assume some version of a stepwise model of social development, and even though it has become fashionable to throw up one's hands when the term "modernization" is invoked, we still find its root assumptions applied casually and pervasively.

In recent years the modernization notion has more frequently appeared in a version in which the developmental state approximating mid-twentieth-century America is termed corporate capitalism. Not too long ago, on the other hand, modernization schemes were the particular enthusiasm of social scientists with rather different political orientations—many of whom sought to explain and channel economic and political development in non-Western nations. (The term "less-developed nations" is a linguistic relic of such frameworks.) Though the moral—and political—agendas latent in these developmental schemes are rather different, the two ways of seeing past economic and social change are in a logical sense rather more similar than their respective advocates might be willing to concede. The problem is not that these general schemes are wrong; it is that they are too imprecise and general to be useful. Obviously the Western world did get from there to here in the course of the past three hundred years; the great majority of us no longer live in peasant villages. But beyond the broadest descriptive categories, the fit between any of our stage-oriented development theories and available data soon becomes obscure.

Nevertheless, middle-level extrapolations of these schemes have been employed to explain an enormous variety of historical and sociological phenomena. We have no body of middle-level theory and empirical data that specifies the linked changes between the most general aspects of social and economic organizations and the smaller worlds of the school, the factory, the business firm, the hospital—not to mention the still smaller worlds of the family and—ultimately—the individual. Similarly, we have no agreed-upon understanding of the relationships among knowledge, ideology, interest, and institutional structures in our bureaucratic society (though few would deny that such relationships exist). Worse yet, contemporary scholarship is marked by a tendency to use assumptions about these interrelationships in place of evidence and the critical building of middle-level theory. Examples of such extrapolations are easily cited. When the farm family enters an industrializing market economy, the family's emotional structure is presumed to shift as the work and roles of husband and wife diverge. Appropriate ideological forms are then elaborated to legitimate these new social realities. An awareness of change produces new ideologies and institutions—prisons, asylums, orphanages—to palliate the resulting anxiety. The shift to an urban industrial society similarly produces new attitudes toward youth and old age.[1] But there is an obvious dilemma here, and that is the extraordinary difficulty of pinning down the relationship implicit in the evasive "produces." Even if we can associate some changes in time, we have been far less successful in establishing causative relationships or specifying the way in which individual experience is shaped by social location or the mediating effects of ideology and institutions.

Finally, of course, historians and sociologists have in recent years become increasingly self-conscious about their interest in the meaning of events to the individuals who live in and through them. This presents a level of analysis not easily amenable to empirical investigation—and thus a particularly tempting arena for the extrapolation downward from larger models of social change to their implications for individuals. During the past generation, demographers and historians have paradoxically also sought to study past social phenomena with a new quantitative precision, but in this they have experienced a good deal of difficulty in moving from the descriptive aggregate to the explanation of change in such data over time—or to the perceptions of those individuals whose past behaviors created those changed aggregates.

More specifically, to return to the study of aging in contemporary society: current historical and social scientific scholarship underlines the fragmented quality of our understanding. Empirical studies are distributed, in general, into three genres. One is attitudinal. What has society in general or specific groups within it—like clergymen or lawyers—thought about the old? A second approach centers on policy decisions and the debates surrounding them. A third kind of study is demographic, seeking to specify the place of the elderly in households and their proportions in society generally. Each one of these approaches can be criticized as incomplete. Attitudinal studies particularly have been the target of methodological strictures; the relationship between attitudes and behavior remains obscure, while it also is no easy task to pin down attitudes in terms of social location. Most of our policy studies also seem narrow; narrow in a rather different style. What are the relationships between policy discussion (and decisions) and interest? And how are particular measures actually enforced? In the case of both attitudinal and policy studies, we have a body of impressionistic empirical data rooted only loosely in social structure and institutional reality. Demographic studies, on the other hand, seek to specify their data sets and the subsequent manipulations of those sets; and they have already told us a good deal about the aging population and its place in the work force and in household constellations. Such aggregate studies are indispensable but at the same time pose at least as many questions as they provide answers. It is difficult indeed to move from descriptive aggregates to the felt experience of individuals in the past.[2] We have become accustomed to scholars making such jumps, from trends in aggregate data upward to more general patterns of change, and downward to changes in social role and social perception—to the way individuals construct and act out their particular reality. But seductive as such hypothetical constructions may be, we must concede their general arbitrariness; they are based less on evidence than on extrapolation from formal assumptions about the implications of social change.

What historians and sociologists need are some plausible frameworks for empirical analysis; frameworks that organically integrate these realms of structure and ideas, behavior and meaning. Data do not speak, and if they are to contribute to theory development, they must be collected in situations that reflect contextual interrelationships and tell us more about the web of social realities that individuals must actually confront. The problem is finding such research opportunities. Several possibilities for such studies suggest themselves: for example, case studies bounded by space and time. We can learn a great deal through the careful analysis of a community sufficiently small and structured so as to allow study of the aged in a multidimensional context.

I should like to devote the remainder of this chapter to describing another strategy of investigation, what one might call the middle-level social system approach—an approach anchored in real places and particular times but transcending the local manifestations of more general social patterns. Three such social systems are particularly relevant to aging. One is social welfare; another, work and industrial structure; and a third is medicine. (If we were concerned with youth or adolescence, education would constitute a similarly prominent social system.) Each one of these twentieth-century social systems necessarily and organically integrates bureaucracy, institutional structures, ideas, economic relationships, demography, and social policy. Each implies the selection of discrete case studies, whether of a factory, a hospital, a social work agency, or the operation of any one of these systems in a particular region or city, yet at the same time suggests ways of thinking about the case study that transcends it. Once we think of the particular unit of empirical investigation as the manifestation of a more general and structured social system, we are forced to consider the ways in which the system's characteristics relate to each other within the more limited context and thus shed light on the system itself, and the way in which it mediates between the most general aspects of social structure and the lives of particular individuals.

These programmatic remarks can be made more concrete by turning to the case of medicine, first specifying some of the chief characteristics of our twentieth-century medical system, and then suggesting some of the ways in which those characteristics structure treatment of the elderly within the system. Research conceived in this light should not only tell us something about the social position of the aged, but—necessarily—illuminate some of the chief aspects of the medical system more generally. In this sense, a study of the aged and medicine is as

much a sampling device for gaining an understanding of medicine as
it is for providing substantive information about the situation of the
aged. For the elderly have had to adjust to the medical system, a system which has done comparatively little to adjust to the special needs
of the aged.

A number of key aspects of the twentieth-century medical care system are particularly relevant to the aged as patients. One is the difference between the public and private sector in the delivery of medical
care: the private area has ordinarily and historically enjoyed a higher
status within medicine, as it has in so many other areas of economic
and institutional life. Second is a characteristic of modern medicine's
intellectual life that might be called reductionism: a reductionism in
the conception of disease and in diagnostic and therapeutic practice. It
is a style of intellectual activity and self-identification that has shaped
not only the public perception of medicine, but the forging of careers
and attribution of status within the medical profession. Specialization
is a third characteristic of modern medicine. It too is obviously related
in institutional and intellectual ways to what I have called medicine's
reductionism as well as to the delivery of medical care. Fourth is the
central role of the hospital in contemporary clinical medicine and of
the acute-care function within the hospital. Fifth is the relationship between all these factors and medicine's economic support system. A sixth
aspect of the medical system particularly relevant to the aged is the
general characteristics of the patient role, especially in an inpatient setting. Obviously these several characteristics of late-twentieth-century
medicine are only separable for analytical purposes; but even conced-
ing this, it still seems worthwhile, at least for the purposes of discussion, to think of these variables as distinct.

Traditionally—and by this I mean before about 1880—the way older
people were integrated into the medical system was a function not primarily of age but of dependence. Social and economic status, not pathology, determined the kind of care one would receive. If an individual (or one's family) were able to pay, a sick person of advanced years
would be treated by a private physician in a noninstitutional setting
(normally the patient's home) just as a youthful or middle-aged person
might have been. In any case, it should be noted, there was nothing
in the way of diagnostic or therapeutic techniques available in the hospital that could not be employed with equal ease in a private home.[3]
Class, and to a lesser degree, geographical location, determined the

kind of medical care one would receive and the point during a particular course of illness at which that care would be called upon. With occasional exceptions, only the poor were treated in an institutional setting. This was almost entirely true before 1880, with the exception of a comparative handful of middle- and upper-class victims of trauma, sudden illness in a strange community, or insanity, for whom a very different sort of ethos might legitimate the institutionalization of relatives.[4]

By 1900, hospitals were becoming both more widespread geographically and somewhat less stigmatizing socially, but in large cities it was still ordinarily the poor who populated voluntary and municipal hospital wards. The almshouse, general hospital wards, and outpatient dispensary were all designed for the working and dependent classes.[5] There were differences, of course, among the potential beneficiaries of such institutional care: voluntary hospitals were originally for the "worthy" poor alone; almshouses, for the more demoralized—even if, in reality, such categorical distinctions were less easily made than in the abstract world of social ideology. Similarly, in terms of medical diagnosis, the boundaries between sickness and dependence were clear: in practice, as every thoughtful contemporary was aware, they were often indistinguishable.

Almshouses, and their historical successors, municipal hospitals, often contained "old folks" wards, demonstrating in practice their administrators' inability to distinguish categorically between sickness and dependence. In many rural counties, even into the twentieth century, the sick, the handicapped, and the dependent generally were placed promiscuously in the local poorhouse. Well into the twentieth century, as Gerald Grob has forcefully argued, mental hospitals fulfilled a similar function. The aged and dependent were often provided with psychiatric labels when they might have been more candidly characterized as old and in the way; with the gradual death of the almshouse, Grob argues, the mental hospital and the state budget undertook a portion of the burden created by the need to care for the aged and dependent.[6] Not disease process, but social location determined how an individual was to be treated and categorized in this already bureaucratized medical care system.

Obviously, the social characteristics of medicine have changed fundamentally in the last century; nevertheless, the way in which treatment of the aged reflects extramedical realities has not. And there are

more specific continuities as well. One relates to the relationship between public and private sectors. Even at the beginning of the nineteenth century, there was a two-track aspect to institutional care; as we
have noted, the "worthy" poor could *in extremis* hope to find a bed
in a private voluntary hospital (and perhaps "outdoor" aid as well).
The "less worthy" had to settle for the stigmatizing and often punitive
care of the almshouse. But when one looks carefully at the patients in
terms of particular institutional populations, and not the ideal types of
social assumption, the key factor separating voluntary hospital from
municipal patients was chronicity, not moral worth.[7] (Allied with this
was one's place in a family constellation; the single, for example, like
the aged, were disproportionately likely to find themselves in a municipal hospital.) And chronicity is, of course, particularly relevant to age;
for the aged make up a large proportion of the chronically ill populations and, if poor, are likely to find themselves in the least desirable
hospital facility. Even now, there are relatively few nonstigmatizing
institutions to care for the aged and chronically ill.

Even within the pre–World War I voluntary hospital, there existed
an internal two-track system paralleling the social abyss that separated
private and municipal hospitals. Pay and "charity" patients normally
occupied very different positions with respect to both accommodations
and deference. Such distinctions mirrored not only prevailing class assumptions but the casually hybrid quality of all our voluntary hospitals
in this period. I employ the term *hybrid* inasmuch as all were private
corporations clothed with the public interest, burdened with public responsibility, and often provided with public support.[8] The two tracks—
labeled pay and charity—within the institution might just as well have
been termed private and public. As anyone familiar with large urban
hospitals is aware, moreover, social distinctions still persist despite the
presumably leveling effect of third-party payment; older distinctions
between ward and private patients have found subtle ways to perpetuate themselves. In some hospitals, for example, one is treated very differently depending on whether one is admitted by a private physician
or by "staff," whether one is poor or rich, black or white, educated
or uneducated, old or young. And, of course, the elderly patient, who
is often poor (and, in any case, separated by age itself from the house
staff members who provide the bulk of treatment), is particularly affected by these differential aspects of inpatient care.

Another and very different aspect of the twentieth-century medical system is what I have chosen to call reductionism—a shorthand way of emphasizing that from the 1820s and 1830s on, the medical world turned with increasing unanimity to the assumption that illness was fundamentally a specific pathological process with—ordinarily—a particular cause, characteristic course, and lesions.[9] Increasingly, medical personnel turned to the laboratory and to the tools and concepts of the so-called basic sciences to study and express these new pathological views; and as the laboratory played a larger and larger role in the intellectual life of the profession's elite, a scientific rhetoric came to characterize the profession's presentation of itself to society generally.

Traditional conceptions of disease had tended to be more general and holistic; little was heard of specific causes, and the diseased state was seen most commonly as a general state of the patient's physiological being—a result of interactions between the patient and every aspect of his or her social and physical environment.[10] The laboratory and the scientist's tools of measurement and analysis played a small role indeed in this world until the second half of the nineteenth century. From the traditional point of view, it was natural to see one disease shifting imperceptibly into another and to emphasize the ways in which environmental—and even psychological—variables might cause sickness or death. Consistently enough, medical casebooks in hospitals and private practice at the beginning of the nineteenth century often failed to indicate a specific diagnosis but simply recorded the patient's general appearance, therapeutics employed, and the eventual outcome. After the first third of the nineteenth century, changes in pathological conceptions underlined and intensified by the discovery of the germ theory shifted medical views toward a more reductionist understanding of illness—one in which individuals were stricken by specific ills with a specific cause—in which social and environmental factors played a far less prominent role. Diagnosis tended increasingly to be made in terms of seemingly "objective" physical criteria—first through the use of auscultation and percussion and the stethoscope, and later with the aid of the clinical laboratory, the X ray and an increasingly diverse array of chemical and physical tests.

The symptoms of pain and debility in an aged patient may not, however, fit easily into this pattern. In earlier periods, death certificates might record "senile debility" or "old age" as causes of death; between the 1870s and World War I, such imprecise terms were gradually banished; death certificates would ordinarily assign a specific—if in a sense arbitrary—cause of death. For such organ-specific and syndrome-specific diagnoses are consistent not only with a reductionist view of disease but with the way statistics and, even more important, insurance claims and, in recent years, cost controls have been managed. In the social world of modern medicine, sickness does not exist in the absence of a categorical diagnosis.

Age, of course, fits all too imprecisely into this way of thinking about disease and the institutional developments—ranging from specialism to the administration of health insurance—that have incorporated and reified this world view. One can see this pattern neatly illustrated in the illuminating failure of geriatrics to thrive as a specialty. This is a subject of concern for any scholar concerned with the evolution of specialism in medicine; we need to explain the failure of certain specialties to develop as much as we need to understand the factors that allow others to flourish.[11] And despite early twentieth-century calls for its encouragement, geriatrics failed to take root in the profession. Not only could geriatrics not call upon some specific crystallizing and legitimating technical innovation—the X ray, the ophthalmoscope, the laryngoscope—it did not fit easily into the even more fundamental lesion and organ oriented pattern of specialization that developed in the first half of this century. If one looks at the practice of a cardiologist or nephrologist today, it can be described as largely geriatric, but such practitioners do not think of it as such. Moreover, the pattern of economic relationships, enshrined in consultation and referral patterns, has similarly failed to assimilate the role of the self-proclaimed geriatrician. In many cases, physicians prominent in geriatrics are at the same time active in some aspect of social medicine—underlining their connection to the less-prestigious public sector of our medical care system.

All of which relates to the third characteristic of the twentieth-century medical system mentioned above—specialism. Following the dictates of both logic and brevity, this factor is discussed here in conjunction with the fourth aspect of our medical system already specified, namely, the dominance of the increasingly bureaucratic, acute-care oriented hospital. For the hospital has in the twentieth century become the key locus for delivery of medical care as it has become a pivotal institutional element in medical education and the elaboration of professional status. The modern hospital has been shaped by the professionalization of nursing and hospital administration as well as by the needs and perceptions of clinicians and the mechanisms of third-party payment.

But at almost no point in this expansion of hospital facilities has there been a concerted and effective questioning of the self-perception and priorities of the medical community; in fact, the availability of financial support from government and insurance schemes after World War II did not bring with it any pressure for the reordering of existing perceptions and policies. These sources of income have only strengthened, legitimated, and made economically viable the acute-care oriented hospital that had already come to play a central role in American medicine by the 1920s. (Funding for hospital construction and medical research, two important sources of direct and indirect federal support after the war, fit neatly into this pattern.) Much of American hospital financing in the past two generations has been on an unquestioned cost-plus basis, a policy unlikely to foster internal criticism of existing social and economic relationships or the intellectual assumptions that justify and explain them. These key assumptions are so familiar that we need to be reminded that they are indeed assumptions: the practice of medicine can most effectively and efficiently be carried out in a hospital; the hospital's armamentarium of technical resources defines appropriate therapeutic standards; and, finally, the hospital itself should be designed, and status and material rewards within it distributed, in ways reflecting medicine's ability to intervene in acute-care situations.

The tenacity of these institutional realities is underlined by the long and inconclusive history of American efforts to modify this acute-care, interventionist oriented medical system. For almost a century, for example, would-be reformers have sought to make hospital forms more flexible—and especially to recognize the need for increased chronic and convalescent care. But despite such concerns, the acute-care model has only fastened itself with ever-increasing firmness upon the general hospital. Institutional competition and growth have similarly developed along such clearly established lines of status, dooming most attempts to diversify and rationalize hospital resources and functions. Regional planning for hospital services was a conception of the late-nineteenth and early-twentieth centuries; it has had surprisingly little cumulative impact. Similarly, the Progressive period saw innumerable calls for the expansion of outpatient care and the delivery of care in the patient's home—policies urged by their advocates as both socially and economically desirable.[12] But arguments emphasizing the unnecessary social and economic costs of an oversupply of acute-care beds could not begin to carry the day against contemporary medical perceptions and ambitions allied with the institutional loyalties of hospital boards and administrators. Neither doctors nor laypeople would willingly settle for what they saw as "second best."

I have been trying to emphasize the rigidity of the system; the way it has predictably and, in fact, necessarily failed to respond to recurrent criticism. It is no accident that similar arguments have been resuscitated in decade after decade—and with consistently meager response. Now, it might be argued that these characteristics of the medical system do not affect the aged alone, that they affect us all as tax- and insurance premium–payers and, ultimately, as patients. It seems apparent, however, that the elderly are specifically and particularly implicated in this unyielding system. Not only are they more likely than younger Americans to experience discomfort and disability, but their ailments are more likely to fit into the nonacute and seemingly nonspecific category—ills that might in fact be cared for in the home or in an appropriate chronic-care facility. But events of the recent past have underlined how poorly our society has supported such services. Even the comparatively wealthy may experience difficulty in securing appropriate nonacute care, while choices for the poor are more discouraging still.

Another characteristic of our contemporary medical system, one not unrelated to the issues just discussed, is the nature of the patient role. Again, this applies not peculiarly to older Americans but to anyone who assumes the sick role and especially that version of it acted out in the hospital. All patients in such settings are in some measure reduced to moral and emotional minors; but the personal costs are even greater to aged patients, and the secondary gains fewer. Medical personnel often function best in acute-care situations in which their skills appear to be immediately efficacious and in which a paradigmatic acute-care scenario is acted out: the course of the disease is diagnosed and monitored, the physician or surgeon intervenes, and—ultimately—the patient either recovers or is discharged with some felt symptomatic benefit. But many aged patients fit uneasily into this pattern, for they often suffer from a variety of ills, many chronic and associated with a psychological penumbra of depression and discouragement. Most important, they cannot be cured. They are patients likely to be referred to as "crocks" or "turkeys" in the hospital house staff's *ad hoc* bestiary. Our culture may not honor age in general; its responses can be particularly insensitive and stigmatizing in a hospital context attuned to expectations (and gratifications) very different from those experiences involved in caring for the chronic geriatric patient.

All of these factors are underlined and made more rigid by prevailing economic relationships—a final aspect of the medical care system relevant to the aged. Most obviously, third-party payment mechanisms have intensified the dominance of medicine's inpatient, acute-care orientation; many physicians as well as commentators outside the profession have in recent years become increasingly critical of the inflexibility of present arrangements. Economic interests of a more specific kind are built into the hospital's high technology—and high capital-intensive—character; in our culture, the pressure to approach social problems through the spending of money on technological solutions has strong roots in both ideology and interest. It can be contended as well that research and training dollars have not been abundantly available in areas related to geriatrics (though, of course, many aspects of fundamental research are potentially applicable to patients of any age). Similarly, state and municipal welfare budgets have never reflected with accuracy the medical needs of an aging population. Not until the passage of the so-called Medicare legislation a generation ago has there been a statutory expression of the special health needs of our older population. Significantly, however, continuing support for this legislation has grown out of its class-blind aspect. This broad relevance has obscured its potentially stigmatizing character as an instance of publically funded medical care.

Responses to Medicare illustrate as well a radically new aspect of the relationship between the aged and America's medical system. This lies in the contemporary realization by many older Americans that they constitute an interest group—certainly in response to federal and state health policy. Such self-consciousness and the political behavior it motivates constitute a new element in contemporary health politics; for in earlier periods there was no such age–oriented political consciousness—just as there was no area of public policy to elicit it. Future steps in American health policy will necessarily reflect the influence of this new political force.

It might be argued that this kind of analysis tells us as much about the medical system (and society generally) as it does about the aged specifically. But this, of course, is the point. We cannot remove the aged from the web of social realities and relationships in which they must inevitably function as patients; similarly, we cannot remove the worker or the primary school student or the dependent mother from their particular social situation. Our problem is to be precise in specifying the relationship between such individuals and the institutions that at once constrain and support them. And that implies an understanding of each key institution both in its general characteristics and particular local features. Let me repeat my original contention that an approach emphasizing the coherence of the middle-level social system—like medicine or education or social welfare—provides a plausible framework for understanding the peculiar configuration of economic, ideological, and bureaucratic factors that constitute each such system. I do not mean to imply that every piece of empirical research must be pursued in such general terms—for there could be no foreseeable end to any such study—but rather that when social scientists or historians undertake an empirical investigation—whether it be of a factory, a mill town, a welfare agency or hospital—they remain aware that their subject must be understood as a concrete manifestation of more general social patterns. It is only by remaining aware of the determining aspect of the middle-level social system that we can force the smallest case study to shed light on more general structural realities.

Finally, let me emphasize that there is obviously something significant about aging; it is a substantive problem of continuing interest. There seems little likelihood that medicine will abolish death—or even growing old—in the near future, while structural changes in the economy pose insistent questions for the future well-being of the aged. Growing old is thus both a biological reality and, necessarily, a social and moral sampling device; to study aging in a particular culture is to study the fundamental structures and priorities of that culture. What makes aging particularly intriguing for the sociologist, anthropologist, or historian is that it makes everything else problematic—a web of institutional and attitudinal possibilities that can be constructed in countless ways. Like childbirth or adolescence, old age is "handled" or framed in different ways by different cultures. In our culture that structured relationship cannot be understood without a prior understanding of those middle-level social systems that mediate so many of the intersections between particular individuals and society.

NOTES

1. This style of analysis has been so widespread in the writing of social history during the past generation that no note can deal adequately with it. Let me point out, for example, how central it is to the burgeoning area of women's and family history—or to the growing interest in social control and the role of institutions such as the primary school, prison, and asylum in the transition from a traditional to an industrial society.

2. For discussions of this elusive issue, see Charles E. Rosenberg, "Introduction: History and Experience," in Charles E. Rosenberg, ed., *The Family in History* (Philadelphia, 1975), pp. 1–11; James A. Henretta, "Social History as Lived and Written," *American Historical Review* 84, no. 5 (1979), 1293–1322.

3. Asepsis did not become a reality until the late 1880s and the 1890s, and even then many surgical procedures were performed in the homes of wealthy and middle-class patients. Nursing and diet were considered a significant aspect of hospital care; but again, these did not imply a necessary role for the hospital, except in the case of those too poor to command such amenities outside an institutional setting.

4. See Nancy Tomes, *A Generous Confidence: Thomas Story Kirkbride and the Art of Asylum-Keeping, 1840–1883* (Cambridge, England, London and New York, 1984); Gerald Grob, *Mental Institutions in America: Social Policy to 1875* (New York, 1973); Morris J. Vogel, *The Invention of the Modern Hospital: Boston 1870–1930* (Chicago, 1980); Charles E. Rosenberg, "And Heal the Sick: The Hospital and the Patient in Nineteenth-Century America," *Journal of Social History* 10 (1977): 428–447.

5. Charles E. Rosenberg, "Social Class and Medical Care in Nineteenth-Century America," *Journal of the History of Medicine* 29 (1974): 32–54; idem, "From Almshouse to Hospital: The Shaping of Philadelphia General Hospital," *Health and Society/Milbank Memorial Fund Quarterly* 60 (1982): 108–154; Harry F. Dowling, *City Hospitals: The Undercare of the Underprivileged* (Cambridge, Mass., 1982).

6. Gerald Grob, *Mental Illness and American Society, 1875–1940* (Princeton, 1983), esp. ch. 7, "The Invisible Patient," pp. 179–200.

7. Jon M. Kingsdale, "The Growth of Hospitals: An Economic History in Baltimore," Ph.D. dissertation, University of Michigan, 1981, p. 406; Rosenberg, "Almshouse to Hospital," p. 151; S. S. Goldwater, *On Hospitals* (New York, 1947), pp. 206–207.

8. This fundamental aspect of the history of medical care has been forgotten in recent years. See the instructive discussion by Rosemary Stevens, " 'A Poor Sort of Memory': Voluntary Hospitals and Government before the Depression," *Health and Society/Milbank Memorial Fund Quarterly* 60 (1982): 551–584.

9. For a brief but insightful discussion of this development, see Owsei Temkin, "The Scientific Approach to Disease: Specific Entity and Individual Sickness," in Temkin, ed., *The Double Face of Janus and Other Essays in the History of Medicine* (Baltimore, 1977; originally published 1963), 441–455. Still useful as an introduction to the subject is Knud Faber, *Nosography in Modern Internal Medicine* (New York, 1923).

10. For a more elaborate discussion, see Charles E. Rosenberg, "The Therapeutic Revolution: Medicine, Meaning and Social Change in Nineteenth-Century America," *Perspectives in Biology and Medicine* 20 (1977): 485–506.

11. On specialization, see George Rosen, *The Specialization with Particular Reference to Ophthalmology* (New York, 1944); Rosemary Stevens, *American Medicine and the Public Interest* (New Haven, 1971). For the problem of geriatrics, see Carole Haber, chapter 4 of this volume, and her *Beyond Sixty-Five: The Dilemma of Old Age in America's Past* (Cambridge, England, 1983), esp. chs. 3–4, pp. 47–81.

12. Charles E. Rosenberg, "Inward Vision and Outward Glance: The Shaping of the American Hospital, 1880–1914," *Bulletin of the History of Medicine* 53 (1979): 346–391.

Selected Bibliography

Achenbaum, W. Andrew. "The Obsolescence of Old Age in America, 1865–1914." *Journal of Social History* 8 (1974): 48–62.

———. *Old Age in the New Land: The American Experience since 1790.* Baltimore: Johns Hopkins, 1978.

———. "Did Social Security Attempt to Regulate the Poor?" *Research on Aging* 2 (1980): 470–488.

———. *Shades of Gray: Old Age, American Values and Federal Policies since 1920.* Boston: Little, Brown, 1983.

Achenbaum, W. Andrew, and P. A. Kusnerz. *Images of Old Age in America: 1790 to the Present.* Washington, D.C.: Smithsonian Institution, National Endowment for the Humanities; Ann Arbor: University of Michigan Institute of Gerontology, n.d.

Achenbaum, W. Andrew, and Peter N. Stearns. "Old Age and Modernization." *Gerontologist* 18 (1978): 307–312.

Amoss, P. T., and S. Harrell. "Introduction: An Anthropological Perspective on Aging," in Amoss and Harrell, eds., *Other Ways of Growing Old.* Stanford: Stanford University Press, 1981.

de Beauvoir, Simone. *Coming of Age.* New Work: Putnam, 1972.

Berkner, L. K. "The Stem Family and the Developmental Cycle of the Peasant Household: An Eighteenth-Century Austrian Example." *American Historical Review* 77 (1972): 398–418.

Burgess, E. W., ed. *Aging in Western Societies.* Chicago: University of Chicago Press, 1960.

Calhoun, Richard B. *In Search of the New Old.* New York: Elsevier, 1978.

Chudacoff, Howard P., and Tamara K. Hareven. "Family Transitions into Old
    Age," in Hareven, ed., *Transitions: The Family and the Life Course
    in Historical Perspective*. New York: Academic Press, 1978.
————. "From the Empty Nest to Family Dissolution: Life Course Transi-
    tions into Old Age." *Journal of Family History* 4 (1979): 69–83.
Clark, M. "The Anthropology of Aging: A New Era for Studies of Culture
    and Personality." *Gerontologist* 7 (1967): 55–64.
Clark, M., and G. B. Anderson. *Culture and Aging: An Anthropological Study
    of Older Americans*. Springfield, Ill.: C. C. Thomas, 1967.
Cole, Thomas. "Past Meridian: Aging and the Northern Middle Class." Ph.D.
    dissertation, University of Rochester, 1980.
Conrad, Christoph, and Hans-Joachim von Kondratowitz. *Gerontologie und
    Sozialgeschichte: Weg zu einer Historischen Betrachtung des Alters*.
    Berlin: Deutsches Zentrum fuer Altersfragen, 1983.
Cottrell, F. "The Technological and Societal Basis of Aging," in C. Tibbitts,
    ed., *Handbook of Social Gerontology*. Chicago: University of Chicago
    Press, 1960.
Cowgill, D. "The Aging of Populations and Societies," in F. R. Eisele, ed.,
    *Political Consequences of Aging: Annals of the American Academy of
    Political and Social Science*. Philadelphia: American Academy of Po-
    litical and Social Science, (1974).
Cowgill, D., and L. D. Holmes, eds. *Aging and Modernization*. New York:
    Appleton-Century-Crofts, 1972.
Dahlin, Michael. "Perspectives on the Family Life of the Elderly in 1900,"
    Gerontologist 20 (1980): 99–107.
Demos, John. "Old Age in Early New England," in David D. Van Tassel,
    ed., *Aging, Death and the Completion of Being*. Philadelphia: Univer-
    sity of Pennsylvania Press, 1979.
Faragher, J. "Old Women and Old Men in Seventeenth-Century Wethersfield,
    Connecticut." *Women's Studies* 4 (1976): 11–31.
Fischer, David Hackett. *Growing Old in America* (rev. ed.). New York: Ox-
    ford University Press, 1978.
Fischer, David Hackett, and Lawrence Stone. "Growing Old: An Exchange."
    New York Review of Books, 15 September 1977.
Freeman, J. T., *Aging: Its History and Literature*. New York: Human Sci-
    ences Press, 1979.
Friedmann, E. "The Impact of Aging on the Social Structure," in C. Tibbitts,
    ed., *Handbook of Social Gerontology*. Chicago: University of Chicago
    Press, 1960.
Goldstein, M. C., and C. M. Beall. "Indirect Modernization and the Status
    of the Elderly in a Rural Third World Setting." *Journal of Gerontol-
    ogy* 6 (1982): 743–748.
Goody, J. "Aging in Nonindustrial Societies," in R. H. Binstock and E. Shanas,

eds., *Handbook of Aging and the Social Sciences*. New York: Van Nostrand Reinhold, 1976.

Graebner, William. *A History of Retirement: The Meaning and Function of an American Institution, 1885-1978*. New Haven: Yale University Press, 1980.

Gratton, Brian. "Boston's Elderly, 1890-1950: Work, Family and Dependency." Ph.D. dissertation, Boston University, 1980.

Greven, Philip J., Jr. "Family Structure in Seventeenth-Century Andover, Massachusetts," *William and Mary Quarterly* 23 (1966): 234-256.

————. *Four Generations: Population, Land and Family in Colonial Andover, Massachusetts*. Ithaca: Cornell University Press, 1970.

Gutmann, David. "Observations on Culture and Mental Health in Later Life," in J. E. Birren and R. B. Sloane, eds., *Handbook of Mental Health and Aging*. Englewood Cliffs, N.J.: Prentice-Hall, 1980.

Haber, Carole. "The Old Folks at Home: The Development of Institutionalized Care for the Aged in Nineteenth-Century Philadelphia." *Pennsylvania Magazine of History and Biography* 51 (1977): 240-257.

————. "Mandatory Retirement in Nineteenth-Century America: The Conceptual Basis for a New Work Cycle." *Journal of Social History* 12 (1978): 77-96.

————. *Beyond Sixty-Five: The Dilemma of Old Age in America's Past*. Cambridge, England: Cambridge University Press, 1983.

Hareven, Tamara. "The Last Stage: Historical Adulthood and Old Age." *Daedalus* 105 (1976): 13-27.

————. "Family Time and Historical Time." *Daedalus* 106 (1977): 57-70.

Hendricks, Jon, and C. D. Hendricks. "The Age Old Question of Age: Was It Really So Much Better Back When?" *International Journal of Aging and Human Development* 8 (1977-78): 130-154.

Holmes, L. D. "Trends in Anthropological Gerontology: From Simmons to the Seventies." *International Journal of Aging and Human Development* 7 (1976): 211-220.

Holtzman, A. *The Townsend Movement: A Political Study*. New York: Bookman, 1963.

Kastenbaum, R., and B. Ross. "Historical Perspectives on Care," in J. G. Howells, ed., *Modern Perspectives in the Psychology of Old Age*. New York: Brunner/Mazel, 1975.

Keith, J. "The Ethnography of Old Age: Introduction." *Anthropological Quarterly* 52 (1979): 1-6.

Keyssar, A. "Widowhood in Eighteenth-Century Massachusetts: A Problem in the History of the Family." *Perspectives in American History* 8 (1974): 83-122.

Kleinberg, Susan. "Aging and the Aged in Nineteenth Century Pittsburgh." Manuscript, Western College, Miami University, Miami, Ohio, 1977.

Laslett, Peter. "Societal Development and Aging," in R. H. Binstock and E. Shanas, eds., *Handbook of Aging and the Social Sciences.* New York: Van Nostrand Reinhold, 1976.

———. "The History of Aging and the Aged," in *Family Life and Illicit Love in Earlier Generations: Essays in Historical Sociology.* Cambridge, England: Cambridge University Press, 1977.

Linford, A. A. *Old Age Assistance in Massachusetts.* Chicago: University of Chicago Press, 1949.

Lubove, Roy. *The Struggle for Social Security, 1900–1935.* Cambridge, Mass.: Harvard University Press, 1968.

McTavish, D. G. "Perceptions of Old People: A Review of Research Methodologies and Findings." *Gerontologist* 11 (1971): 90–101.

Maxwell, R. J., and P. Silverman. "Information and Esteem: Cultural Considerations in the Treatment of the Aged." *Aging and Human Development* 1 (1970): 361–392.

Myles, John F. *Old Age in the Welfare State: The Political Economy of Public Pensions.* Boston: Little, Brown, 1983.

Palmore, E. B. "Sociological Aspects of Aging," in E. W. Busse and E. Pfeiffer, eds., *Behavior and Modification in Late Life.* Boston: Little, Brown, 1969.

———. *The Honorable Elders: A Cross-Cultural Analysis of Aging in Japan.* Durham, N.C.: Duke University Press, 1975.

Palmore, E. B., and K. Manton, "Modernization and the Status of the Aged: International Correlations." *Journal of Gerontology* 29 (1974): 205–210.

Parsons, Talcott. "Age and Sex in the Social Structure of the United States." *American Sociological Review* 7 (1942): 604–616.

———. "The Kinship System of the Contemporary United States." *American Anthropologist* 45 (1943): 22–38.

Philibert, Michel A. "The Emergence of Social Gerontology." *Journal of Social Issues* 21 (1965): 4–12.

———. *L'Echelle des âges.* Paris: Seuil, 1968.

Pratt, Anthony. *The Gray Lobby.* Chicago: University of Chicago Press, 1977.

Putnam, J. K. *Old Age Politics in California.* Stanford: Stanford University Press, 1970.

Quadagno, Jill. *Historical Perspectives on Aging and Social Policy: Work and Family in Nineteenth Century England.* New York: Academic Press, 1983.

Rebel, Hermann. "Peasant Stem Families in Early Modern Austria: Life Plans, Status Tactics and the Grid of Inheritance." *Social Science History* 2 (1978): 255–291.

Roebuck, Janet. "When Does Old Age Begin? The Evolution of the English Definition." *Journal of Social History* 12 (1979): 416–429.

Roebuck, Janet, and Jane Slaughter. "Ladies and Pensioners: Stereotypes and Public Policy Affecting Old Women in England, 1880–1940," *Journal of Social History* 13 (1979): 105–114.

Roscow, I. *Socialization to Old Age*. Berkeley: University of California Press, 1974.

Sheehan, T. "Senior Esteem as a Factor of Socioeconomic Complexity." *Gerontologist* 16 (1976): 33–40.

Simmons, L. "Aging in Preindustrial Societies," in C. Tibbitts, ed., *Handbook of Social Gerontology*. Chicago: University of Chicago Press, 1960.

―――. *The Role of the Aged in Primitive Society*. Hamden, Conn.: Archon Books, 1970.

Smith, Daniel Scott. "Parental Power and Marriage Patterns: An Analysis of Historical Trends in Hingham, Massachusetts." *Journal of Marriage and the Family* 35 (1973): 419–428.

―――. "A Community-Based Sample of the Older Population from the 1880 and 1900 United States Manuscript Censuses." *Historical Methods* 11 (1979): 67–74.

―――. "Life Course, Norms and the Family System of Older Americans in 1900." *Journal of Family History* 4 (1979): 285–298.

Smith, Daniel Scott, Janice L. Reiff, and Michael Dahlin. "Rural Push and Urban Pull: Work and Family Experiences of Older Black Women in Southern Cities, 1880–1900," *Journal of Social History* 16 (1983): 39–48.

Smith-Rosenberg, Carole. "Puberty to Menopause: The Cycle of Femininity in 19th-Century America," in M. Hartman and L. Banner, eds., *Clio's Consciousness Raised*. New York: Harper and Row, 1976.

Spicker, Stuart, Kathleen Woodward, and David Van Tassel, eds., *Aging and the Elderly: Humanistic Perspectives in Gerontology*. Atlantic Highlands, N.J.: Humanities Press, 1978.

Stearns, Peter N. *Old Age in European Society: The Case of France*. New York: Holmes and Meier, 1976.

―――. "Old Women: Some Historical Observations." *Journal of Family History* 5 (1980): 44–57.

―――. "The Modernization of Old Age in France: Approaches through History." *International Journal of Aging and Human Development* 13 (1981): 297–316.

―――., ed. *Old Age in Preindustrial Society*. New York: Holmes and Meier, 1982.

Stone, Lawrence. "Walking over Grandma." *New York Review of Books*, 12 May 1977.

Thomas, Keith. "Age and Authority in Early Modern England." *Proceedings of the British Academy* 62 (1976): 205–248.

United States Senate, Special Committee on Aging, *Fifty Years of Social Se-*

curity: *Past Achievements and Future Challenges*, Serial No. 99-C.
  Washington, D.C., U.S. Government Printing Office, 1985.
Van Tassel, David, ed. *Aging, Death and the Completion of Being*. Philadelphia: University of Pennsylvania Press, 1979.
Waters, John J. "The Traditional World of New England Peasants: A View
  from Seventeenth-Century Barnstable." *New England Historical Genealogical Register* 130 (1976): 3–23.

Index

Contributors

W. ANDREW ACHENBAUM teaches in the Applied History and Social Sciences program at Carnegie-Mellon University. He is currently completing *Social Security: Visions and Revisions*, for the Twentieth Century Fund.

THOMAS R. COLE is Assistant Professor of History and Medicine at the Institute for the Medical Humanities, University of Texas Medical Branch, Galveston. Dr. Cole's articles have appeared in *American Quarterly*, *Hastings Center Report*, and *Gerontologist*. He is now preparing historical studies on the culture of aging in the United States and on aging in American autobiography.

WILLIAM GRAEBNER, Professor of History at the State University of New York College at Fredonia, received the Frederick Jackson Turner Award from the Organization of American Historians for *Coal-Mining Safety in the Progressive Period: The Political Economy of Reform* (1976). His second monograph, *A History of Retirement: The Meaning and Function of an American Institution, 1885–1978*, was published in 1980. Professor Graebner is currently working on a history of youth subcultures in Buffalo in the 1950s.

BRIAN GRATTON, Assistant Professor of History at Arizona State University and author of *Urban Elders: Family, Work and Welfare among Boston's Aged, 1890–1950* (1985), is interested in both the historical and the contemporary labor-force activity of older men and women.

GERALD N. GROB is Professor of History at Rutgers University and author of a number of studies on the history of mental illness including *Mental Illness and American Society, 1875–1940* (1983). He is currently conducting a study of mental health policy since 1940.

CAROLE HABER is an Associate Professor in the Department of History at the University of North Carolina at Charlotte. She is the author of several articles on the history of old age in the United States and *Beyond Sixty-Five: The Dilemma of Old Age in America's Past* (1983).

TAMARA HAREVEN is Professor of History at Clark University, Research Associate at Harvard University's Center for Population Studies, and Editor, *Journal of Family History*. Her most recent books are *Family Time and Industrial Time* (1982) and *Aging and the Life Course in Interdisciplinary and Cross-Cultural Perspective* (edited with Kathleen Adams, 1982).

JOHN MYLES, a member of the Department of Sociology and Anthropology at Carleton University, is the author of *Old Age in the Welfare State: The Political Economy of Public Pensions* (1983).

JILL S. QUADAGNO, Associate Professor in the Department of Sociology at the University of Kansas, is the author of *Aging in Early Industrial Society: Work, Family and Social Policy in Nineteenth Century England* (1983). Her present research concerns the historical development of old age security in the United States.

CHARLES E. ROSENBERG, Professor in the Department of History and Sociology of Science at the University of Pennsylvania, has written widely on the history of American science and medicine. He is currently completing a study of the hospital in America from 1800 to 1920.

DANIEL SCOTT SMITH is a member of the History Department of the University of Illinois at Chicago and editor of *Historical Methods*.

During the 1983–1984 academic year, he was NEH Senior Fellow at the Newberry Library, Chicago, and a Fullbright Fellow at the University of Lund, Sweden. His research has encompassed various aspects of historical demography.

PETER N. STEARNS, Heinz Professor of History at Carnegie-Mellon University and editor of the *Journal of Social History*, has written two books on the history of old age plus several articles on retirement and social security policy. His current research concerns the history of emotions.

DAVID VAN TASSEL, of Case Western Reserve University, has ranged widely in his work as historical scholar and teacher. He founded the National History Day exercises and has edited two previous volumes on the humanities and issues of old age, which gave shape to earlier historical work in this field.